for Delilah,
who completed me

BOUGHT,
Borrowed
& *Stolen*

RECIPES & KNIVES
FROM A TRAVELLING CHEF

Design by Natasha Coverdale • Photography by Andrew Montgomery

conran
OCTOPUS

A. Meg.

LOVE TO
EAT

Contents

Introduction

It doesn't matter where you are in the world, once you've assumed fire, the other two essentials for cooking are knives and ingredients. Much has been written about ingredients but this book puts the tools of our trade in the ascendancy and for the first time gives them the starring role they deserve.

When I started at cooking school I had a healthy, respectful admiration for my shiny new blades: any trainee will tell you that the day they get their first knife is a day of enormous pride. But as the years went by and I gathered more and more from trips abroad, my fascination grew not in the physical properties of a knife (science was never my strong suit) but in what they represent. For depending on where you are in the world, a knife can be anything from the most basic way of gaining your food to a precision-crafted piece of engineering. All my knives mean something to me: some emotional, some cultural, some just blow me away with their amazingness, but point to any of them and I'll tell you a story.

At first, I started bringing knives back from places I'd visited just kind of in an ad hoc way: if I saw one I was attracted to, I'd pick it up. Then when I'd amassed a few, I started looking at them next to each other, and there it was, plain and simple: the knives told the story of the place. And I was hooked.

Huge machete-like things from Burma for cutting crops; ceramic-bladed ones from chic Milan (from the shop where Giorgio Armani buys his knives); a unique, single piece of cold-plunged steel made for specifically breaking down an eel from the masters of precision in Kyoto; sleek, perfectly engineered ones for filleting fish from Scandinavia (made by Porsche); a pâtisserie knife from France that has a fierce, serrated edge that doubles as a palette knife; a lethal and extraordinary butcher's chopper from China ... and so on. Some hewn roughly for basic use, some crafted and shaped for accuracy.

Mostly I gather kitchen knives; I hesitate at the word 'collect' as that implies that they are not for use - and I certainly do use them all ... except maybe that Brazilian pig leg boner as I can't seem to negotiate it in a butchery context - the rest are all in circulation. Sometimes, though, I pick something up that doesn't technically count as a kitchen knife, usually because it is too stunning to walk on by. The only rule I truly tried to stick to was no hunting knives (and I even broke that in the Philippines, but with just cause). I reckon there's enough violence in our world that I want no connotations of that in my kitchen or indeed this book. My knives are impressive, cultural, beautiful and, for the most part, just plain useful.

Julia Child said it plain and simple when she fessed up: 'I am a knife freak'. Well, she's not alone.

As for the recipes - I grew up travelling around: that's not to say our family were hippie Nomads; my early life in Hammersmith, London couldn't have been further from it, but my dad was an historian, writing historical atlases covering from the year dot to modern times, and so our 'holidays' were basically his research trips. I'll never forget the bemused looks I got from my classmates when, aged eight, I started a new school and asked them how many ruins/fortresses/cathedrals/temples had they seen on holiday?

Larkin may say they fuck you up, but those trips with my parents had a profound effect on me, and made me the chef I am today. But whereas my old man would seek out the most obscure outposts of the Roman Empire, or the oldest monastery bell in Asia, or the exact place where Vasco da Gama set out from, when I travel I seek out a different side of their culture, every bit as old as their history, but of an altogether more digestible form.

As youngsters both my sister and I were encouraged to keep diaries, though it became clear pretty quickly that mine were less about the culture we'd seen, as each entry started with what I'd had for breakfast, and went on to catalogue the rest of my day's food intake. From street snacks to smart restaurants, buffets to bistros - I just started writing it all down.

That was all before I became a chef, and after I'd taken up my metier the focus of them geared up a notch: early mornings were spent at fish markets, afternoons lazily grazing through menus whilst extensively sampling the local wines and stickies, and afterwards a hunt for the best ice-cream in town. All in the name of research. And as I ate I jotted down in my diary anything particularly yummy, interesting, fun or new to me (sometimes along with a really crap picture to help jog my memory).

So this is the first cookbook I've written that aren't my recipes: it's a book of things I've eaten all over the world that moved me, and I've tried to recreate using my notes, that dodgy picture and my taste memory: hence the title (the knives being the bought part).

The whole business of eating can mean so many different things in different places around the world: to Jews it's closely tied to religion; in the west it's subject to fashion and fad and in many parts of Africa it's quite simply a lifeline. Anywhichway it always reflects a country's culture: it's a blueprint of where they're at and the journey that got them there.

Some of the recipes I've chosen for this book are ones that I think are particularly relevant when you keep that in mind. Going beyond the national dish, they are recipes that represent a taste of their culture, past as well as their present. Others are in here because I'd never tasted anything like it before, or they are show stopping in their simplicity. There may be huge glaring omissions of a country's classics but this is just my story of what I ate. All of them are knock-your-socks-off yum and all of them are dishes that the people who fed me are hugely proud of.

I'm indebted to and hugely appreciative of those people who first cooked these dishes for me, and can only hope they know how much pleasure they've given. Because from what I've seen, wherever you are in the world, there's no better way of giving people joy than by handing them a plate of food made with love ... and watching them love it too.

Two other points about the recipes: The number of recipes in each chapter is not at all reflective of how much I liked the food from that country - it's simply a reflection of how much I ate (which is just a marker of how long the trip was and whether I've been back).

And secondly, for culinary purists, you'll have to forgive me where I've altered them a bit, but these recipes must be cookable, so in some places I've adapted methods or swapped ingredients to make them more accessible ... and in the odd case just downright possible at all. All recipes have been tested using a fan-assisted oven.

A CLASSICAL MAP
of
ASIA MINOR

Being a partial revision by permission of
Messrs John Murray of J. G. C. Anderson's
Map of Asia Minor
by
W. M. CALDER and G. E. BEAN

Scale 1: 2,000,000
English Miles

Roman Miles

Roman Roads, certain or probable course
Provincial Boundaries, 63-72 A.D.

Geographical summary: Straddles the continents of Europe and Asia. Many bordering neighbours: Armenia, Azerbaijan, Bulgaria, Georgia, Greece, Iran, Iraq and Syria. High central plateau (Anatolia), narrow coastal plain; several mountain ranges.

Population: 77.8 million.

Religion: Muslim 99.8%, other 0.2%.

Ethnic make-up: Turkish 70–75%, Kurdish 18%, other minorities 7–12%.

Life expectancy: 69.5 male, 74 female.

External influences: The biggest foreign issue modern Turkey has had to deal with is the diminishing of its once magnificent and enormous Ottoman empire. At its height in the 16th and 17th centuries it stretched east into Anatolia, west as far as the Balkans, south over the Arabian peninsula and into parts of Africa and north to the Caucasus. Although shrinking through the 18th, 19th and early 20th centuries, it wasn't formally dissolved until 1922, leaving Turkey with the same land mass as the

FACT FILE

present day. Fell out badly with Greece over ownership of Cyprus in the '60s, a dispute that continues to drive a Green Line through the capital, Nicosia.

The essentials of their cooking: It's really a grill culture primarily, but slow-cooking veg are also a feature. Plenty of freshness and herbs all round. Great with pastry.

Food they export: Hazelnuts, flour, prepared nuts, pastry, chocolate, tomatoes, raisins.

Top 5 favourite ingredients: Lamb, aubergines, yoghurt, honey, olives.

Most famous dish: The kebab.

What to drink: Efes Pilsen (brewed in Izmir) and raki – fierce aniseed in a cloudy haze. Excellent muddy coffee, often flavoured with cardamom.

Best thing I ate: Pine honey by the spoonful.

Most breathtaking moment: Sailing into Istanbul at dawn.

Don't ask for…: Greek yoghurt.

Turkey ⋆

I've been to Turkey three times and I kind of feel like I've done it backwards. The latest visit, just a couple of years ago, we arrived into Istanbul by boat from Athens, a tall ship no less, taking in Troy the day before, then sailing in at dawn. As we crossed the busy Sea of Marmara traffic, watching the unmistakable domes of Aya Sofia and the Blue Mosque dominate the horizon - each complete with fairytale minarets - it felt undoubtedly the right way to view this incredible city for the first time. Coming in by sea feels majestic, mystical and timeless, with so few visible giveaways of the modern world.

My actual first time was when I was thirteen, and we went on a family holiday to look at the Roman and Byzantine sites that litter the coast from Izmir to Antalya.

My dad was an historian and had an unsurpassable passion for the Romans, so, as opposed to all my friends who spent holidays on beaches, this was a fairly regular way of passing the summer for us. I remember clambering up some amazing ruins that scorching August: a stadium with giant steps in Aphrodisias, the Lycian tombs at Myra carved into vertical rock faces, and the entire city of Ephesus were all one giant playground for me.

But even though it doesn't sound like I was particularly respectful, I was definitely in awe. Ephesus in particular struck a chord, as St Paul, after whom my school was named, supposedly lived and preached there, and also it was home to one of the Seven Wonders of the World, the Temple of Artemis. Less than a week later I was at the site of another: the Mausoleum of Halicarnassus at Bodrum, and even as a youngster I realized how impressive this was, and remember being properly amazed that I was this close to the stuff of legends.

My dad and I went back to Turkey some years later, just for a long weekend to Istanbul to photograph something for his research in the National Museum. It was January and the snow on the minarets made them look even more fairytale as we stomped round town, Pa giving me a quick-hit tour of the must-sees, and me making him go round the souk and duck into coffee shops where I'd suck on a hookah and he'd smile magnanimously.

And then back to the last time: at the end of our Athens-Istanbul cruise we had a few days there, and this time a city that had been sleepy with winter was bustling and alive in the heat of summer. We explored this city that has a toe in Asia and a hand in Europe more thoroughly, staying in the old town prison that had been converted to a hotel, eating our way round the Golden Horn and letting it work its way into my heart as one of my favourites in the world. It was magical and moving going back to the same places: Topkapi Palace (I'd only remembered the kitchen), the lost Imperial Cistern built by Justinian, and the city's second mosque, Sultan Ahmet Camii. But of course it was at the extremely powerful and moving Aya Sofia, standing on the balcony looking out over so much splendid detail and religious iconography, in the exact spot where I'd stood with my dear old dad, that was my emotional undoing.

Pine Forest
Picnic Knife

I didn't mean to collect knives - it wasn't like my Smash Hits sticker collection in the '80s, where I searched endlessly for the drummer of Haircut 100. In the most basic sense of that most overused word of our times, it happened organically.

My mum bought this knife in a little hardware shop in a forgotten town because we were going to have a picnic and needed a knife. When I look at it now, it's like that bit in *Raiders* where Harrison Ford has to choose the cup that holds the Holy Grail - the cup of a carpenter: compared to some of the other weapons of finery in my collection, it is so basic and really has no home among my professional tools, yet I love it so much because when I look at it and hold it, I'm right back there.

That holiday was one of the last we had as a family, and this simple knife takes me straight back to that uncomfortable picnic on an inconvenient slope in the middle of the biggest pine forest I'd ever seen (pine honey - yum, but steep gradients and picnics are not an ideal pairing, as it's a constant struggle to stop your lunch rolling away).

I don't remember how it came back with us but it's stayed with me for a quarter of a century, slowly getting more battered, wobbly and loved.

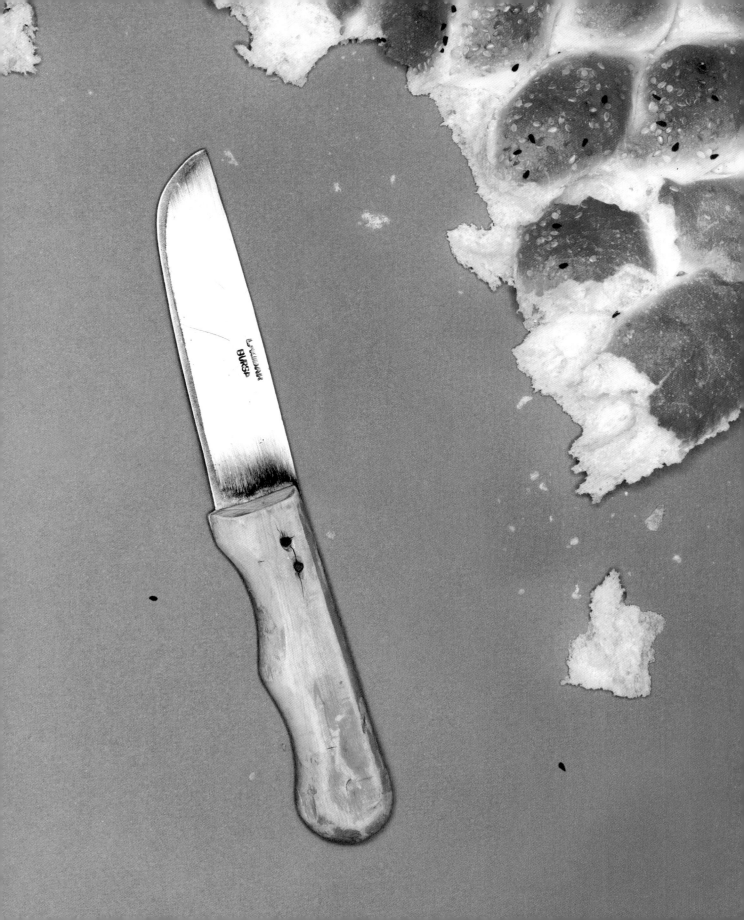

Turkish Recipes

Zeytin Ezmesi
Turkish Tapenade

Çoban Salatası
Shepherd's salad

Fırında Yoğurtlu Ispanak
Spinach & Yoghurt Bake

Patlıcan Kebabı
Lamb & Aubergine Kebabs

Süt Jöle ile İncir
Milk Jelly & Figs

Turkish Tapenade

Makes a smallish bowlful,
and can be thrown together
in 15 minutes

125g/4oz stoned olives (Enver used
black but it's up to you)

30g/1¼oz shelled walnuts

1 clove of garlic, roughly chopped

a couple of pinches of the following
spices: chilli flakes, ground cumin,
ground coriander, dried oregano
and sumac

100ml/3½fl oz extra virgin olive oil

juice of ½ a lemon, or more to taste

20g/¾oz flat-leaf parsley, finely
chopped

salt and pepper

One of the prettiest restaurants we ate at in Istanbul was Asitane,
specializing in old Ottoman cuisine, where the tables are in a little
courtyard, overlooked by the Byzantine Chora mosque. Seeing I was
making all kinds of notes as we ate, the chef, Enver, came out to
chat, had a drink with us and kindly shared his recipe for this rather
different (and I think more interesting) kind of tapenade. According
to him it had eleven spices, but with only the handful I've put in it
you get the general idea.

Great as a snack on toast or crackers, and blinding with fish.

Put the olives, garlic, spices and salt and pepper into a food processor
and whiz briefly to combine. Then add the walnuts and pulse for just a
few seconds so they are left in slightly chunkier pieces.

Scoop it all into a bowl and stir in the oil, lemon juice and parsley.

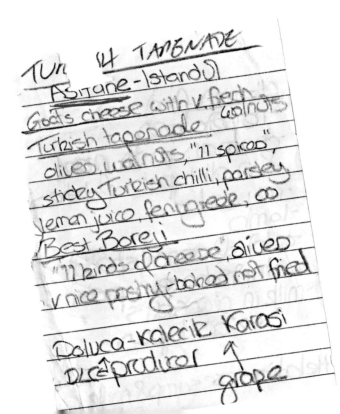

Coban Salata
Shepherd's Salad

Serves 4-6, and takes less than 30 minutes

600g/1lb 2oz good-quality, ripe tomatoes, quartered, seeded and diced small

1 large green pepper, diced small

1 red onion, diced small

2 green chillies, diced small (seeds in or out - up to you)

½ a cucumber, seeds scraped out, diced small

a big handful of flat-leaf parsley, finely chopped

a medium handful of mint, finely chopped

1 fat clove of garlic, finely minced with salt

60g/2½oz stoned olives, roughly chopped

juice of 1 lemon

75ml/3fl oz extra virgin olive oil

100g/3½oz salty sheepy cheese, like feta (very optional)

salt and pepper

The translation of this crunchy, tasty salad betrays its simplicity, though that of course means there's nowhere for bad ingredients to hide: don't bother making it unless you've got good, ripe-smelling tomatoes.

No prizes for seeing the similarity between this and a Greek salad, but don't underestimate the joy of having everything chopped up small.

Mix the tomatoes, pepper, onion, chillies, cucumber, herbs, garlic and olives in a bowl. Season liberally, squeeze over the lemon juice, then drizzle over the oil. Taste to check salt and pepper levels as well as the oil/acidity balance.

Crumble the cheese over the top, if you fancy it, but I've rather come to the conclusion it's better without.

Spinach & Yoghurt Bake

Serves 6 as a side dish, takes
30 minutes to make and a bit less
than that to cook

1kg/2lb whole leaf spinach (or the
same weight of frozen, defrosted)

60ml/2½fl oz extra virgin olive oil

---

3 onions, roughly chopped

---

4 cloves of garlic, sliced

---

1 teaspoon chilli flakes

---

a squeeze of lemon juice

400g/13oz strained yoghurt
(such as Greek, but don't say that
to the Turks)

---

salt and pepper

I'd been to Istanbul before, but on this trip we were shown round by a rambunctious carpet-selling friend of a friend called Ismet. We shared an appetite for good food and good times, and bonded over meals in his favourite places. The people next to us at a really excellent, not at all posh Formica-tabled restaurant called Sefa had a plate of this and it caught my eye. Damn tasty it is too, especially with grilled meats like lamb, chicken and steak.

If you're using fresh spinach, wash it, throwing away any really thick and gnarly stalks.

Heat the oil in a big, wide pan, drop in the onions and put a lid on - you want to soften them without colouring.

After a few minutes, stir in the garlic along with a good pinch of salt, and once you can smell the garlic frying turn the heat up to high and chuck in the spinach in big handfuls, adding more as each batch wilts (and if you are using defrosted stir it in now, along with 200ml/7fl oz water). When it is all in, put on a lid and cook for a few minutes until the spinach has collapsed and heated through. Take the lid off, stir and turn the heat down.

Leave it cooking for another 20 minutes or so, stirring occasionally, until it's a very muted, almost swampy green, and pretty much all the liquid has evaporated (give it a few minutes of hard simmering at the end if necessary to dry it out).

Preheat the oven to 170°C/340°F/gas mark 3½. Taste and season with salt, pepper, half the chilli flakes and some lemon juice.

Turn the spinach into an ovenproof dish (I used an oval dish 20 x 25 x 5cm/ 8 x 10 x 2 inches, so shoot for something roughly that size) and level the surface. Spoon on the yoghurt, spread it evenly and sprinkle with the rest of the chilli flakes.

Bake for 20-25 minutes, until the yoghurt is just set and browning a touch at the edges.

Lamb & Aubergine Kebabs

Makes 2 big ones, and takes less than 30 minutes

2 peppers - your choice on colour
400g/13oz minced lamb
3 cloves of garlic, minced
1 onion, grated and squeezed out
a couple of big pinches of dried mint, crushed chilli flakes and ground cumin
2 slender aubergines, each weighing roughly 250g/8oz, trimmed at each end
2 tomatoes, halved for the barbecue/griddle or quartered into wedges for under the grill
extra virgin olive oil
strained yoghurt to serve (don't call it Greek - that would rightly annoy the Turks)
couple of large flatbreads
salt and pepper

We were in a little pavement restaurant that our friend Ismet had taken us to on a back street in Istanbul, quietly enjoying far and away the best kebab experience I'd had for years, when my food-appreciation bubble was burst by some particularly mad and memorable guitar playing by a man who sang in chicken noises (which, believe it or not, is actually different to singing like a chicken).

In Turkey they use a particular kind of sticky chilli flakes that have been oiled and roasted, definitely worth seeking out next time you're passing, but of course regular chilli flakes do pretty much the same job.

Preheat the grill or get the barbecue good and hot.

Grill the peppers whole, either on the barbecue, directly over the flame of the hob or under the grill, then put them in a bowl covered with clingfilm to cool.

Use your hands to mix the lamb, garlic and onion with the dried mint, chilli, cumin and seasoning. Divide unequally into 4, with 2 of the balls being a bit larger than the others.

Cut each aubergine into 3 pieces, keeping each set of three separate, and season the cut sides of the aubergines. Rebuild each aubergine vertically, as a kind of tower, with the balls of meat interspersed so that the larger one is stuck between the two larger chunks of aubergine. Stick two skewers through each tower and put them under the grill or on the barbecue.

Drizzle the tomatoes with oil and salt, and get them cooking as well, with the cut side directed towards the heat.

The kebabs need to be turned quite frequently and will probably take about 20-25 minutes (get on with peeling those peppers); they are ready when the meat is browned and the aubergine blackened on the outside.

Stir some salt into the yoghurt, drizzle with oil and sprinkle with more chilli flakes.

To eat, scrape the soft aubergine flesh out of the burnt skin, and squish it into softened flatbreads along with the lamb, tomatoes and peppers. Top it off with a splodge of the seasoned yoghurt and get stuck in.

Milk Jelly & Figs

Serves 6, needs about 15 minutes to make and a minimum of 3 hours to set: overnight is safest

---

enough gelatine to firm-set 500ml/17fl oz liquid (should be 5-6 leaves or 15g/½oz, but check the packet)

500ml/17fl oz whole milk

50g/2oz icing sugar

---

1 tablespoon rosewater

---

6 really ripe figs (though if they turn out to be a bit disappointing you can always bake them in a medium oven with a drizzle of honey for 15-20 minutes, to intensify their flavour)

---

honey (optional) - Turkey is famous for its delicious pine honey, so if you've got any honey that is slightly fragrant in the back of the cupboard that you once brought back from holiday, reach for it now ... though of course any will do

---

They're keen on a milk pudding in Turkey, and in fact my first trip there as an thirteen-year-old was totally blown apart by some chronic food poisoning brought on by one such dessert. Bodrum may mean crusader castles and yachting to some, but it has very different memories for my sister and me.

Quarter of a century later I was ready to try again, so in a different part of this amazingly diverse country I ordered this pudding and felt so very fine after it that I had another one. It's a light, sophisticated eat, but has nuances of nursery food, though with a sexy texture (not often you see 'nursery' and 'sexy' in the same sentence, thank God!).

Line a smallish, shallow tray around 18 x 25cm/7 x 10 inches with clingfilm.

Soak the gelatine in cold water. In a small pan, heat the milk until it is steaming then turn the heat off. Whisk the gelatine leaves into the milk one by one, then the icing sugar, then the rosewater, and leave to cool. Pour into the prepared tray and refrigerate overnight or for a few hours until set.

Cut carefully into diamonds (this is easier if you keep them small) and serve with quartered figs, Turkey's national fruit. If, like me, you tend to like a bit of sweetness, you can squiggle honey over if you want.

New York City

When you come into the city from JFK and catch your first glimpse of the Manhattan skyline from the BQE (Brooklyn-Queens Expressway), it's impossible not to get a surge of excitement. Although I've done it so many times now, I still feel that 'whoosh' and a buzz runs through me, just like the first time when as a twenty-six-year-old I'd decided to make this city my new home. I didn't know New York at all - hadn't been there since I was nine - but having done five years in London restaurants I was ready for a change, and it just seemed the right place to go.

So I went over on a covert reckie, as U.S. Immigration doesn't take kindly to folks trying to solicit work in their country. The way I could get round the law was by convincing someone to sponsor me, which it's fair to say involved an amount of bravado that I can't quite believe I was capable of. I'd done a bit of research, talked to some friends and targeted eight restaurants that I thought I'd like to work in. Some just weren't interested, but I did get a few trial shifts both uptown and downtown, the trouble being that once I'd explained to them that they'd have to wade through a fair whack of paperwork from Immigrations they quite reasonably lost interest. But with the kind of luck that youthful confidence seems to generate, one of my top three, the de Niro-owned Tribeca Grill, called me back, and somehow they agreed to jump through all the necessary hoops.

Mission accomplished, I came back home and got busy submitting my 100-page application (a basic work of fiction with the odd grain of truth to hang it on), hassling the restaurant to do their end and my lawyer to do mine before I was at last granted a Type-R visa for being 'an alien of extraordinary ability in the culinary arts'. I passed a truly seminal year and a half in the city, living in Park Slope, Brooklyn with a cool American chick I knew from London called Jodi. Both work and playtime were formative and life-altering experiences: trying to hold my own as sous-chef in the male, Hispanic Tribeca kitchen, which was permanently hysterically busy - 500 covers a night - due to the royalty of the owner, balanced by taking advantage of the best going-out town in the world.

Being an excited stranger in the city I really made the most of what it had to offer, going to concerts and operas in the Lincoln Center, outdoor movies in Madison Square Park, and the Frick became my favourite private art collection in the world.

Having quiet time at the Temple of Dendur in the Met became essential, as did walks round the Cloisters, all the way up beyond 190th Street, that struck a familiar chord with my European upbringing. Having been a fan of pubs for many years, I fell in love with bars: I loved the quiet afternoons of my chosen local, just off Christopher Street, of course, as well as their bawdy jazz-filled evenings. The ethnic restaurants were so much more diverse than London was then, from Latvian to Peruvian via Angolan, all to be explored. Life was a blast, even just the day-to-day stuff like the simple joys of stoop culture: how can a doorstep be so much more fun just because it's in New York?

In my blood; under my skin; written on my bones; captured my heart: pick any and all of these corporeal clichés and that's how I feel about New York. Even if I'm not long back from a visit, I'm already earmarking some month in the not too distant future to return. It's a familiar friend now, albeit one that I have a slightly unhealthy crush on, but flicking back through a diary from my early days there, when I was apartment-less, sofa-hopping, short of old mates and just a touch homesick, I found a pained, slightly paranoid, scrawled note-to-self that says: 'This city can sense your nervousness - don't let it eat you.'

Fact File

Geographical summary: Located on the Eastern Atlantic coast, at the mouth of the Hudson River. Comprises five boroughs, Brooklyn, Queens, the Bronx, Staten Island and Manhattan, separated by various waterways including the Harlem, Hudson and East rivers. Central Park is 341 hectares (843 acres) and the city has more skyscrapers than any other in the world.

Population: 8.4 million.

Religion: Hard to get exact data on this one, but broadly speaking approximately 40% Catholic, the next biggest group is Jewish, and Protestants come in at around 10%.

Ethnic make-up: This also isn't straightforward: 98% of the city population self-defines as being of one race: half white, quarter Black or African American, 12% Asian and the rest from all over the place. HOWEVER, of the total city population, 27% report as Hispanic/Latino, and they may be of any race, i.e. some of the folks who define themselves as white might also be Hispanic/Latino, and the same applies to crossover of the other groups. Hey, it's New York, so this one was never going to be simple.

Life expectancy: 76 male, 82 female.

External influences: The Dutch settled first, then of course it was Brit territory for a while, but the New York of now is the culmination of influences from so many world cultures … and that's part of what makes the magic.

The essentials of their cooking: They don't cook at home much: generally everything is eaten out, to go or delivered. But once you're on the streets they have it all, from greasy to goodness, fine dining to hotdog stalls, and there's a restaurant from just about everywhere in the world.

Top 5 favourite ingredients: Beef (burgers, steaks, salt beef), cinnamon, shrimp, bagels, kosher pickles (made with kosher salt).

Most famous dish: Hotdog or burger … hard call.

What to drink: Coffee by the pint (iced in summer), proper cocktails (the city runs on vodka and everyone orders by brand name), pissy beer and alcohol-free cider (who knew!).

Best thing I ate: A dish of foie gras with a tasting of world salts at Thomas Keller's restaurant, Per Se.

Most breathtaking moment: The first time I walked over the Brooklyn Bridge, entering Manhattan via that great Gothic gateway, mesmerized by the geometric shapes that the cables threw.

Don't ask for…: A friendly face on the subway.

Artisanal Heels & Arches

I bought these two some five years apart - the smaller one was the first, but I enjoyed it so much, particularly its gently arcing back, that on another visit to the city I picked up a second one. This time I chose one which, being longer, accentuated this curve even more, as well as having a completely killer heel. I love a good heel on a knife, need it in fact, and this is the handsomest in my set.

As I've said elsewhere in this book, the more metropolitan the city, the harder it is to find a knife of character, as everyone gets all obsessed with the big, flashy brands. But as soon as I saw this, it was quite clearly the work of a craftsman: the chap responsible for these hand-forged beauties is a blacksmith by trade and an ex-farrier to boot, with a suitably grizzly beard for a bloke whose best friend is an anvil.

Michael Moses Lishinsky operates under the name Wildfire Cutlery - note the initials on the blade, and even though I bought them in New York (extraordinarily at the back of Dean & Deluca) he works out of Oregon. Like all proper artisans he's had no regard for shortcuts or modern whims, and instead has simply gone out to make the best tools he can. All his knives are full tang, which means the metal from the blade extends all the way through to the heel, making them much stronger.

Most unusually the knife is made of heat-treated carbon steel, not the omnipresent and more convenient rustproof stainless, so you have to dry it after every use (and I tend to oil mine too), but for that small must, you get the benefit of a knife that stays much sharper for longer. Below the generous, sturdy brass bolster the eco-harvested rosewood handle is finished with olive oil. It's incredibly smooth and sexy to hold, darkening over time with the natural oils in your skin, which is why my smaller one is further down the line. There are two kinds of discreet, flush rivets, and don't miss the bit of fancy footwork in the bottom one, just as a quiet little show-off of how well he knows his craft. Great job, Michael.

FAIRWAY

"LIKE NO OTHER MARKET"

CATERING
PARTY PLATTERS

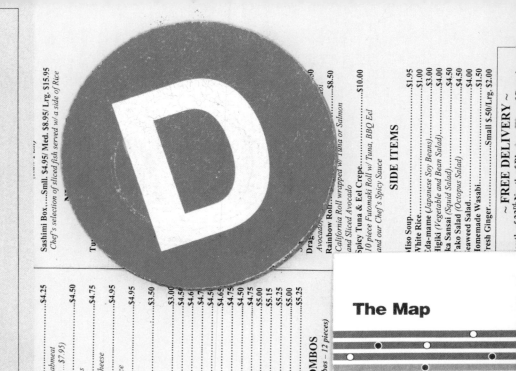

Sashimi Box.....Sml. $4.95/ Med. $8.95/ Lrg. $15.95
Chef's selection of sliced fish served w/ a side of Rice

Rainbow Roll................................$8.50

Drag
Avocado
Rainbow Roll
California Roll wrapped w/ Tuna or Salmon
and Sliced Avocado
Spicy Tuna & Eel Crepe..................$10.00
10 piece Futomaki Roll w/ Tuna, BBQ Eel
and our Chef's Spicy Sauce

SIDE ITEMS
Miso Soup	$1.95
White Rice	$1.00
Eda-mame (Japanese Soy Beans)	$3.00
Higiki (Vegetable and Bean Salad)	$4.00
Tako Sansai (Squid Salad)	$4.50
Tako Salad (Octopus Salad)	$4.50
Seaweed Salad	$4.00
Homemade Wasabi	$1.50
Fresh Ginger	Small $.50/Lrg. $2.00

~ **FREE DELIVERY** ~

$4.25
$4.50
$4.75
$4.95
$4.95
$3.50
$3.00
$4.6
$4.7
$4.5
$4.65
$4.75
$4.50
$4.75
$5.00
$5.15
$5.25
$5.00
$5.25

Crabmeat
...($7.95)

Cheese

COMBOS
Combos – 12 pieces

The Map

To Hudson Falls

SHELL

New York

Featuring Metropolitan and Downtown New York
City • Albany • Buffalo • Niagara Falls • Rochester
Schenectady • Syracuse • Troy • Utica

857 5721

ry Frank's

Where to
Hit, Buy it,
Eat it
in
York

THE
BEST
HOT
DOG
IN
Newyork

thor

POLITE
NEW YORKER

Gray's Papaya

E 46787481 E

5 B 5

THE UNITED STATES

ONE DOLLAR

KATZ'S§
DELICATESSEN®
205 E. HOUSTON ST.
NEW YORK, N.Y. 10002

SHIPPING

Visit our w

ARE YOU THINK
WE SHIP HARD S
PHONE OF
WE ACCEPT VISA, M
"SEND A SALAMI T

SALAMI — $9.15/lb.   sizes: 2, 3 and 5 lb.
HARD SALAMI — $14.15/lb.   sizes: 1.5, 2.5, 3.5 lb.
(sold by weight/sizes are approximate)
KNOBLEWURST/GARLIC SAUSAGE — $9.15/lb.
(average size of each ring is 1.5 lb)
SPECIALS/KN
WHOLE PIECE
WHOLE PIECE
size: u
SLICED PASTRA
RYE BREAD —
OR TURK
ASSORTED PIC
KNISHES — Po
Broccoli, Spina
FRANKFURTE
CHEESECAKE
CHOCOLATE
CHOCOLATE
TRAY OF MINI
NOVA SCOTIA
Only SALAMI ar
be shipped eith
Everything else
the weight of th

delivery orders during peak hours.

Gift Certificates Available

WEIGHT
2 lbs.
additional lbs.
(approx.)

Mugs

NYC RECIPES

PEANUT BUTTER PROTEIN SHAKE

BRUNCH HASH

OATY BUTTERMILK PANCAKES

THE REUBEN

JEAN'S HOT ARTICHOKE DIP

GREEN APPLE & CHICORY SLAW
WITH BLUE CHEESE DRESSING

HOW TO SALT BEEF

PUMPKIN & GINGER DOUGHNUTS

WE ARE HAPPY
TO SERVE YOU

The Unicorn Tape

a Tart...

NEW YORK

Berkshire Berries

Peanut Butter Protein Shake

Makes 2 big boosting glasses in about 3 minutes

2 small bananas (or one big)

50g/2oz natural whey protein

6 tablespoons peanut butter

4 tablespoons Greek yoghurt

400ml/14fl oz semi-skimmed milk

a handful of ice

New Yorkers love a supplement: whole chains of shops are devoted to them, and they even sell little baggies of pep-up pills next to the gum at checkouts. As a rule, I'm against them, as I think you should be able to get everything you need from a decent diet, but my chef friend Ethan made this for me when I was very pregnant on the grounds that it would be good for me (i.e. the baby).

The reason I've included it is not only because it reflects how people really eat (which is what this book is all about), but also because I think it tastes great even if you're not pregnant.

You can also make it with ice cream instead of the skimmed milk, but this is the healthier version.

Put all the ingredients into a blender and blitz until smooth and frothy.

Brunch Hash

Serves 4, and takes around 30 minutes

500g/1lb potatoes (i.e. 2 large ones), diced

3 tablespoons light oil

2 tablespoons butter

2 onions, diced 2.5cm/1 inch square

4 really thick slices of salt beef*, weighing about 75g/3oz each, large diced or roughly broken into big pieces

1-2 tablespoons Dijon mustard, to taste

a big handful of flat-leaf parsley, chopped

4 medium cooked beetroot (about 200g/7oz), diced

4 spring onions, sliced

4 eggs

a good pinch of chilli flakes

salt and pepper

*If you're really good you will have made your own - see page 41.

This, or something like it but a bit greasier, was the first thing I ate when I went on my illegal job-hunting mission to New York. I'd met up with an old buddy who took me for breakfast in this tiny little joint on Second Avenue, just to the left of the theatre where Stomp has been playing for decades. It's really just a greasy spoon, run by Egyptians, but I'll never forget how unfeasibly exciting it was sitting at cramped stools at the bar, just a couple of feet away from the brusque short-order cook flipping his homefries and shouting in a heavy accent about eggs easy over or sunny-side up. I was hooked.

This is one of the yummiest brunch dishes out there: such a quick and easy cook - I dare you to make a hash of it!

Cover the potatoes with cold salted water, put on a high heat and bring to the boil, then simmer until almost tender and drain.

While the spuds are cooking, heat half the oil with half the butter in a large, heavy pan and fry the onions over a medium heat until they are softening and starting to brown. Chuck in the drained potatoes, add the rest of the oil, turn the heat up to maximum, and fry for a few more minutes, until the potatoes are just starting to pick up some colour.

Season, stir in the beef, mustard and parsley and lastly add the beetroot, turning it in carefully so as to avoid everything going pink. Once the beetroot is warm - just a minute or two - turn the heat off and stir in the spring onions.

Fry the eggs in the rest of the butter, then season and sprinkle with chilli flakes. Divide the hash into 4 portions and put an egg on top of each.

Oaty Buttermilk Pancakes

'Enough for 4 big appetites', says Dorian. Knock up the batter in 5, leave to rest overnight then allow 15 minutes in the morning to finish it all off

240g/7¾oz plain flour

1 teaspoon bicarbonate of soda

1 teaspoon baking powder

1 tablespoon sugar

a pinch of salt

1 large egg

500ml/17fl oz buttermilk (or 500ml/17fl oz milk mixed with 2 tablespoons lemon juice)

150g/5oz porridge oats

2 tablespoons unsalted butter, melted

light oil, for greasing

8-12 rashers streaky bacon (unsmoked), grilled until crispy

1 punnet of blueberries

maple syrup, for pouring

As a Sunday treat my lovely flatmate Jodi would make us breakfast from a very battered book called *Pancakes* by Dorian Leigh Parker. The author said it was her father's recipe that she used to make at college in the 1930s, which may explain why there is a bit more integrity and substance to the pancakes, as opposed to the fluffy ones usually served these days. I find those modern American pancakes a bit dull, really just a sweet sponge for oceans of maple syrup, but these, by contrast, are filling and substantial - a proper start to the day.

You can get buttermilk in most supermarkets, but you can also make it by mixing 2 tablespoons of lemon juice into 500ml/17fl oz of milk and leaving it for 5 minutes.

This recipe involves a rest overnight, which is perfect if you don't have much time in the morning; you can just get up and start cooking. Once made, the batter keeps for 3 days.

In a big bowl stir together the flour, bicarbonate of soda, baking powder, sugar and salt. Separately whisk the egg and buttermilk, then add the wet ingredients to the flour mixture and stir to combine, then refrigerate overnight.

When you're ready to get going, fold the oats and melted butter into the batter with as few strokes as possible - it doesn't matter if there are a few streaks of butter left. Choose a thick-bottomed frying pan, skillet or griddle and lightly grease it. Make sure the pan is hot before you pour in the batter, but keep the flame underneath gentle.

Use a ladle to scoop in the batter - one holding about 4 tablespoons or 60ml/2½fl oz makes a good-sized pancake - and cook in batches. The first side is done when big bubbles appear on the surface and the pancake looks set around the edges - it will take around 3 minutes and should be golden-brown underneath. Flip them over and cook the other side for a similar amount of time. Serve immediately, with grilled bacon, blueberries and maple syrup. (If you want to keep the pancakes hot while you make the others you can put them into a warm oven, but they're a bit more magic straight from the pan.)

The Reuben

To make a sandwich you need about 10 minutes and ...

several slices of corned/salt beef*

2 slices of bread, preferably rye, lightly toasted

butter

American mustard

a big dollop of sauerkraut, water squeezed out of it and then warmed

a few slices of Emmenthal/Swiss cheese

a dill pickle, sliced

*Which you can either buy or do the right thing and make your own, see page 41

I'd never heard of a Reuben when I arrived in New York, but I'd go as far as to say that now I couldn't live without them. They may not be my death row meal, but they're definitely my desert island sandwich. Try it with thinly sliced pickled onions, too.

As the Croque Monsieur is to France, so is the Reuben to New York. Here's what goes into it - it's up to you to balance these ingredients as you like.

Preheat the grill to hot.

Warm the beef through, either under the warming grill or in a frying pan over a medium heat with a couple of tablespoons of water.

Spread 1 piece of toast with butter and the other with mustard. Pile the meat on the buttered toast, followed by sauerkraut, then Emmenthal.

Grill until the cheese has melted and then top with pickle and the other piece of toast. You must cut it in half to see its inner beauty.

Jean's Hot Artichoke Dip

Makes a medium bowlful, and is thrown together in 10ish minutes, then from there it's a 35 minute cook

---

250g/8oz cooked artichoke hearts (from the deli counter/jar in oil - tinned tend to be very watery)

40g/1½oz Parmesan, coarsely grated

---

1 clove of garlic, peeled and chopped

---

2 eggs, beaten

200ml/7fl oz double cream

¼ teaspoon cayenne

½ teaspoon celery salt

---

juice of ½ a lemon

---

a handful of finely chopped parsley

---

pepper

I was one of two women in the thirty-strong brigade of Tribeca Grill, the other being a young Mormon commis from Salt Lake City called Jean. We did time together on the line, being a source of support to each other through all the Hispanic male banter.

I left and we lost touch, but recently I was reading up on the hot new restaurants in NYC and I was chuffed to see that one of them, Vinegar Hill House in Brooklyn, was hers. I belled her up, we got together, and she let slip this recipe, saying it was going down a storm with her patrons. This is fantastic party food, in a keys-in-the-bowl '70s way.

Preheat the oven to 180°C/350°F/gas mark 4. Put the artichokes, Parmesan and garlic into a food processor and blitz roughly to an uneven chunky paste. Break in the eggs and blitz again, very briefly - just a few seconds. Finally add the cream, cayenne, celery salt, lemon juice and pepper and pulse once or twice more, trying to keep the texture as rough as possible.

Butter a soufflé dish (roughly 15 x 8cm/6 x 3 inches). Pour into the dish and put it in the oven for 35-40 minutes until golden brown and slightly domed on top but still a little wobbly in the middle. Serve with/on small toasts or crackers, sprinkled with chopped parsley.

Apple & Chicory Slaw with Pecans & Blue Cheese Dressing

Serves 6-8, and takes 20 minutes

100g/3½oz Gorgonzola (piccante not dolce, if anyone asks)

---

4 tablespoons crème fraîche

---

juice of ½ a lemon

3-4 bulbs of chicory, sliced

---

2 Granny Smith apples, quartered, cored and sliced

75g/3oz pecan nuts, lightly toasted and roughly chopped

---

a big handful of dried cranberries

---

pepper

We used to do a slaw like this at Tribeca Grill, and it just sums up American salads: a creamy slaw with lots of crunch and a cheesy dressing, partnered with their national nut and favourite dried berry. Not as healthy, it's true, as a vinaigrette dressing but very easy eating and proteinous, too.

Once cut, both the apple and the chicory will oxidize and go brown pretty quickly, so if you're making it ahead of time, keep them in iced water and only dress just before serving as they will lose their bite.

Whiz or beat together the cheese, crème fraîche and lemon juice with a good grinding of black pepper. Add enough water so that you have a mixture with the consistency of double cream (about 50ml/2fl oz).

Toss the chicory, apples, nuts and cranberries (saving a few of these last two for the top) lightly with the dressing, as you want the colours to still come through. Finish with the last of the pecans and berries on top.

How to Salt Beef

Makes around 12 generous slices. Takes naff-all work to get it going, then 1 week brining followed by 4 hours simmering

---

1.8kg/3½lb piece of silverside (though brisket is also commonly used) and I'd bother to get it from a butcher

---

For the brine

450g/14½oz salt beef cure pre-mix (which is 10g/⅓oz sodium nitrite, then 175g/5oz white sugar and 275g/9oz table salt)

10 cloves

6 allspice berries or ½ teaspoon ground allspice

a small handful of black peppercorns

2 tablespoons coriander seeds

2 tablespoons mustard seeds

a few bay leaves

6-8 cloves of garlic, crushed with the side of a knife

90g/3¼oz soft brown sugar

For the cooking liquid

2 onions, peeled and halved

2 large carrots, cut into big chunks

7 bay leaves, broken up

1 teaspoon caraway seeds, roughly broken up in a pestle and mortar

½ tablespoon peppercorns, roughly cracked with the side of a knife

---

Salt beef and corned beef are the same thing, so named because the salt used to come in little pellets known as 'corns' and were a way to make the meat last longer without going off. The traditional preservative used was sodium nitrate (aka saltpetre) but nowadays it's hard to get hold of because it can be used to make explosives, and its common replacement is sodium nitrite. The reality is that you don't really have to use either, but firstly your meat won't last as long, and secondly it won't be an appealing pinky colour, but browny-grey. I'll leave that one with you, but from experience the easiest thing to do is buy the cure mix all together (I've used www.weschenfelder.co.uk in the past), though of course if you can get hold of sodium nitrite you can make your own.

The other question not in the title is 'Why to Salt Beef'. Well, it's a satisfying, easy process that makes a very economical and pride-inducing result ... but if you really need me to talk you into it this recipe is not for you.

Put the cure mix (or the individual components) into a large pan with 2 litres/3½ pints of water, the cloves and ground allspice if using. Put all the other whole spices into a mortar, including the whole allspice berries, then smash them roughly and briefly with the pestle and chuck into the pan. Scrunch in the bay leaves, add the garlic and sugar, and bring quickly up to the boil with a lid on, then turn off the heat and leave to cool.

Once completely cooled, soak the beef in the brine for a week, turning a couple of times. On the allotted day of readiness, rinse it well and soak in fresh water for 1 hour, changing the water a couple of times until it stops tasting salty.

Now move the beef into a large pan, cover with fresh cold water, put a lid on the pan and bring to the boil. Give it a good skim, add the onions, carrots, bay, caraway and peppercorns, and turn the heat right down to minimum. The beef should be cooked for about 4 hours - so gently that there are no bubbles - with the lid on throughout. Keep it submerged in liquid during cooking, topping up with boiling water if necessary.

Cool in the water, then drain, and it's up to you if you want to weight it and press it overnight: makes it much easier to slice thinly, but this isn't a New York deli, and flaky, chunky slices are more real-looking to my eye.

Pumpkin & Ginger Doughnuts

Makes about 20 and takes
1 hour 30 minutes (including a
30 minute break for rising time)

150ml/¼ pint whole milk

5 teaspoons (15g/½oz) fast-acting
dried yeast

100g/3½oz sugar, plus 1 teaspoon
extra

1kg/2lb plain flour, plus extra for
kneading and rolling

1 tin (460g/14¾oz or thereabouts) of
mashed pumpkin (or make your own by
roasting 650g (1¼ lb) peeled pumpkin
or squash, foiled, in a medium oven
for 40 minutes, then mashing it)

½ teaspoon ground cinnamon

½ teaspoon salt

1 egg, beaten

4 tablespoons melted butter

2 tablespoons plain oil (groundnut,
veg, sunflower)

1-1.5 litres (1¾ - 2½ pints) oil, for
frying

For the glaze

a knob (around 1 teaspoon) butter

75ml/3fl oz milk

175g/6oz icing sugar

1½ teaspoons ground ginger

75g/3oz ginger, washed and unpeeled

½ teaspoon vanilla extract

The second time I lived in New York I rented an apartment in a big tenement block on the Lower East Side, in the old Jewish neighbourhood. It always smelt of chicken soup, which I find a comforting smell and was the reason I took the flat, but the minute you stepped outside the air was filled with a different kind of yum. Just round the corner was the fantastic Donut Factory, and as Hallowe'en is a very big deal over there they did these as a special.

Heat the milk gently until it's just warm to the touch, then whisk in the yeast and the 1 teaspoon of sugar and leave to stand for 20 minutes, until frothy.

In a large bowl mix the flour, pumpkin (or squash), cinnamon, salt and sugar, then pour in the yeast mixture, beaten egg, melted butter and the oil then bring it all together to make a soft dough. Turn out on to a well-floured surface and knead with floured hands for about 5 minutes, adding more flour as necessary so that it doesn't stick to you or the surface.

Roll out the dough to a thickness of about 2cm/¾ inch and use two circular cutters, one with a diameter of 8cm/3½ inches and one with a diameter of 4cm/1¾ inches, to make your rings. Use the trimmings to re-roll, then leave them to rise for 30 minutes.

Knock up the glaze by melting the butter in the milk and whisking in the icing sugar, ground ginger and vanilla extract. Coarsely grate the ginger root and squeeze the juice into it too - you can re-use the fibres for tea/hot toddies.

Pour the oil into a wide, thick-bottomed pan to a depth of about 2.5-3cm/1-1¼ inches. Heat it up until hot but not nearly smoking, then turn the heat down to medium. Slide one of the doughnuts in first, just to check the temperature is right: it should fizzle and float up to the surface, very gently bubbling away. Cook them in batches for 5-7 minutes total, turning halfway through so they are evenly golden brown all over, then take them out with tongs or a slotted spoon and put them on a wire rack.

When they're cool enough to pick up, dip them into the glaze on both sides and tuck in not long after: there's not many ills in the world that can't be cured with a warm doughnut.

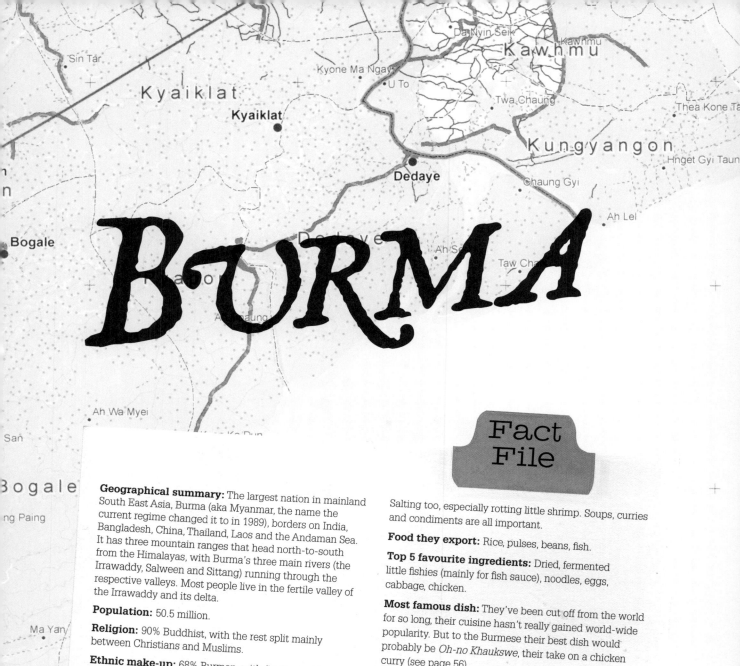

BURMA

Fact File

Geographical summary: The largest nation in mainland South East Asia, Burma (aka Myanmar, the name the current regime changed it to in 1989), borders on India, Bangladesh, China, Thailand, Laos and the Andaman Sea. It has three mountain ranges that head north-to-south from the Himalayas, with Burma's three main rivers (the Irrawaddy, Salween and Sittang) running through the respective valleys. Most people live in the fertile valley of the Irrawaddy and its delta.

Population: 50.5 million.

Religion: 90% Buddhist, with the rest split mainly between Christians and Muslims.

Ethnic make-up: 68% Burman, with (in descending order) Shan, Karen, Rakhine, Chinese, Indian and Mon making up nearly all of the remainder.

Life expectancy: 62 male, 67 female.

External influences: British in three stages throughout the 19th century, during which time large numbers of Indians were brought in to work as civil servants, and Chinese were encouraged to immigrate and stimulate trade.

The essentials of their cooking: Wok-like pans over fires on the ground for simmering and frying. Lots of salads.

Salting too, especially rotting little shrimp. Soups, curries and condiments are all important.

Food they export: Rice, pulses, beans, fish.

Top 5 favourite ingredients: Dried, fermented little fishies (mainly for fish sauce), noodles, eggs, cabbage, chicken.

Most famous dish: They've been cut off from the world for so long, their cuisine hasn't really gained world-wide popularity. But to the Burmese their best dish would probably be *Oh-no Khaukswe*, their take on a chicken curry (see page 56).

What to drink: Mandalay beer, lots of water.

Best thing I ate: Weirdly I had my first taste of caviar in Burma, at colonial favourite The Strand Hotel in Rangoon. When I looked on the bottom of the tin it was six months out of date, but it still tasted great to me!

Most breathtaking moment: Without a shadow of a doubt looking out over the 10,000 stupas scattered over the site of Pagan.

Don't Ask For…: A free election.

Through all the bad press it gets, it's easy to forget that Burma is a truly beautiful country. I went as my father's companion with my uncle and aunt, so it wasn't so much with my youthful revolutionary hat on as a middle-class sightseer. Apart from a couple of nights in Yangon, or Rangoon as we call it, most of the trip was spent cruising upstream from the ancient capital Pagan past Mandalay to Bhamo, which is just 25 miles due west of the Chinese border.

We were travelling on a magnificent old pandaw, Scottish-built in 1946 for the Irrawaddy Flotilla Company, which had been slowly decomposing in a Rangoon boatyard until its restoration to its former glory just a year before we took our trip. It felt like good old colonialism at its best, not least because I was the youngest person on the boat by some thirty years - most of my fellow travellers were old boys with their wives, revisiting places they'd served in during the war. Partly because of this wartime connection, complete with colonial undertones, and partly because after the military coup of '62 the new government closed down the borders, the whole trip really did feel of a bygone age. I've been to much poorer places but never to anywhere so unaffected by the rest of the world, which gave it a very weird but serene timelessness.

The Irrawaddy is the main artery and provides a central core of activity, in the way that the Nile does in Egypt, but it is also sacred, like the Ganges is in India. Travelling up it at a sedate pace was the most wonderful way to view how the rural Burmese live, as well as the ever-changing, breathtaking landscapes. It's been a Buddhist country for 2,000 years, and as well as the constant smiling presence of lads as young as four done up in burgundy-coloured monk's garb, the main feature of their fervour was an extraordinary number of temples and stupas. Some were newly whitewashed and painted, some made from bricks and clay, and a handful were brilliantly gold-leafed, catching the sun resplendently for all to see.

As we pottered up the river we took in the little towns and villages that have been untouched by the modern world, on occasion visiting a craft workshop (they're big on baskets and pottery), or elephant logging, or going to have a look at a school (their hoopy, circular alphabet makes ours look so angular and unfriendly), or the market ... and inevitably a stupa or two. My favourite was the cheroot factory ... apart from the very young girls rolling the tobacco leaves in near dark conditions for God knows how many hours. We saw a lot of child labour, but having said that, the kids were pretty smiley and looked healthy, blissfully unaware of their right to an education or even to playtime.

And the hours in between were spent peacefully watching life on the river. Huge rafts of logs being transported downstream, with huts built on them so they looked like little floating villages; exotic flowers and brightly coloured birds; villagers washing and children playing in the river; fishermen with their baskets in the water full of catch; majestic, pointy stupas; all against the backdrop of dramatic dawns and thrilling sunsets.

Life on the Irrawaddy really did feel like such a step back in time that Kipling himself might have been in the next cabin to us when he wrote:

Come you back to Mandalay,
Where the old Flotilla lay:
Can't you 'ear their paddles chunkin'
*   from Rangoon to Mandalay?*
On the road to Mandalay,
Where the flyin'-fishes play,
An' the dawn comes up like thunder
*   outer China 'crost the Bay!*

I can't say this was the first knife that I brought back from a foreign country, but I can say it's the one that started my obsession. The picnic knife from Turkey was technically the first, but I don't recall making any real efforts to gain it or get it back, it just kind of somehow came with us.

But this mighty machete was different. We were right up by second defile at a little village and I saw this fine blade hanging in an open-sided shack that passed for the local ironmonger's. A fair amount of disbelieving eye-narrowing went down before the deal was done, and from his toothsome smile afterwards, I have a feeling he did well, which is all right and proper as far as I'm concerned. And then it was all mine to bring back through customs.

I have to say that although size isn't everything, this beauty is very impressive ... two foot long and heavy, too. I guess from the agricultural terrain we were in that its primary use was crop-hacking, but it could easily be for slaughtering and I'd be none the wiser. At that time I hadn't honed my brief down to knives of a culinary nature only, so no rules broken there.

It's the utilitarian homemadeness that really appeals: it came from a place where a tool is just a means to an end, nothing more - it has no airs and graces. There are little bungs driven down between the body of the blade and handle bolster to keep it firm; the eye at the top for hanging it up is pure genius - all knives should have one! - and there are metal cuffs at the top and bottom of the handle, so no tricky rivets required. Finally, for the personal touch, there are even a couple of words in that extraordinary circular, loopy language of theirs on one side that I'm told translate as 'Win's Special', Win being the craftsman's name, and Special being how he felt about it. Me too.

But in truth what I love most is that it reminds me of the last big trip I did with my dad, and of what a kind and understanding father he was to indulge his non-conformist daughter by purchasing such a thing. Little did he know that by doing so he had let me loose down a path that would lead me on so many adventures all over the world, and indeed eventually to the publication of this book.

'Win's Special'

BURMESE MACHETE

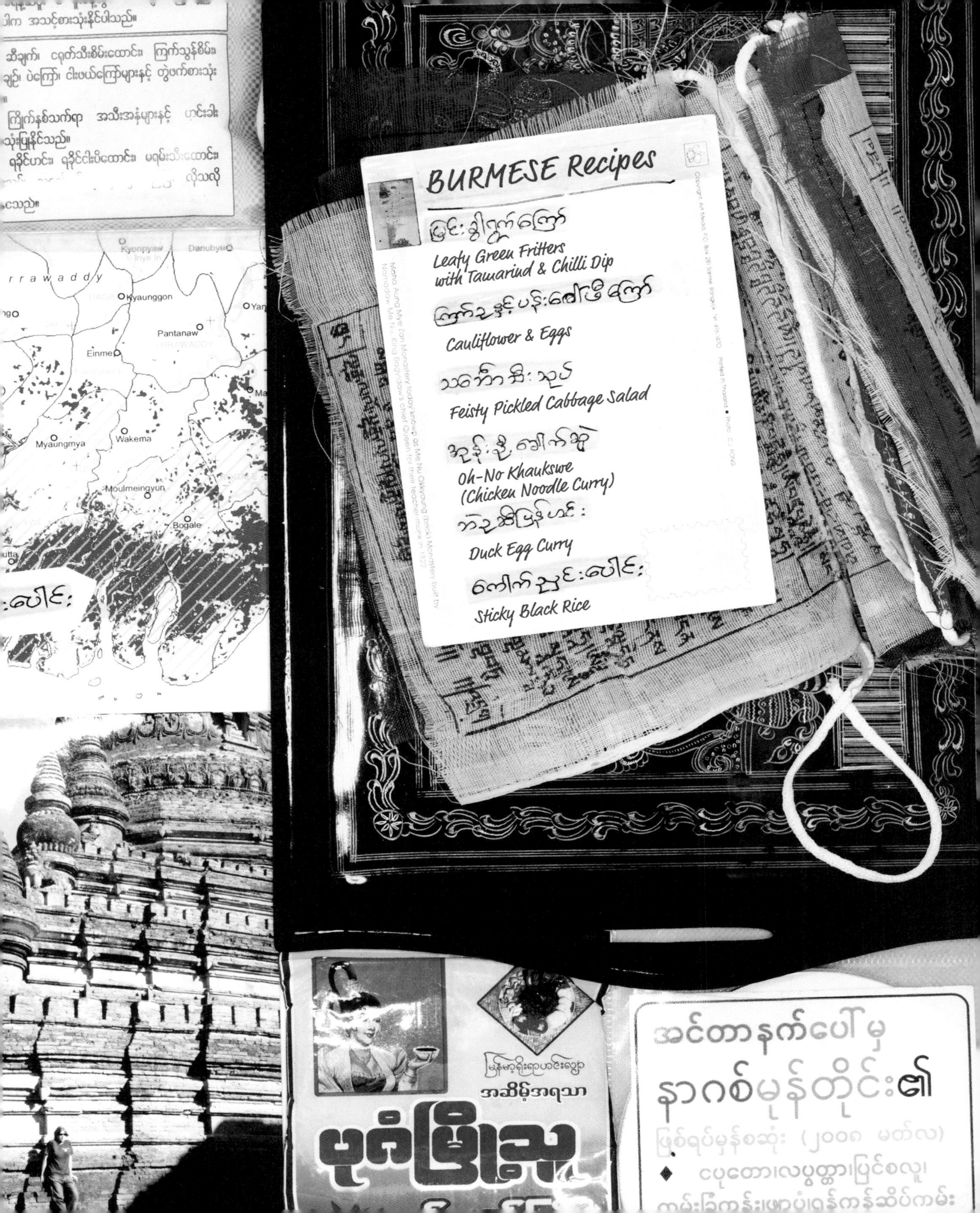

BURMESE Recipes

ြင်း ချို့ကွက်ကြော်

*Leafy Green Fritters
with Tamarind & Chilli Dip*

ကြာဇံနှင့် ပန်းဆောင်ဖီ ကြော်

Cauliflower & Eggs

သေက်ာ စီး သုပ်

Feisty Pickled Cabbage Salad

အုန်း နို့ ခေါက်ဆွဲ

*Oh-No Khaukswe
(Chicken Noodle Curry)*

ဘဲ ဥ စိမ်း ြပုတ် ဟင်း

Duck Egg Curry

ကောက် ညှင်း ပေါင်း

Sticky Black Rice

Leafy Green Fritters with Tamarind & Chilli Dip

Makes 10 fritters,
and takes 15 minutes prep
and 15 minutes to cook

For the batter

75g/3oz flour, preferably gram, but plain will do

200g/7oz plain yoghurt

½ teaspoon turmeric

½ teaspoon ground coriander

½ teaspoon salt

For the dip

2 tablespoons tamarind paste or syrup

½ teaspoon fish sauce

1 round shallot, very finely diced

a handful of coriander, with stalks, finely chopped

juice of ½ a lime

1 large green chilli, seeds and ribs in, diced tiny

1 litre/1¾ pints groundnut oil

250g/8oz leafy greens, like bok choi or pak choi, with stalks, washed and cut just a couple of times into rough 5cm/2 inch pieces

One evening our boat moored at a village, or maybe even a town (it's hard to tell after dark when there's no electricity and you arrive by boat), and I jumped ship looking for a place a girl could get a beer. Suffice to say, no such place existed for women, foreign or not, so I settled outside a café on a box-stool on the dirt road and ordered some tea.

At the next box arrangement a group of men were eating something fried and I used the international language of 'I'll have some of that please' to investigate further. This, or something like it once I'd taken apart the flavours, is what arrived. Basically it's the cousin of an onion bhaji, but more interesting and less greasy.

Tamarind really is a trick worth keeping in your fridge: it lasts for ever and brings a rich, fruity sourness to many a dish. You can buy it in supermarkets now in the form of a treacle-like syrup, or from ethnic shops in block form, either with or without seeds (though it's much easier to use without). To make the block into a paste, just pick out any seeds and mix well with a couple of tablespoons of hot water, squishing it with the back of a spoon, or whiz in the spice grinder until it's smooth.

Mix the batter ingredients together in a large bowl and whisk with around 3 tablespoons of warm water to make a thick, smooth batter.

In a separate bowl, stir together all the ingredients for the dip, and add a little water if it's a bit firm; it depends on the kind of tamarind used - you'll probably need to if you started with the block form.

Heat the oil in a wide (20cm/8 inch), thick-bottomed pan of at least 5cm/2 inch depth on a low to medium heat.

Briefly dry the greens, then throw them into the batter, giving it all a good stir so that the batter becomes like a sticky binding. Test the temperature of the oil by scooping a small amount of the mix into a spoon then use your fingertip to slide it into the pan. If it sinks, the oil is not hot enough. If it comes up to the surface and fizzles immediately, it's ready.

Once the oil is OK, load up a dessertspoon with the mix and do what you did before, repeating till you have 5 of them in there (or as many as your pan fits comfortably). Fry for 4-5 minutes, turning over once or twice, until golden brown, then drain on kitchen paper whilst you get the rest of them going. Sprinkle with a touch of salt and serve with the dip.

Cauliflower & Eggs

Serves 4 as a side, and is on the table in 15 minutes

---

1 medium head of cauliflower

2 tablespoons light oil, like peanut

1 small onion, thickly sliced

1 tablespoon soy sauce

3 eggs, beaten with a little water

a big handful of chives or spring onions, chopped/sliced

salt and pepper

Deliciously unfancy and uncomplicated, which makes it a great side to a dish of curry and rice, but I've also really enjoyed this for breakfast (and if you think that sounds odd, my wife's favourite breakfast is broccoli on toast).

Cut the cauliflower into florets, put them in a bowl, cover with cold water and leave to soak.

Heat the oil in a wok or a wide frying pan and fry the onion until just softened. Drain but don't dry the cauliflower and chuck it in, along with the soy sauce.

Toss over a high heat for a few minutes until it is dry, then add 3 tablespoons of hot water and cover. Cook a little longer, until the cauliflower is nearly tender, then take off the lid and pour in the eggs.

Season and stir for a minute until the eggs have set, then sprinkle over the chives or spring onions and add a splash more soy, to taste.

Tin-Baw-Thee Thoat
Feisty Pickled Cabbage Salad with Crispy Shallots

Serves 4 over a relaxed and fulfilling 30ish minutes

125ml/4fl oz rice wine vinegar

2 tablespoons sugar

3 bird's-eye chillies, seeds in and sliced

350g/11½oz fresh white cabbage (as opposed to one that's been in the back of the veg drawer for months), cut into thickish slices

500ml/17fl oz groundnut/veg oil, for deep-frying

2 big banana shallots, sliced into rings about 1cm/½ inch wide

a small handful of plain flour

3 spring onions, sliced diagonally

⅓ of a cucumber, diced

a handful of mint, roughly chopped

a big handful of peanuts, finely chopped

salt

My dad and I ate this in a little restaurant in Rangoon entirely lit by candles (there had been a power cut) and directly opposite the longest reclining Buddha you could imagine - easily the length of a football pitch, with inscriptions on the soles of his gigantic feet. He was housed in what looked like a makeshift corrugated iron open-sided shed, but even in such inauspicious surroundings he emanated calm, beauty, and strength. Very moving and magical, especially all twinkly with tea-lights.

It was too hot for my dad (the salad, not the temperature), but I liked it. Who knew a cabbage-based salad could be quite so interesting...

Put the vinegar into a wide pan over a high heat and add 60ml/2½fl oz of water, the sugar, chillies and a big pinch of salt. Put on the lid and bring to the boil.

Drop in the cabbage, replace the lid and bring back to the boil. As soon as it begins to bubble, whip the lid off and cook for 2-3 minutes, stirring occasionally until there is just a little bit of liquid left. Tip the cabbage, with its liquid, on to a small tray/large plate to cool down.

In a small saucepan, heat up the oil for deep-frying. Break up the shallot slices into individual rings and pop them into a colander. Chuck the flour over them and toss, so they are lightly coated and the excess falls away.

Drop the shallot rings into the hot oil in batches, separating them as you go, and cook until nicely brown - a little past golden - about 3 minutes. Drain on kitchen paper and season with salt immediately.

Toss the cabbage (and remaining liquid) with the spring onions, cucumber, mint and peanuts, and taste for seasoning: salt or soy, depending on your preference.

Transfer to a pretty dish and scatter with the crispy shallots.

Oh-no Khaukswe
Chicken Noodle Curry

Serves 6-8, and takes about 1 hour 30 minutes, but well worth it

---

1 chicken (weighing about 1.5kg/3lb), legs & breasts removed and skinned, then legs split into thighs and drummers (DIY or ask the butcher, but you need the carcass and wings as well)

---

1 tablespoon turmeric

---

4 tablespoons light oil, plus a bit more for frying

---

a couple of handfuls of rice vermicelli noodles

---

3 teaspoons chilli flakes

---

3 red chillies, sliced

---

2 cloves of garlic, chopped

---

1 large onion, chopped

40g/1½oz gram flour

---

1 x 400ml tin of coconut milk

1½ tablespoons fish sauce

400-600g/13oz-1lb 2oz egg noodles (depending on the number of people)

2-4 eggs, hard-boiled and sliced

4-5 spring onions, green part only, thinly sliced

3-4 limes, cut into wedges

---

salt

All Asian countries have their own brand of curry, and all are different. The curries we are most familiar with in the UK are Indian and Thai, and Burmese ones contain elements of both while being distinctly their own. Simple and tasty in the base, but as was often the case in Burma, it's the accoutrements that raise its game to a higher echelon.

It's economical but tastes rich.

Put a pot, big enough to hold the whole chicken, on a high flame with a splash of oil. Brown the carcass and wing, then pour about 2 litres water over to cover, bring to the boil, skim and reduce to a simmer.

Mix the turmeric with an equal amount of salt then sprinkle it all over the breasts and legs. After 20 minutes simmering drop these into the stock, bring back to the boil, then simmer fast for 15 minutes. Take out the breasts and put on a tray to cool, keeping the legs and wings in there for another 12-ish minutes, before transferring them to the cooling tray, too. Leave the stock busily reducing away and shred the meat once it's cool enough.

Heat some oil in a wide pan - around 3cm/1¼ inches, enough for shallow frying. When it is really hot, drop in the vermicelli, poke them around for the few seconds until they have puffed up then turn the oil off, use a slotted spoon to take them out of the pan and drain on kitchen paper. Once the oil has cooled down a bit, put a low heat underneath it and tip in the chilli flakes. Swirl for 3 or 4 minutes, taking care not to burn them, then pour the chilli oil into a bowl to serve with the noodles later.

Heat the pan again, this time with around 2 tablespoons of oil, and fry the chilli, garlic and onion for a few minutes, then add the shredded chicken and stir and fry for a couple more minutes. Strain on the yellow stock, which should now be about 1 litre/1¾ pints. Mix the gram flour with 3 tablespoons of water to a smooth paste. When the stock is simmering, stir in the gram flour paste, then the coconut milk. Cook the egg noodles as per packet instructions. After about 10-15 minutes more of the curry gently simmering, have a look at the consistency: it shouldn't be too thin, but this is supposed to be a wet curry. Turn off the heat and season with fish sauce and salt.

Serve in shallow bowls: a pile of warm egg noodles with the curry ladled over the top, and sliced eggs, spring onions, crispy noodles, chilli oil and lime to embellish.

Duck Egg Curry

Serves 4, in under 45 minutes

6 duck eggs

125ml/4fl oz light oil (such as peanut/grapeseed)

2 banana shallots (or 4 regular), peeled and sliced into thin rings

2 onions, peeled and chopped

½ teaspoon turmeric

2-3 bird's-eye chillies, sliced very small

4 cloves of garlic, finely chopped

½ a thumb of ginger, washed, gnarly bits trimmed (but don't peel), finely chopped

1½ tablespoons tomato purée

1 tablespoon curry powder

250g/8oz okra, trimmed and cut into thirds/halved, or little ones left whole

3 medium tomatoes, chopped large

½ teaspoon shrimp paste (optional but authentic, though if you want to keep it vegetarian just add a bit more salt)

a handful of chopped coriander

salt

You don't tend to see egg curries much on menus over here, but all over Asia they are common and pleasingly easy on the tum. Over the course of our trip we encouraged the chef on our boat to give us a lesson in Burmese cuisine, and when this appeared everyone declared it damn tasty.

Recreating it back home, I discovered there's an unusual and particular pleasure to be had in frying hard-boiled eggs!

Serve with rice and salad like the Feisty Pickled Cabbage Salad on page 55.

Bring a pan of water to the boil and carefully lower in the duck eggs. Cook them for 4-6 minutes, depending on size, then drop them into the sink to crack the shells and run them under cold water.

Heat the oil in a wide saucepan. When it's hot, drop in the shallots, breaking them up into rings. Once they are a deep golden brown (5-8 minutes), use a slotted spoon to transfer them on to kitchen paper and sprinkle immediately with salt.

Put the duck eggs into the hot oil and lower the heat. Fry them for 3-4 minutes, turning them to brown on all sides, then take them out of the pan and sit them on kitchen paper, too.

Keeping the pan on a medium heat, add the onions, turmeric, chillies, garlic and ginger and fry for a few minutes, until it all starts to soften, then stir in the tomato purée so that the onion is well covered in it. Cook for a minute or two before adding the curry powder and then stir that in well, too.

Add the okra with a big pinch of salt, followed by the tomatoes, and give it all a good stir. Dissolve the shrimp paste in 500ml of hot water, pour it into the pan and bring to a fast simmer. Let it bubble away busily for around 10 minutes without a lid to reduce, then lower the eggs back into the pan giving them a prod so they are mostly submerged in the liquid. Put the lid on and simmer for just another couple of minutes so that the eggs warm through, then turn the heat off and give it a 3 minute rest.

Finish by sprinkling a little salt on each egg and scattering on the shallots, with roughly chopped coriander on hand to top off each serving.

Sticky Black Rice

Makes a small jam jar
which is enough to transform
about 6-8 servings of rice.
Takes 10 minutes prep,
20 minutes to cook and keeps
in the fridge for months

For the paste

75ml/3fl oz peanut oil (other light
oils would do)

300g/10oz shallots, sliced

60g/2½oz fermented black beans

6-8 cloves of garlic, roughly chopped

½ a thumb of ginger, trimmed and
chopped

1-2 bird's-eye chillies, sliced thin

To serve

long-grain rice (about 75g/3oz
per person)

spring onions, green part only,
sliced on the oblique

some ripe tomatoes, sliced

quartered limes

Strange as it may sound, this dish was my strongest food memory from Burma - I'd just never tasted anything like it, and the balance of the deep flavours from the paste, contrasted with the fresh zinginess of the finishers (spring onions, lime juice and tomatoes), made this a complete revelation. The paste was usually served on a small dish on the side to rice and grilled meat or fish, then you mixed it yourself, but you can also add it to stir-fries, veggie or meaty, to jazz them up a bit.

The black beans that form its base are not related to the Mexican kind but are salted, fermented soy beans, which is why this paste has a slight aroma of smokiness and miso: you can easily pick them up in Asian stores, some supermarkets or there's always online.

The first time I had this was in a little café within the site of Pagan: ancient capital, home of 10,000 stupas and one of the most magical places I've ever been to. Ever.

First get your rice going according to the instructions on the packet.

Next get started on the paste: heat the oil in a wide saucepan and gently fry the shallots - stir regularly and keep the lid on for about 10 minutes to soften them without colouring (cooking them like this will really allow their sweetness to come through).

Meanwhile tip the beans into a sieve and run cold water over them for a minute, then leave to sit.

Stir the garlic, ginger and chillies into the shallots and fry gently for about 5 minutes, then tip in the beans.

Lower the heat right down, keeping the lid on, and cook for a last 5 minutes.

Blitz to a smooth, shiny purée, using a few splashes of water to bring it together if it's not moving, and then transfer to a sterilized jar (unless you're using it all today).

Bang it hard on the table to knock out all the air, then pour in a touch more oil, just to create a sealing, oxygen-proof layer on top.

When you're ready to eat, there's no need to warm it through, just serve at room temp with hot rice, sliced toms, green onion slivers and lime.

Technically the kind of work visa I had for the States meant that I could only be employed by the restaurant that had sponsored me, but after a year and a bit in New York, and despite having a hell of a lot of fun, I was gripped by the same restless spirit that was the professional mark of my twenties. Luckily, within the same group, they had a place in San Francisco, and in a desire to take in the full breadth of this mighty country's cooking, I begged and pleaded and they finally agreed to transfer me.

To be fair, it wasn't only for the geographical span that I wanted to head West Side, there were two other factors in my mind: firstly, California was getting a reputation as being the home of provenance: long before the word 'organic' was ever stamped on a box here, the roots of this thinking were being sown in fields in the verdant land of the Bay Area. I was there in '97, but a lady called Alice Waters had been quietly preaching these simple but relatively unknown ideas since the '70s, and whereas now this notion is commonplace, it really wasn't that long ago that beef was beef and that was that.

And the other reason? I needed to see how gay it was these days.

So having only just really got myself sorted in New York, I upped stakes, shipped a few bits over and started again. I already had a job, but within days of arriving I realized things at the Bank of Allegra weren't all rosy: two big city moves in eighteen months had pretty much wiped me out. I was 6,000 miles from home, my credit cards maxed out, didn't know anyone there to borrow from and had exhausted my dad's patience, so for the first time in my life I was well and truly broke. My back was against the wall, so there was nowt to be done except set a strict budget at $10 a day and go out and find a second job.

So my days fell into a happy, frugal pattern: from 6 a.m. to 8 a.m. I worked as a butcher, learning to break down whole animals into six-ounce portions (skills I've been glad ever since that I have), then I'd jump into my job as line cook (sauté) at Rubicon, sister restaurant to Tribeca Grill and with celeb owner/partners like Robin Williams and de Niro. Once a hustling, bustling lunch service was out the way - and that place was really busy - I'd clean down and five evenings a week I'd go straight to a very progressive restaurant called Jardinière, for the evening shift, which would finish up about midnight.

On days off I would go and see my friend Kate, who worked at a little dairy, the brilliantly named Cowgirl Creamery, just over the Golden Gate Bridge in Marin County, and learn a bit about making cheeses (stretching mozzarella is a particular memory); and I even got to hang out in the kitchen at Alice Waters's legendary Chez Panisse, learning how to make prosciutto and really getting to grips with how the history of an ingredient defines its flavour.

Due to a family situation back home (let's call it The Birth of Alfie), my West Coast 'stage' came to a bit of an abrupt end. I'd never worked so hard and been so broke, but one thing's for sure: I learnt more about cooking in the few months I was there than I did in all my time in New York.

SAN FRANCISCO

FACT FILE

Geographical summary: At the northern tip of the San Francisco Peninsula, surrounded by the Pacific Ocean and San Francisco Bay. Prone to earthquakes; famous for its hills. Various factors combine to make up several microclimates within the city, which is why it's also known for its fog.

Population: 815,358 (*2009 estimate*).

Religion: (*Information was only available for the state of California, not San Francisco*) Roughly speaking, the three largest are Catholic with approximately 23%, Jewish 6% and Muslim 2.9%, with various Protestant groups (including Methodist and Episcopal) making up most of the rest.

Ethnic make-up: 98% of the city population self-defines as being of one race: 54% white, 30% Asians, 6.5% Black or African American, with Pacifiic Islanders accounting for the remainder. HOWEVER, of the total city population, 14% also report as Hispanic or Latino, and they might be a part of any of the above groups. As with New York, this is the nature of big cities, especially American ones.

Life expectancy: (*Again, this is for California: San Francisco information not available*) 76 male, 80 female.

External influences: Lots of Mexicans came over the Rio Grande, and strong culinary Asian influences, too.

The essentials of their cooking: It's a healthy cuisine, so lots of good raw juices, salads and fruit. 'Fine dining' still strongly French-influenced, and some of the best Mexican outside of Mexico. Grilling is good – indoor or barbecue – and general respect for ingredients.

Top 5 favourite ingredients: Meyer lemons, tomatoes, fresh cheeses (ricotta, goats'), great salad leaves, anything local for fish and meat.

Most famous dish: Fortune cookies began here.

What to drink: Vibrant juices and smoothies; organic soy lattes with the caffeine on the side; gross vitamin drinks from powdered supplements (seaweed, etc); a lot of surprisingly expensive but excellent Californian wine; beer from micro-breweries. And enough water to keep you looking young for ever.

Best thing I ate: At Chez Panisse I had a very simple pizza of local Sonoma goats' cheese, a scattering of excellent Californian almonds and a handful of watercress grown up the road that redefined pizza for me, while also underlying the cruciality of provenance.

Most breathtaking moment: You'll never forget your first sight of the Golden Gate Bridge – just an awesome piece of engineering.

Don't ask for…: The local plonk – damn they take their wine seriously!

SUCTION-
free
chef's
KNife

I was sitting at the bus stop after my morning shift, heading for my evening shift at the other restaurant, and when the bus arrived I bent down to pick up my worn and trusty knife roll and it had gone. Tears of frustration and tiredness rolled down my cheeks: as you can gather by now, my knives have always been important to me and I immediately felt lonely, bereft and a very long way from home. It was like Delilah had come along and cut off my hair. These were so much more than knives to me: like the scars on my arms they represented my professional culinary journey thus far - time served, if you like - and suffice to say that my confidence was seriously shaken.

By next payday I'd regrouped and after my shift I went down to Japantown: every major city has a Chinatown but I'd never heard of a Japantown before and it seemed like the right place to start again. Money was tight for me then, so more than ever I chose my knife very carefully. My need was for an everyday knife, a common chef's knife if you like, but of course it had to be just a bit different ... and I'd never seen a knife with holes in it before.

About those holes and the escalated ridge that runs in between them: the aim is, I'm sure, that as you're chopping your veg (at super-speed, like they do in Japan) these features help to break the suction, so that each new slice doesn't stick to the done side of the blade but falls on to the board, thus allowing for a cleaner chop.

Which is why it's the only knife in my drawer specifically for right-handed people, as you feed whatever you're cutting in with your left hand towards the left-hand side of the blade, and the done side is to the right.

To be honest, I've never really noticed them making a ton of difference to my chopping, but because of the spirit of resilience in the face of adversity I had that day as I started to rebuild my pride and joy, and the fact that I've never known the value of a dollar more than at that time, this knife is most holy to me.

Note: you can tell I was feeling a bit nervy about having any more of my knives pinched, because after I'd bought it I went straight to an engraver's and with a very shaky hand carved my initials just above the heel (as if that really would make any difference…).

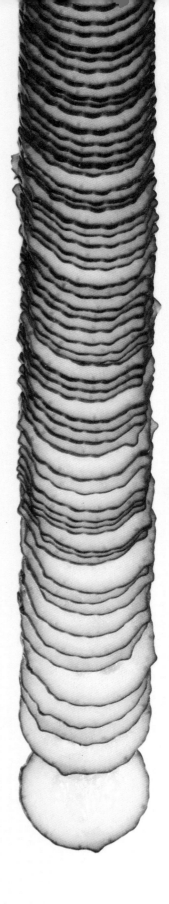

SAN FRANCISCO RECIPES

Warm Jerusalem Artichoke, Pecorino
& Rocket Salad

Paul's Basil Pancakes
with Cherry Tomato Ragoût

Asparagus & Morels on Toast

Pissaladière

High-Kicking Quail,
Slow-Cooking Lentils

Chinese Confit Duck with Noodles

West Coast Ricotta Cake

Mint Julep Crush

Warm Jerusalem Artichoke, Pecorino & Rocket Salad

Serves 6 as an starter/ accompaniment (very nice with fish), takes 10 minutes to throw together and a 45-minute cook

---

1kg/2lb Jerusalem artichokes, scrubbed (smaller ones are better - they can get ridiculously enormous by the end of the season)

---

3 tablespoons extra virgin olive oil, plus a little extra for roasting

---

a big handful of rocket

1-2 tablespoons good wine vinegar (I've used chardonnay, though also nice with red wine or even sherry)

40g/1½oz pecorino, finely grated

---

lemon juice

---

salt and pepper

I learnt a lot in Frisco food-wise, but few things have been more continually time-saving than the lesson that you don't need to peel Jerusalem artichokes. But this isn't just about laziness - cooking them in their skin means you get two flavours out of one cook: a deliciously nutty outside and a ridiculously creamy middle.

Preheat the oven to 180°C/350°F/gas mark 4.

Lay the scrubbed artichokes on a baking tray, drizzle with extra virgin olive oil, sprinkle with salt and roast for about 45 minutes, turning after half an hour. They're ready when they're golden and squidgy when pressed.

Let them cool down a bit but whilst they're still warm, cut in half or quarters if they're whoppers, toss with the rocket, oil, vinegar, pecorino, a good squeeze of lemon and some salt and pepper.

Paul's Basil Pancakes
with Cherry Tomato Ragoût

Starter for 4 (12 little pancakes) and takes 10 minutes to get it ready then a 30-minute cook.

For the ragoût

20g/³⁄₄oz butter

150g/5oz shallots, sliced

2-3 cloves of garlic, thinly sliced

220ml/7¹⁄₂fl oz tomato juice or passata

200g/7oz vine-ripened cherry tomatoes

1 teaspoon balsamic vinegar

a touch of sugar (optional)

For the pancakes

75g/3oz brioche (slightly stale works just fine)

125ml/4fl oz double cream

2 eggs, beaten

20g/³⁄₄oz basil leaves, washed

a handful of spinach leaves (about 40g/1¹⁄₂oz), washed

40g/1¹⁄₂oz plain flour

1 tablespoon butter

a few splashes of extra virgin olive oil

salt and pepper

To serve

a ball of buffalo mozzarella (about 200g/7oz), sliced

Paul was my Europhile sous-chef at Rubicon, a restaurant owned by Robin Williams, among others. I was working there the morning after he won his Oscar for Best Supporting Actor in *Good Will Hunting* - he came down into the kitchen and gave us all a bottle of Champagne. Unexpected and very appreciated by his hard-working team.

In California in the '90s I feel certain they would have served this with a squiggle of balsamic reduction on the plate ... thank God that trend seems to have bitten the dust.

Melt the butter in a pan over a medium heat and cook the shallots with the garlic for a few minutes. When they start to sizzle but before they begin to brown, turn the heat down to minimum and put on a lid. Stir from time to time for about 8-10 minutes until they are well and truly softened, then set the lid aside and pour in the tomato juice. Simmer slowly for 12-15 minutes to a fairly thick sauce, seasoning along the way. Lob in the cherry tomatoes and cook for 5-ish minutes, until their skins have split and they are just cooked, not collapsed. Turn the heat off, stir in the balsamic vinegar, and taste: you may want to add a touch of sugar, depending on the tomatoes.

While all that is going on, mush the brioche into the cream using the back of a spoon, then gradually stir in the eggs. In a blender, whiz together the basil, spinach and the soaked brioche until pale green and very smooth. Scrape it into a bowl, sift then fold in the flour and give it a decent shot of both salt and pepper.

Only start cooking the pancakes when the ragoût is ready.

In a large heavy-based frying pan over a medium heat, melt a teaspoon of the butter into a splash of olive oil. When the butter starts to sizzle, gently dollop in a desert spoon of the mix per pancake - you should be able to get at least 4 in the pan. Turn them over after 1-2 minutes and fry the other side until very lightly golden - it's good to have a bit of goo left in the middle, so they should be in and out of the pan in 3 minutes. Drain quickly on kitchen paper and cover with foil to keep warm as you get on with the rest. Serve with the ragoût and a couple of slices of mozzarella.

Asparagus & Morels on Toast

Serves 2 in less than 30 minutes

30g/1¼oz (big knob of) butter

3 shallots, chopped

2 cloves of garlic, chopped, plus an extra whole one

6-8 spears of asparagus, woody ends trimmed

125g/4oz morels

75ml/3fl oz white wine

1 tablespoon chervil or tarragon, chopped, and a few extra sprigs for the top

2 tablespoons double cream

2 slices of toast (sourdough is ideal)

extra virgin olive oil

2 big wedges of lemon

salt and pepper

Most people rightly think of wild mushrooms as an autumnal thing, but the gods gave us morels bang on the same time as asparagus (late spring/early summer) for a good reason. Together they do a crossover job of new green and deeper earthy that makes for a multi-layered kind of deliciousness.

Put a frying pan on a medium heat and melt the butter, but don't let it brown. Add the shallots and chopped garlic and soften over a low heat for about 10 minutes.

Peel the spears of asparagus using a potato peeler, working from just under the tip to the base of the stem. Cut the stems into 2cm/¾ inch pieces up to the tips and then split each tip lengthwise.

Trim the morels and cut into rings. Once the shallots are tender, add the mushrooms to the pan and when they have been on the heat for about 5 minutes, pour in the wine. Turn the heat up, season with salt and pepper and cook with a lid on for a couple of minutes, then take the lid off so that the wine reduces.

After another minute or so add the asparagus, chervil and the cream, keeping the heat high. Let the liquid reduce down again for a scant couple of minutes and turn the heat off.

Rub the toast with the whole clove of garlic, then drizzle with extra virgin olive oil. Spoon the mushroom and asparagus over the toast and serve with a big wedge of lemon on the side.

Pissaladière
Onion & Anchovy Tart

Makes 1 big tart - about
9 good-sized pieces.
Takes a couple of hours
all told, but with some
rests in there for you and
the dough

For the dough

325g/11oz plain flour

½ teaspoon salt

½ teaspoon fast-acting dried yeast

1 whole egg + 1 yolk

80ml/3fl oz extra virgin olive oil

For the filling

100ml/3½fl oz extra virgin olive oil

2kg/4lb red onions, sliced

5 cloves of garlic, roughly chopped

15g/½oz thyme on the branch, tied
in a bunch with string

125g/4oz anchovies, drained

50g/2oz black olives, stoned

salt and pepper

While not naturally a pudding kind of a girl, I've always loved playing with dough. This classic and classy French tart is made all the more special by the fat in the dough being olive oil, not the usual butter. This dough recipe was taught to me by a chef there who apparently got it from a man with a dog who knew someone who had apprenticed with Joël Robuchon. And it's this stolen, light dough that makes the work, as well as the magic, but to save time next time (and there will be a next time after you've made it once) you can double the quantities and freeze half.

To make the dough, mix the dry ingredients in a kitchen mixer for a few seconds on medium (or do it by hand - not a lot more sweat). Whisk together the eggs and oil with 80ml/3fl oz of water and drizzle into the dry ingredients, mixing all the time to combine.

Turn the dough out on to a well-floured surface and knead for about 4 minutes, until it feels soft then leave in a warm place for about 1 hour.

For the filling, heat the oil in a big, wide pan and cook the onions over a high heat, stirring so they don't brown. After a few minutes add the garlic, bunch of thyme and seasoning. When the volume has reduced a bit and the onions are starting to collapse - about 10 minutes - turn the heat down to medium and put on a lid, stirring from time to time, taking care to mix in any bits stuck to the bottom of the pan (as long as they're not burnt).

After about 20 minutes, the onions should be caramelized so take off the lid and cook for about another 10 minutes to dry them out. If the onions are still bleeding water you can drain them in a sieve for a while, as they should be moist but not dripping

Preheat the oven to 200°C/400°F/gas mark 6. Roll the dough out quite thinly and lay it on a large baking sheet (about 35cm/14 inches square or the equivalent area if rectangular - whatever fits into your oven best), leaving any extra dough hanging over the edges. Give it a mini-prove on the tray for about 15 minutes, then prick all over with a fork. Chuck the thyme, then spread the onions all over the dough, leaving a small frame around the edge. Arrange the anchovies in a lattice pattern over the top and finish by studding with olive halves.

Brush the pastry edges with olive oil and trim the overhang off with a knife. Cook in the oven for 25 minutes and eat at atmospheric temperature.

High-Kicking Quail, Slow-Cooking Lentils

Serves 4 as a main, and takes 30 minutes to get it going, then a 45 minute break as the lentils cook, then less than 30 minutes to finish it off

---

60ml/2½fl oz extra virgin olive oil, plus a bit more

1 heaped tablespoon butter

4 rashers of streaky bacon, sliced

1 large onion, peeled and diced small

2 carrots, peeled and diced small

2 sticks of celery, diced small

3 fat cloves of garlic, sliced with a big pinch of salt

a couple of bay leaves

a bunch of thyme (about 15g/½oz), tied up with string

150g/5oz Puy lentils

300ml/½ pint red wine

600ml/1 pint chicken stock

8 quails

2 big handfuls of watercress

a small pot of crème fraîche

salt and pepper

Having always thought of them as more French than anything else, I was surprised to find out that the quail is the state bird of California. I'm not sure how much this impacts on the consciousness of most of its inhabitants, but one aspect of local produce all the folks of the Golden State are aware of is wine; so being true to the area and the original recipe (which is what this book is all about), I use a Californian zinfandel for this dish. But really any ballsy red will do.

In the '90s, when I was cooking over there, at the top end most restaurants were still absolutely infatuated with French food (and the precision cutting that comes with it), and this recipe combines their love of these things.

Preheat the oven to 170°C/340°F/gas mark 3½.

Heat the oil in a heavy-bottomed pan that can go into the oven and melt the butter into it. Add the bacon, onion, carrots, celery, garlic, bay and thyme and fry on a medium heat for a couple of minutes, then season with a little salt and quite a lot of pepper and put on a lid. Cook for 10-15 minutes, stirring from time to time, letting the veggies really soften up, but don't let them brown.

Tip in the lentils, stir well for a minute, then pour in the wine. Turn up the heat to bring to the boil, then simmer until all the wine has reduced away. Add the stock, and if the quails came with necks, cut them off and put them in with the lentils for added flavour.

Cut a piece of greaseproof paper a bit larger than the pan lid and rest it on top of the liquid (in poncy French world this is called a *cartouche*). Put the pan in the oven for around 35-40 minutes, until the lentils are cooked but still have a bit of bite, then take it out and turn the oven up to 200°C/400°F/gas mark 6.

Take off the *cartouche* and put the pan on the hob over a medium heat to reduce the liquid - you want it to be more like a binding sauce than soupy - this will take about 10 more minutes, then turn the heat off and let the lentils rest while you cook the quails.

You can either cook the quails in 2 heavy-based, ovenproof frying pans or seal them in two batches in the same pan then transfer the birds to a roasting tray - it all depends on if you have a couple of suitable pans; an average, large-ish frying pan holds 4 quails. Heat the pan or pans

on a high flame and put in a splash of olive oil. On each quail, make a little cut just along the underside of the bone of one lower leg and push the shin of the other leg through it so that the legs are crossed and when you line them all up they look a bit like can-can dancers (or so I thought, and hence the name for this recipe).

Drizzle the birds with olive oil and a good sprinkling of salt. When the pan or pans is/are really hot, lay the birds in on their sides. Brown them on one side for a couple of minutes, then turn them over and brown the other side. Finally, brown the breasts and put them in the oven breast-side down. If you are using two pans, put them straight into the oven for 6-8 minutes (depending on size of bird and whether you like your meat pink), switching over the position of the pans in the oven halfway through cooking. If you have sealed them in two batches, transfer all 8 birds with their juices to a roasting tin, breast-side down, and roast for 8-10 minutes.

Once cooked, move the quail on to another dish and rest them the other way up (with their legs in the air). Roughly chop the watercress and stir it into the lentils along with any juices that have come out of the rested quail. Now is the time to season the lentils carefully - quite a bit of salt.

Spoon the lentils into large, warm, shallow bowls, nestle a couple of quails on top and finish with little blobs of crème fraîche dotted around them.

Chinese Confit Duck with Noodles

Serves 8. It'll take you about 15 minutes to get the legs curing, which, after they've sat overnight take a couple of hours unsupervised cooking time in the oven. Once out it's about 30 minutes to get supper on the table

For the confit

40g/1½oz good salt (sea salt is best)

½ tablespoon fennel seeds

10 cloves

1 teaspoon chilli flakes

3 whole star anise

2 tablespoons Szechuan peppercorns

4 duck legs,

700g/1lb 6oz duck fat

around 300ml/½ pint groundnut or sunflower oil to top up

For the noodles

250g/8oz egg noodles

2 heads of broccoli, cut into bite-sized pieces

2 tablespoons toasted sesame oil

2 red chillies, sliced

1 bunch of spring onions

2 tablespoons soy sauce

San Francisco has an enormous Chinese population: vast numbers came over in the 19th century and were put to work building railways and digging in the gold rush: Chinatown SF is the oldest in North America.

The thumping heart of this recipe is the spice mix that you cure the duck in, a fragrant and also earthy blend which I learnt from a fourth generation Chinese-American chef while working there. The flavours in this dish are not so much strictly authentic Chinese, but what happens when one cuisine is made to live in a different culture. Just as with Italian American food which, while obviously being tied in to the mother country, is markedly different from what you really eat in Italy.

This is a great dish for when a bunch of mates are coming round - informal but totally impressive and all the duck work can be done way in advance, the day before even, just leaving you with a 30 minute gateway to duck & noodle heaven.

Blend the salt, fennel seeds, cloves, chilli flakes, star anise and Szechuan peppercorns in a spice grinder/food processor until coarsely ground, or if you're a real masochist pulverize them in a pestle and mortar. Sprinkle a quarter of this mix on to the bottom of a roasting tray and lay the duck legs on top, skin side down (try to find a tray that they fit into fairly tightly). Pat the rest of the spice mix on to the flesh side of the legs. Cover and refrigerate for a minimum of overnight - up to 2 days is fine.

When you're ready to get going, preheat the oven to 160°C/325°F/gas mark 3. Take the duck legs out of the cure and pat them dry, gently brushing off the majority of the mix.

Clean and dry the tray and put the legs back in skin-side up. Pour over the duck fat, then top up with oil so that the legs are completely covered. Put the tray into the oven and after 30 minutes turn the temperature down to 140°C/275°F/gas mark 1 and cook for another 2 hours.

Lift the duck legs out and set aside (the oil is completely re-useable; just strain it through a sieve lined with a J-cloth, and only use it for dishes that you don't mind tasting vaguely Chinesey). When you can handle the duck, peel off the skin and slice it into 1cm/½ inch thick ribbons. Pick the duck, put the meat in a bowl and for extra brownie points make a stock with the bones for a rainy day - stocks last for months in the freezer and can form the backbone of many emergency meals.

Prepare the noodles according to the instructions on the packet and 3 minutes before they are done drop the broccoli in with them too: a scant couple of minutes - don't overcook it.

Heat the sesame oil in a wok until just about smoking and add the duck skin and chillies. Toss vigorously over a high heat for 30 seconds until the skin is crisp, then add the duck meat and the spring onions. Stir-fry (as in literally stir and fry) for a couple of minutes, encouraging the duck to break up and shred a bit as it gives a good texture once we're all in. Add the noodles (not in a clump), broccoli and soy sauce and keep tossing over the heat for another minute or so, until everything is well combined. Taste for seasoning, adding a splash more soy or sesame oil if necessary.

West Coast Ricotta Cake

Makes 10 slices, and is about a 30-minute make then 1 hour cooking time

---

175g/6oz caster sugar

---

10 eggs, separated

---

zest of 6 lemons

---

1 teaspoon vanilla extract

125g/4oz ground almonds

175g/6oz plain flour

---

2 teaspoons baking powder

---

1 teaspoon salt

450g/14½oz ricotta

I can't remember her name - it may have been Amy - and she was the pastry chef at the restaurant I worked at. This was one of their long-standing, best-selling desserts, and she very kindly gave me her recipe, unaware that twelve years later I would publish it in a book under my own name. Shame.

Preheat the oven to 160°C/325°F/gas mark 3, and line a springform cake tin, 23cm/9 inches in diameter and 7cm/3 inches deep, with buttered greaseproof paper.

Either by hand or in a kitchen mixer, beat the sugar and egg yolks until very light and fluffy, then stir in the lemon zest, vanilla and almonds.

Mix the flour with the baking powder and salt, then sift and fold them into the eggy base using a wooden spoon or spatula. Crumble in half the ricotta and do a bit more gentle folding.

Whisk the egg whites to the old firm peak stage and fold half into the mixture - it's a lot of folding, I know, but this is all about the air. Repeat with the remaining ricotta followed by the rest of the egg whites, then turn into the tin.

It will probably take at least 45 minutes to cook in the oven, but check it after 40 as you don't want it to overcook - it's ready when it's risen and golden, and a skewer comes out clean or very nearly.

Cool completely in the tin and dust with icing sugar.

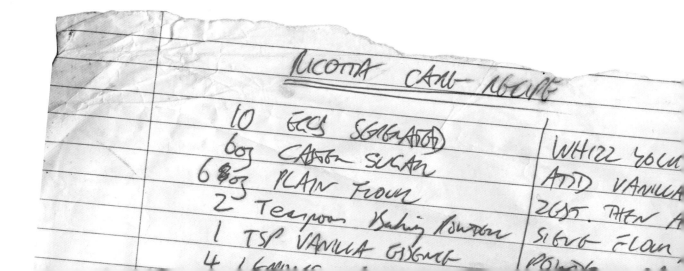

Mint Julep Crush

Makes 6 long, cool drinks in about 15 minutes

12 longish stalks of mint, leaves and top sprigs picked

9 tablespoons caster sugar

crushed ice

300ml / ½ pint Bourbon

For most of my time in San Fran I worked two jobs, but before I started my evening job I had a run of a great couple of weeks where I'd finish my shift after lunch service at 2.30 (after a 6 a.m. start) and head straight to the cocktail bar next door with my fellow line cook Sandy. Day after day we'd be merry by 3.30, slaughtered by 4.30 and crashed out in bed by 6p.m., then it would all start again. Happy days indeed.

We'd always have a couple of these to kick off: Sandy was from the South, and was most firm that it was the best daytime drink ever, being the tipple associated with the Kentucky Derby, where she assured me it was served in silver cups!

Split the mint into three piles: top sprigs, the rest of the leaves and the bare stalks. Put the sugar in a pan with 300ml / ½ pint of water, the stalks and around half the mint leaves, tearing them a bit as you drop them in. Leave to infuse on a low heat for 5 minutes, then set aside to cool.

Strain the syrup into a jug and add the bourbon - this can all be done ahead of time and stored in a glass bottle.

When you're ready to go, share the rest of the mint leaves, also torn, between 6 glasses and muddle with a bit of crushed ice - you can do this with the end of rolling pin or fashion your own muddling device.
Fill each glass with more crushed ice, pour over the boozy syrup and finish with the sprigs of mint.

third Cy

The Brazil I saw was full of the beautiful people. It's fair to say I was suffering from an acute broken heart at the time, and therefore had pretty low self-esteem, but even so ... my, these folks were gorgeous. The busy white sand beaches around Porto Seguro were packed every day with perfect bodies playing volleyball, doing capoeira or simply parading their perfectness (though it is slightly heartening to note that Brazil is number three in the world for plastic surgery).

Our time was spent in the state of Bahia, the fifth largest (out of twenty-six) in Brazil, and supposedly one of the poorest, but that side of it wasn't wholly apparent from what I saw. What I did see was a truckload of Carnival, or to be more precise about 150 truckloads, all bouncing with heavy bass and sparkly sequinned girlies.

In my day I've done my share of partying, but among these pros I got out-partied and partied-out every night for the duration of the festivities. I'd read that Carnival in Rio was a five-night affair, so there was nothing to do but knuckle down, learn some samba steps and try very hard to keep my sorry white ass up with the locals.

And so passed our time in Porto Seguro: I'd arrived in the country in a fairly tender state, in need of some R & R and general wound-licking time, but after doing the right thing each night and seeing five dawns on the trot I was practically committable. Relief washed over me as I woke up from my final tripped-out reverie and stumbled down to an afternoon breakfast, desperate for some calm. I was met by a room full of beaming smiles and I was informed how lucky we were that in this hedonistic corner of Bahia, *their* Carnival went on for *seven* days! Fear doesn't touch the sides of the shiver that ran through me.

That was just too much for us, so my friend Bridget and I packed our shared quarter of a liver and remaining brain cells (plus a couple of peacock feathers, because you never know in Brazil) and headed for Salvador, the capital of Bahia and supposedly a cultural mini-Mecca for art and music.

Whether I was just so pleased with my narrow escape from Sodom and Gomorrah, or whether it really is that lovely, who knows, but I fell for Salvador with its 400-year-old Portuguese architecture and clusters of little galleries and art shops. In the evening the old part of the city, known as the Pelourinho, came alive with music - not the artery-twanging kind that I'd just been experiencing, but lyrical guitar playing, in the Portuguese tradition but more mellow for its Brazilian interpretation.

Having hardly eaten at all for the first part of our visit, we more than made up for it here, as Salvadorians have a proud culinary tradition. Just as our stomachs had been starved, so had our cultural needs, but a few days in this charming city sorted us out in all departments. I'd been expecting the postcard beaches and full-on Carnival, but the gentle, thriving soul of Salvador had been unexpected: I could leave now with some kind of equilibrium restored, both internally and in my view of Brazil.

BRASIL

Geographical summary: Covers nearly half of South America, and is the continent's largest nation, bordering the Atlantic Ocean to the east and every nation on the continent except Chile and Ecuador. Brazilian Highlands, or plateau, in the south and the Amazon River basin in the north. Amazon rainforest the largest in the world. Tropical or subtropical climate almost throughout.

Population: 194 million.

Religion: Three-quarters Roman Catholic and 15% Protestant, but where I was there was a strong following of Candomblé, a religion of African origin where spirit-gods are venerated.

Ethnic make-up: Just over half white, nearly 40% mulatto, 6% black and the rest a mix.

Life expectancy: 69 male, 76 female.

External influences: The Portuguese came in the 15th century and started bringing slaves over from Africa about a century later; it is estimated that over the following 300 years around 3 million Africans were brought over to work the land. Both of these two mass arrivals have shaped modern Brazil.

Traditional cooking methods: Lots of grilling, and a strong culture of raw & fresh – salads and fruit. They like a slow-cook too, in black clay pots known as *moquecas* that are fired and traditionally sealed with mangrove sap.

Food they export: Soya beans, chicken, coffee, beef and veal, sugar.

Top 5 favourite ingredients: Fish and seafood (especially prawns), fruit (papaya, watermelon, guava), peppers, palm oil (especially in Bahia, where there is a strong African influence) and, as with all countries with some Iberian connection, the Pig is King.

Most famous dish: *Feijoada* (see page 96).

What they drink: Lots of super-fresh fruit juices, also guarana-based drinks. Surprisingly, Antarctica beer.

Best thing I ate: *Moqueca de camarão.*

Most breathtaking moment: Carnival was one very long breathtaking and breath-releasing moment.

Don't ask for…: The music to be turned down.

Clearly there was nothing to buy in Porto Seguro during Carnival apart from pink feathers and party toys, so my knife quest had to wait until we went to Salvador. Walking past a hardware shop I saw this in the window and, attracted by its frankly weird-ass shape, went in to investigate. My Portuguese is only good for kitchens, and to say that the storekeeper spoke broken English is kind, but between us both making animal noises and pointing to parts of our body I ascertained that it was for doing something to a pig's leg.

When I got home I took it down to my butcher, Stentons, where John is the guru and Perry his trusted apprentice. We all had a good look and a think, and tried to break down a pork thigh with it in a post-mortem-like way, but none of us could see how having the handle so high above the blade helped, and indeed what that extension of the blade below the handle was for, except cutting ourselves. So with help from my Brazilian friend Rosangela, we wrote to the makers, Tramontina, for clarification.

And this is what they wrote back:

'Tramontina, together with an expert cuts of pork to one of the largest refrigerated in Brazil and the world, developed this model knife to meet a need for greater ease and enjoyment in doing the boning or dismemberment of the parts that compose a pork shank.

As the ham and a piece of very thick, and as a function of the geometry of the blade, the highest position of the handle facilitates the movement and precision that makes the person with the knife to the leg bone.

The question of why the knife blade extends even below the hilt, and as a function of the handle need to be very near the ends of the blade, with the objective mentioned above and that greater mastery of the movements of the blade thereby offering a better use in the ham boning.'

Everyone clear on that then? So I tried again, this time with the confidence that I was at least attempting the right manoeuvre, namely to bone-out a leg of pork, and completed the mission with enough huff and puff to blow the house down.

It is true that butchery varies wildly from country to continent, and all I can surmise is that all those expert butchers in the Brazilian meat industry know something that me, John and Perry don't. One thing's for sure though, when I go back to Brazil I'm taking me knife with me and getting a demo - until then it remains the strangest-looking and least used knife in the drawer.

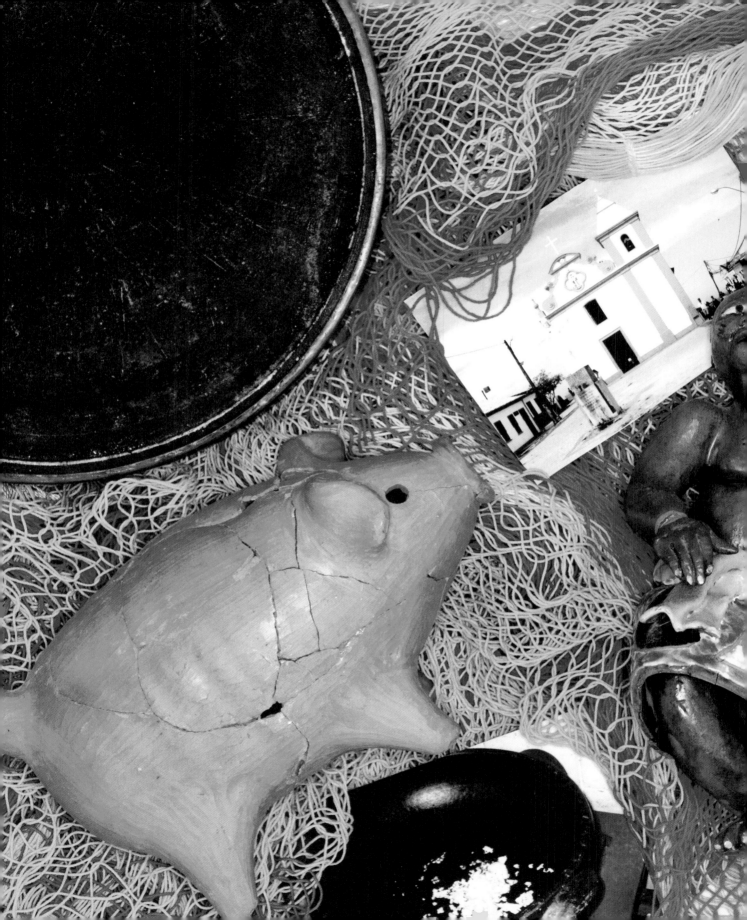

BRAZILIAN RECIPES

Brazilian Breakfast Juice

Panquecas de Queijo
Sweet Goats' Cheese Pancakes

Salad for a Barbecue
(aka 'Mayonnaise')

Moqueca de Peixe e Camarão
Seafood Stew

Feijoada
Black Beans Braised with plenty of Pig

Arenque
Fresco: os olhos devem estar brilhantes e a carne bem firme. É ótimo em grelhados, frito, assado e em recheios. Muito bom para saladas.

Enlatado: quando vier em molho e tomate, aqueça um pouco e sirva com torradas ou vegetais. Use também frio, em saladas. Se estiver em molho de mostarda, é excelente para torta de peixe, coberta com purê de batatas e levada ao forno.

Atum
Fresco: a carne, rosada para vermelho, é de consistência firme e gordurosa. Muito saborosa, tem poucas espinhas. O atum fresco pode ser conservado no frigorífico por no máximo dois dias. Para que a carne adquira bom sabor, tempere-a com meia hora de antecedência. Para cozimento, deixe-o no lume de 10 a 30 minutos, conforme a espessura da posta. É ótimo para caldeiradas, ensopados e gratinados.

Enlatado: use como o salmão, acompanhado de m... ses, saladas, em recheios ou patês.

Bacalhau
Fresco: escaldado, frito ou grelhado. Para evita... parta, quando frito, é bom empaná-lo bem.

Defumado: cortado em filetes e curtido em s... empregado escaldando-se em água ou leite e s... manteiga ou com molho.

Congelado: não precisa descongelar. Frite o... como se estivesse fresco, apenas deixando u... de tempo do que o normal para o fresco. Se... grande, corte-a antes e use normalmente. O... antigo de conservação de alimentos, o fuma... expô-los ao fumo de madeira, o que, além... confere-lhes um sabor especial.

Abadejo
Fresco: este peixe é ótimo para dietas dev... teor de hidratos de carbono, ou ainda mu... pessoas com problemas digestivos. A car... textura delicadíssimos. A maior parte das... badejo não tem escamas e a pele deve se... esfregada, a fim de eliminar a película ás... receita, pode-se retirar a pele. Ótimo gr... no forno. Muito bom também para ens...

Camarão
Fresco: cozinhe durante 10 minutos e... ensopados ou molhos. Pode ser frito p... conservar o camarão fresco no freezer... Para limpá-lo, puxe a casca, por baixo... cabeça, e a tripa das costas do ventre,... com um palito. As cabeças e as casc... deixadas em salmoura e reaproveitad... Enlatado: empregue-o como se esti...

Pargo
Peixe ótimo para cozer e assar.

Pescada
É ideal para cozer ou fritar. Em fil... numa uma grande variedade de pr...

Peixe-espada
É cozido em postas. Pode ser fri...

Polvo
Fresco: é um dos moluscos de... muito saboroso, conforme o n... do polvo deve ser lustrosa e lig... cheiro, suave. Para prepará-lo... base, lave em água corrente e...

Brazilian Breakfast Juice

Makes 4 glasses in under 10 minutes

1kg/2lb chunk of watermelon

1 papaya

2 guavas (if you can find them - can be tricky to track down)

juice of 1 lime

a few drops of guarana, or empty out a capsule (optional but authentic)

a handful of ice cubes

Fresh fruit is mind-blowing in Brazil, and it's an important part of their daily diet. Makes our apples and pears seem pretty flat with all those vibrant colours and mad shapes that flourish in a hot climate.

Papayas have an enzyme that makes them very digestible - according to some nutritionists they are the best thing you can possibly have first thing in the morning, which is exactly what you need after another night on the tiles.

Peel and roughly chop the fruit, then blend everything together.

Take the seeds out of the papaya and guava (watermelon too if you're feeling fussy). Drink immediately, preferably on or near a beach.

Panquecas de Queijo *Sweet Goats' Cheese Pancakes*

Makes 6-8 in a relaxed and fun 45 minutes

90g/3½oz sugar

5 guavas, or 4 tall, hard pears, peeled, quartered, seeds removed then cut big bite-size pieces

2 tablespoons honey

50g/2oz butter

250g/8oz soft, young, rindless goats' cheese

more fruit, to serve

For the batter

165g/5½oz plain flour

a pinch of salt

1 heaped tablespoon sugar

2 eggs, beaten

250ml/8fl oz milk

In Arraial d'Ajuda, busy nights meant that breakfast became our most important meal and we would stare blankly at the sea, waiting for the lady owner to restore us to normality through nourishment.

We had these with poached guava, but tall hard-ish pears also work well.

Tip the sugar into a pan with 300ml/½ pint of water and bring to a simmer. Slip in the pieces of fruit and poach gently, covered with a lid (about 8-10 minutes for pears and 20-25 for guavas). Lift the cooked fruit out and put aside, then stir the honey into the syrup and let it slowly bubble down until you have about a ramekins worth of syrup.

To make the batter, mix the flour, salt and sugar. Stir in the eggs and milk, then move to a whisk and add a little water to make it the smooth consistency of single cream. Heat a knob of butter in a shallow frying pan or skillet until it sizzles, then swoosh it round the pan and up the sides. Pour in enough batter to just cover the bottom of the pan when you tip it around. Cook the pancake until browning at the edge on the first side, then flip. You should get 6 to 8 out of the batter; just remember to re-fizzle butter in the pan in between each pancake.

Stir the cooked and cooled pear/guava into the goats' cheese to make a soft mixture. Put a sausage-shaped portion of mix into the middle of each pancake, then roll them up. The cheesy middle is supposed to be room temp, but you need the syrup to be properly boiling as you pour it over the pancakes to warm them. Serve with your favourite fresh fruits.

Salad for a Barbecue
aka 'Mayonnaise'

Serves 6 as a side dish, and is
30 minutes easy cooking

500g/1lb potatoes, diced into rough
2.5cm/1 inch cubes

---

2 or 3 carrots, chunky sliced/diced,
plus another 1 or 2, thinly sliced,
for pretty round the edge

---

2 cobs of sweetcorn, shucked

---

3 handfuls of frozen peas

---

5 spring onions, finely sliced

---

a handful of flat-leaf parsley, finely
chopped

For the mayo

2 egg yolks

1-2 cloves of garlic, peeled and
minced with a big pinch of salt

---

3 tablespoons lemon juice

---

1 teaspoon Dijon mustard

200ml/7fl oz light olive oil

100ml/3½fl oz extra virgin olive oil

---

salt and pepper

Everyone has their own version of this salad: the famous Russian,
'Salad Olivier' in Iran, newies and mint here. They all seem slightly
'70s and very kiddie, but in reality what's not to like? We had it many
times, sometimes with raisins and apples in, or shredded chicken,
which turns it into an easy meal for children.

Of course you can just use a bottle of mayonnaise rather than making
your own ... but it's well worth the extra five minutes, which really is
all it takes if you do it in a food processor.

Put the potatoes into a pan with just enough water to cover them, plus
a big pinch of salt, and bring to the boil with a lid. Turn the heat down
and simmer steadily for about 5 minutes, until just tender, then tip in the
carrots, sweetcorn and peas. Turn the heat up high and put the lid on.
As soon as the water comes back to the boil, drain the veggies and run
them under cold water for a couple of minutes, until cooled. Leave them
to drain dry.

While the vegetables are doing their thing, knock up the mayo.
Whiz the egg yolks, garlic, lemon juice, mustard and seasoning in
a food processor until pale. Gradually drizzle in both oils until all
incorporated, then finish with salt and pepper - it's essential to taste
it for correct seasoning.

Mix the cooled vegetables with most of the spring onions and parsley,
saving a few for the top. Stir in as much mayo as you like: I tend to only
use about half this amount, but it's hard to make a smaller quantity in
the food processor and home-made mayo is always welcome in my fridge
- lasts for up to 5 days. If you're feeling properly Brazilian, decorate
with sliced carrot as well as the rest of the spring onions and parsley.

Moqueca de Peixe e Camarão
Seafood Stew

Serves 4, and takes 30 minutes
action (ideally with 1 hours
marinade first) then around
15 minutes to finish it off

---

4 steaks (on the bone) from a large,
flat fish (halibut, plaice, turbot,
etc.), each weighing about 175g/6oz

3 cloves of garlic, minced finely
with a big pinch of salt

4 limes

a big handful of coriander, chopped

60ml/2½fl oz extra virgin olive oil
(plus a splash more)

60ml/2½fl oz palm oil or olive oil

3 red onions, sliced

1 tablespoon tomato purée

5 vine-ripened tomatoes, roughly
chopped

2 green peppers, sliced

1 x 400ml tin of coconut milk

4 tablespoons plain flour, seasoned
with salt and pepper

300g/10oz king or tiger prawns,
fresh, raw, peeled (but leave the
tail on) and de-veined

long-grain rice, to serve

salt and pepper

Moquecas are a speciality of the Bahia region in the north of Brazil,
which is where I was staying, and you can have a moqueca of just about
anything, as the name comes from special pot it's cooked in.

As with any regional classic, there are a host of versions, all with a similar
theme, but very different riffs. This recipe is based on one given to me
by the vibrant Mrs Maria Graça Fish (she married a Yorkshireman), who's in
charge of Food, Music and Culture at the Brazilian Embassy in London.

Great for when you've got friends over, as it's easy and impressive but
most usefully you can do a lot of the recipe the day before.

Rinse the fish steaks and pat them dry. Put them into a dish with the
garlic, the juice of 2 limes, salt, pepper and most of the coriander (saving
a bit for the end) and leave to marinate for 1 hour at room temperature,
or longer (i.e. overnight) in the fridge.

Put half the olive and palm oils into a wide saucepan and fry two-thirds
of the onion slices over a medium high heat until softened and slightly
caramelized - up to 10 minutes. Add half the tomatoes and half the
peppers and cook for a few more minutes, until softened.

Stir in the tomato purée, coat everybody well and then tip in half the
coconut milk. Simmer gently for 10 minutes, season, then blitz to a thick
purée in a food processor or a blender, and set aside.

About 30 minutes before you want to eat, heat the rest of both the oils
in a wide saucepan on a high heat (and get the rice on). Put the seasoned
flour on a plate and pat the fish steaks in it on all sides. Lower the steaks
into the very hot oil and fry for 3-4 minutes on each side, until golden
brown. Lift them out, add a splash more oil (if it needs it) and tip in the
last of the onions, peppers and tomatoes. Stir on high for about
5 minutes, then add the blitzed mixture and the rest of the coconut milk.
Adjust the seasoning as it comes to a simmer, then slide the fish steaks
back into the pan, just submerging them in the liquid, and cover with a lid.

After 4 minutes, scatter in the prawns (stick the lid back on) and cook
for another 3-5 minutes until the prawns are pink. Taste and adjust the
seasoning. Finish with the rest of the chopped coriander, and serve with
rice and pieces of lime.

Feijoada
Black Beans Braised with plenty of Pig

Serves 8+, and requires some overnight soaking, then takes about 1 hour to get on, followed by around 4 hours cooking time.

1kg/2lb black beans, soaked overnight

---

2 bay leaves

---

1 tablespoon lard or extra virgin olive oil

---

2 onions, diced large

---

6 cloves of garlic, peeled and roughly chopped with a big pinch of salt

---

3 shots (125ml/4fl oz) cachaça (a fierce Brazilian spirit) or clear rum like Wray & Nephew

---

6 pieces of rind + juice of 1 orange

---

chopped flat-leaf parsley and spring onions

Meat (essential)

300g/10oz pork ribs (smoked or fresh), cut into 8cm/3 inch chunks

---

100g/3½oz beef jerky, or 200g/7oz *carne seca* if you can find it

---

300g/10oz pancetta, cut into cubes

200g/7oz cured sausage (Portuguese smoked is best, or use chorizo sausages thickly sliced)

Meat (not essential)

---

1 pig's trotter, split in half - ideally salted, but fresh is fine, too

---

salted pig snout and tail

This is one of the oldest, tastiest and most famous dishes in Brazil, coming from the age before refrigeration so ingeniously relying on three ways of preserving meat (curing, air-drying and smoking) as well as dried beans.

The snout, tail and trotter (which, you buy salted, not fresh) aren't essential, and you don't have to eat them - they're mainly flavour-adders. They are, however, very good at that job, as well as being fun to track down if you get a kick out of that kind of thing.

Improves it massively if left to sit for a day or three ... even a week.

If you are using salted snout, tail and trotter, wash them in water twice and then soak them for 2 days, changing the water occasionally. Drain and rinse them, put them into a pan of fresh water, and simmer completely covered for about 1 hour 30 minutes.

Drain the soaked beans, put them into a pan and cover them with cold water. Add the bay leaves and fresh pork ribs (if using). Bring to the boil, then reduce the heat and simmer for about 1 hour till the beans are starting to soften, topping up with water as necessary to keep everything nicely covered before adding the beef jerky/*carne seca* and smoked ribs (if using). Simmer for another 30 minutes, until the beans are just about cooked.

Once the jerky is in, heat the oil or lard in a medium-sized pan and fry the pancetta, onions, garlic and sausage/chorizo for about 15 minutes, until well softened and beginning to caramelize. Use a slotted spoon to scoop out all the meat and most of the onions, leaving just a few in the pan with the fat, and add the meat to the pot of beans which should now be pretty much there. Lift out about a coffee mug-full of beans, tip into the remaining onions, mash them together and mix this back into the beans. If you did the snout, tail and trotter, tip the entire contents (i.e. bits + stock) into the beans now too, and if you didn't pour in 1 litre or so of water enough to keep it from sticking through the final leg. Cook over a low to medium heat for another hour and 30 minutes, adding the orange peel, juice and cachaça after an hour.

By now the whole dish should have come together and not have much liquid left - it should be a thick, creamy, rich dish of pig and bean-ness. Taste for seasoning and serve with rice, kale, oranges, hot sauce (all pretty key) and to be truly authentic, farofa (toasted cassava flour) too.

Madeira: an island for newly-weds and nearly-deads, so we were told by a mate after we'd booked it, and sure enough I've never seen a departure gate so full of silver hair and drip-dry cream-coloured jackets. We'd been looking for some October sun and neither the purse strings nor the time off were stretching to truly foreign climes, which is how we'd settled on the unlikely destination of Madeira.

Over the years there had been numerous trips to the Portuguese mainland: a bizarre teenage week mucking around on a golf course in Albufeira; a villa with my sister's family near Lagos; what turned out to be a very rock and roll long weekend in Lisbon with a particularly feisty ex, and the inevitable beach holiday on the Algarve. But I was aware that on all these other trips, Portugal itself was slightly peripheral: I was definitely in Portuguese airspace but not in full explorer's mode, as the nature of the holidays was of a different kind: brainless chill-out (except for Lisbon, which I loved, but really spent most of the time rowing or crying to fado, an education in itself). Madeira was different - I was in a mood to absorb.

The island benefits from the Gulf Stream, giving it a sub-tropical climate, which accounts for the exotic flowers that famously flourish there. The sea around is not a placid one - the full force of the Atlantic crashing into the rocks makes for a craggy coastline and a bumpy swim, but on dry land the air is mostly warm and welcoming, though we did have a couple of days when the mists descended and it felt like we were living in a cloud. You can drive easily round the island through mountainous woods - Madeira actually means wood in Portuguese - exploring the towns and landscapes, and there's excellent food to be had: we didn't eat badly once.

Funchal, the capital, was first descended upon in the 15th century, after Henry the Navigator dispatched his best men in search of new conquests. It is built around the natural port, and rather pleasingly named after the abundance of fennel they found growing in the area. Apart from enjoying the pace of life, enhanced by a few glasses of their local tipple, the done thing to do is to ride the cable car up to the picturesque village of Monte that overlooks it, take a turn around the park and climb the stairs to the pilgrimage destination of Nossa Senhora do Monte. Then you wait to get accosted by a group of lost-looking gondoliers - all dressed in white with boaters on - who encourage you to get into their baskets on wooden runners and hurtle down the cobbled narrow streets back to sea level at a speed that makes you want to cuddle your coccyx. I guess every town needs a good way to have a laugh at the tourist's expense.

They've been making Madeira here for hundreds of years: legend has it that on a sailing trip a barrel came loose of its strappings and rolled around on deck in the sun for weeks. The crew figured they might as well try it and discovered that the wine had fortified and sweetened with the conditions, and so started a profitable industry.

I've always liked the stuff - excellent to cook with and I enjoy its old-timers connotations. When you start going back through the vintages, comparatively it's not that expensive for one so old: we had glasses from both our birth years, as well as the summer of '69 and, for a random taste of history, 1934, the year Hitler became Führer.

The hotel we were staying in, the once grand and very grandly named Reid's Palace, now subsists in a rather endearing way on couples of a certain age, which was entirely in keeping with our relaxed Madeira-sipping afternoons and gentle perambulations around the numerous botanical gardens. It definitely didn't feel like our usual action stations holiday, and could so easily have felt laughably geriatric ... but it didn't, it was just a perfect change of pace and refreshingly restorative.

PORTUGAL

FACT FILE

Geographical summary: The most westerly country on the European mainland and borders only with Spain. The land consists of highland forests in the wetter and cooler north and rolling lowland in the hotter south. The Madeira Islands are a Portuguese archipelago positioned about 580 kilometres (360 miles) west of Morocco in the northern Atlantic Ocean. They are an autonomous region of Portugal, with Madeira Island (the largest island of the group), and Porto Santo being the only inhabited ones.

Population: 10.7 million.

Religion: Over four-fifths Roman Catholic; less than 3% other Christians and the rest unknown or atheists.

Ethnic make-up: 95% Portuguese, approximately 5% ethnic minorities.

Life expectancy: 76 male, 82.5 female.

External influences: Apart from a brief union with Spain (1580–1640), Portugal remained independent, but it's basically been downhill all the way since their Golden Age, the 15th century, when Henry the Navigator and Vasco da Gama didn't so much put them on the map as drew the first draft.

The essentials of their cooking: There's a lot of grilling going down, though they're fond of a fryer, too.

Soups and stews are popular and slow-cooked; puddings (including the excellently named *pudim*) tend to be nursery-ish. Strong flour culture: breads and pastries.

Food they export: Wine, beer, sugar, olive oil, tomatoes, pastry.

Top 5 favourite ingredients: Fish and seafood (especially *bacalhau* – salt cod – their favourite), olive oil, rice, tomatoes, pork.

Most famous dish: To all intents and purposes piri piri, though technically this is actually of African origin, named after the bird's-eye chillies with which it's made.

What they drink: Plenty of wine – green-tinged whites (*vinho verde*) and dark reds. Coral and Sagres beers. And Madeira for all occasions, from dry to sweet: sercial, verdelho, boal and malvasia (aka malmsey).

Best thing I ate: For the sheer fun of it, those *espetadas* (see page 108).

Most breathtaking moment: I had my first helicopter ride in Madeira – that vertical take-off takes a bit of getting used to.

Don't ask for…: A penalty shoot-out with England.

Rural
&
Real

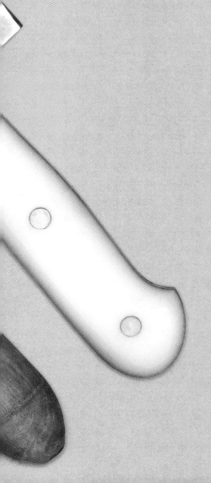

Without meaning to sound too greedy, I bought two knives in Madeira, both of which it turns out were made on the mainland.

The more attractive of them is by a small cutlery maker in the Évora province, Joaquim Franzino, with a rounded olive-wood handle. It's a personal belief of mine that a knife isn't truly yours until it's drawn blood, but with this knife I had a first: catering a wedding in Greenwich Park, intently slicing fifteen legs of lamb to feed a party of 200, it was the blunt side of the blade that split the callous on my forefinger and there was nothing I could do as my blood trickled into the perfectly pink juices running from the saltmarsh lamb. Show must go on.

The second looks a lot more pedestrian but over the years has proved itself extremely useful and versatile. This is actually v.2 of the same knife: I'd purchased exactly the same one in the corner of a small fish market one very early sunny morning outside Lagos, and immediately felt pleased with the weight and grip of it … and that white handle just worked in a fishy context: very cool and smooth to grip. But when I got back home to work my favourite sous-chef told me he was leaving, heading back to Brazil, and I did the thing that any decent head chef would do and gave him the knife, knowing that it would serve him well in many circumstances.

Some years later we were in Madeira, and remembering how much I'd briefly bonded with the white-handled knife from Portugal, we knocked around a few hardware stores in Funchal just on the off-chance that I might run into it again. There was no joy in any of the ironmongers, but having asked around I was pointed in the direction of a '70s-looking slightly under-populated department store and with no expectations at all went to the upstairs kitchen department and there it was. Same knife, same maker, and it was like being reunited with an old friend that you never thought you'd see again.

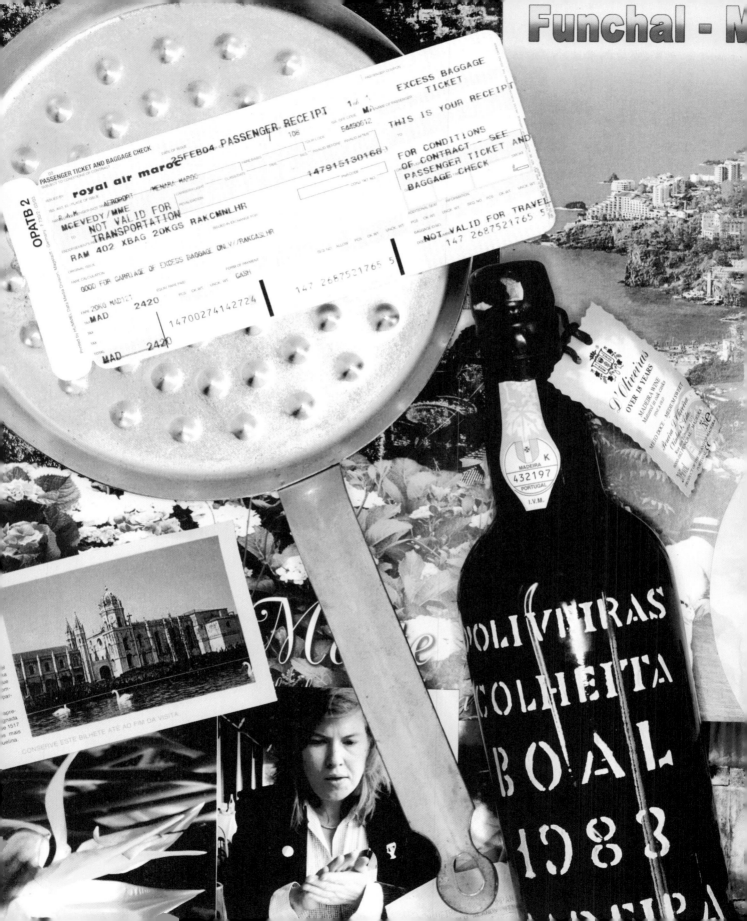

PORTUGESE RECIPES

Caldo Verde
A Soup of Greens, Spuds and a bit of Pig

Clams Açorda

Grilled Lapas
Limpets – or mussels/clams

Espetadas com Milho Frito
Swords of Meat with Fried Polenta

Caldo Verde
A Soup of Greens, Spuds and a bit of Pig

Serves 4, and involves about 45 minutes easy cooking

60ml/2½fl oz extra virgin olive oil

2 small onions, peeled and diced

4 cloves of garlic, minced with salt

650g/1lb 5oz potatoes, peeled and cut into big chunks

1 litre/1¾ pints light chicken stock (as in half strength)

20 thickish slices of *fuet/salchichón* (or any skinny salami - not the one with peppercorns on the outside)

200g (7oz) kale, Cavolo Nero or outside leaves of Savoy cabbage, finely shredded

As a testament to how popular this delicious soup is, in any veg market in Portugal you'll see hanging bags puffed up to busting with super-finely shredded dark cabbage leaves sold specifically for making industrial amounts of caldo verde.

Heat the oil in a heavy casserole pan and gently cook the onions until tender. Add the garlic, stir and then tip in the spuds. Season with salt and pepper, pour on the stock, turn up the heat and cover with a lid. When it is boiling, drop in the *salchichón*, put the lid back on and turn down to a busy simmer.

After about 15-20 minutes, the potatoes should be starting to fall apart. Break them up roughly with the back of a spoon before stirring in the cabbage and more seasoning. You might need to adjust the consistency by adding some water at this point.

Turn the heat down to low and keep cooking with the lid on until the greens collapse, about 10 minutes, but don't let them lose all their integrity and goodness. Let sit for 5 minutes before serving.

Clams Açorda

Quick supper for 2 in 30 minutes

150g/5oz really crusty white bread

3 tablespoons extra virgin olive oil, and more for drizzling

a big handful of coriander, roughly chopped (including stalks)

2 cloves of garlic, peeled and chopped

500g/1lb clams

1 small onion, finely chopped

300ml/½ pint dry white wine

1 egg, beaten

salt and pepper

You'll see many variations on the *açorda* theme in Portugal: the most memorable one I had was just clams, but they really use any seafood - prawns, mussels, squid - so you can, too.

Preheat the oven to 170°C/340°F/gas mark 3½.

Tear the bread into pieces roughly the size of a squash ball and spread them on a baking tray. Drizzle liberally with olive oil and put them into the oven. Bake for 15 minutes, giving them a shuffle and turn a few times.

Whiz the coriander, garlic and a couple of big pinches of salt in a food processor with the 3 tablespoons of olive oil to make a paste (or use a pestle and mortar).

Heat a wide pan on a high flame and chuck in the clams, onions and wine. Cover and simmer for a few minutes until the clams open.

Use a spoon to pick out and discard any clams that haven't opened, toss in the toasted bread chunks, then pour in the egg and stir well.

Put a lid on for a couple of minutes until the bread has softened, then whip it off, give it a stir and reduce busily for 2-3 minutes. Turn off the heat and mix in most of the herb paste, keeping back about a tablespoonful.

Season, then serve immediately with the rest of the coriander paste spooned over the top.

Grilled Lapas (or Mussels/Clams)

Serves 2, and all done in
15 minutes

2 portions of shellfish (around
500g/1lb for 2 people)

½ a glass of water or white wine

a big handful of flat-leaf parsley,
leaves picked and finely chopped

4 cloves of garlic, chopped

5 tablespoons butter, softened

a few handfuls of rock salt,
for serving

salt and pepper

On top of a hill, within sight of the sea, I had this riff on the old seafood-garlic-parsley-butter theme with limpets (*lapas*), which were properly sea-tasting and had a very absorbing texture. For some reason I've yet to see limpets for sale in this country, so the obvious substitutes for recreating this taste of Madeira are clams or mussels. Regular clams are more of a hassle, as they are so small, so you'll have an easier life either using big clams (anything from a large American hardshell to an armande, which is mid-size) or mussels, in which case go for fresh British rather than the big and usually tough frozen green-lipped New Zealand ones. Basically opt for whatever is freshest on the day ... or splash out on a shellfish combo and do a mix of both.

Because I live under the mistaken belief that my kitchen is a Tardis, I brought back some special limpet-grilling pans, but you can use any grill pan and then transfer them to a plate with rock salt on it, so they sit nicely.

Get a wide pan big enough to hold the shellfish good and hot, then drop them in along with the water or white wine. Cover the pan with a lid until the clams have just opened, then quickly tip them on to a plate to cool.

Preheat the grill to high. Break off and chuck away the half of the shell that doesn't have the goodies nestling in it, and fit the other halves into the grill pan, open faces upwards.

Mix together the parsley, garlic, butter, salt and pepper. Use a teaspoon to share it between the open shellfish (using more on the bigger ones) and put them under the grill for about 3-4 minutes, until golden and the smell of garlic and hot seashells fills the room.

Unless you, too, happen to be the proud owner of bespoke limpet-grilling pans, cover the bottom of the serving plates with a couple of centimetres/an inch of rock salt. As soon as the beasts are done, move them across (caution: the shells will be mighty hot) and give them a little shimmy to nestle in the salt, thus avoiding spilling their liquid gold.

Espetadas com Milho Frito
Swords of Meat with Fried Polenta

Fun and filling times for 6-8. Allow 30 minutes for the meat prep (though your friendly butcher could do most of this for you), then marinating time of your choice. The actual cooking can all be done in 45 minutes.

For the chicken

1kg/2lb chicken breasts

5 bay leaves, slightly crushed

3 cloves of garlic, crushed

60ml/2½fl oz extra virgin olive oil

juice of 1 lemon (about 60ml/2½fl oz)

pepper

For the beef

1.5kg/3lb hunk of sirloin

5 bay leaves, slightly crushed

3 cloves of garlic

60ml/2½fl oz extra virgin olive oil

60ml/2½fl oz red wine vinegar

pepper

For the polenta

extra virgin olive oil

250g/8oz quick-cook polenta

light oil for frying

salt and pepper

Espetadas are very large kebabs particular to Madeira and Portugal; basically a yard of grilled meat per head.

Clearly you aren't going to have the *espetada* kit, but I'd still go for this dish using the longest kebab skewers you can find, as it makes for a really fun lunch, and interactive food is the best.

In a cliff top restaurant on the north coast of the island, chicken and beef were both served to us, and the presentation was impressive to say the least: the chicken *espetada* had a scrunched-up butter wrapper at the hook end (i.e. the top) of the skewer, so that when they were dangling on the stand the butter from the paper melted down on the meat, keeping it moist and glistening. The beef one relied on chunks of beef fat interspersed with the meat for doing the same job. As the meat rested on the vertical skewers, these tasty fatty bits combined with the meat juices to drip on to the bread underneath, which was then used to wrap the meat in. Nice.

I appreciate this is not the easiest thing to recreate at home, but it was just too spectacular and delicious not to include in our culinary report from Madeira - really all you need is some very long kebab sticks, a grill (preferably open), some kind of fashioned stand and quite a lot of robust red wine to help the proceedings along.

Cut the chicken breasts in half lengthwise and then 3 times crosswise so that each breast makes 6 pieces.

Trim the fat and skin off the sirloin and cut it into 3cm/1¼ inch chunks. You should be left with about 1kg/2lb of cubed meat and 500g/1lb of fat. Cut the fat into squares of about 3cm/1¼ inches as well.

Put the beef into one bowl and the chicken into another. Add the bay, garlic and olive oil, and lots of ground black pepper to each bowl, then add the lemon juice to the chicken and the vinegar to the beef. Leave the meat in the marinade for 1-2 hours or overnight if you're that forward thinking.

To make the polenta thins, heat a litre/1¾ pints of water with a good sprinkling of salt and a splash of olive oil. When the water is at a rolling boil, pour in the polenta, whisking as you pour. Cook for about 3 minutes, stirring with a wooden spoon. Check the seasoning. Oil a baking tray that will hold the polenta in a layer about 1-2cm/½-¾ inch thick. Spread the polenta on to it and level the surface with a palette knife. Leave it to set and cool for about 30 minutes.

Thread the meat on to skewers, packing it closely. Intersperse the beef chunks with the squares of fat, which will melt during cooking and make the meat taste yummy. The chicken skewers should be started with a piece of crumpled butter paper (which does the job of the beef fat), followed by the meat.

When the polenta has cooled, cut it into squares about 3cm/1¼ inches across. To fry the polenta, use a thick frying pan with oil about 1cm/½ inch deep over a medium high heat. Drop in the squares of polenta in batches and fry for about 5 minutes each side, until crispy. Drain on kitchen paper and keep warm in a low oven.

Season the meat well before cooking it on the barbecue or under the grill - it's really hard to give barbecuing cooking times, but mine take about 8 minutes on both sides, plus a little rest on your homemade stand with the warm flatbread underneath the skewers for their juices to drip on to. Have a bowl or basket of the crisp polenta thins to the side and serve with an undressed salad of intense leaves, like rocket or watercress, and some ripe tomatoes.

The first time I went to Morocco was Christmas Day 1995, when I was twenty-five: I'd cooked lunch for family and friends, served it up, then departed for the airport with my girlfriend, leaving them to enjoy. Starting the trip in this slightly eccentric way, from goose and sprouts to Christ-free Casablanca in a matter of hours, accentuated the difference between our world and this new, magical one that enraptured me then, and has never subsequently disappointed. I had no idea that somewhere so different could be so close - it seemed almost cheating that in three and a half hours you could be in an enchanted place, refreshingly unfamiliar and definitely not in Europe any more, Toto.

I always hire a car, and I always underestimate the distances, leaving us on one occasion a crazy day's driving to get from the Sahara desert to Marrakech, over the High Atlas mountains, in order to catch our flight home. We made it, just, but both us and the car were in tatters when we arrived, due to a blowout and, separately, a teeny-weeny crash. Essentially, though, driving here is fun and easy, as the roads tend to be straight and just disappear into the horizon: there's no better way to cover distance and take in as much as possible of the goodies on offer.

There's adventure to be had in every size of location, from a truck-stop shack to the teeming Djemaa el Fna, the main square of the capital, with its sizzling stalls and wagons of teeth for sale. Provincial cities like Rabat and Meknes have crowded and atmospheric souk-filled medinas, enclosed by old city walls - nothing like the Roman ones I'd grown up with - and guarded by impressive kasbahs. The best of all of these is Fes, the central city of Morocco for so many years and still just a little stuck in those times.

Smaller towns, like the mysterious Chefchaouen, pocketed in the mountains in the north, are famed for their murderous ways when Christians passed by only 100 years ago. After dark you definitely feel like you're on their turf, with the menfolk coming out of the hammams on to the gas-lit streets, looking like Obi-Wan Kenobi in their swishing djellabas. Anywhere you care to stop for a cup of sweet tea you'll find something to absorb you, even if it's just a boy with some goats or the beauty of the landscape. One day you're waking up with Berbers to the sound of camels clambering up the sand dunes, and the next in full winter warmers surrounded by snow.

For those who like their food, it's inspirational: being a stone's throw from the European mainland we share many of the same ingredients, but the attitude and basic principles of their cooking are a world apart. The same for the architecture - the Moors are my heroes, with their ludicrously intricate carved mosques, brightly coloured geometric *zellij* (tiles) and astounding inlaid marble.

As you can probably tell by now, Morocco holds a truly special place in my heart: it was my first holiday with my wife-to-be, and on that trip everywhere we went felt like it was sprinkled with stardust. Rose-tinted specs, you say? Well, that seemed only appropriate as we were in the Vallée de Dadès, the source of their much-loved rosewater.

Morocco

Fact File

Geographical summary: Situated at the top of Africa; borders with Spain to the north, Algeria to the east and south-east, and Mauritania to the south. About the size of California. The Atlas Mountain range is the largest in North Africa. Northern regions have a Mediterranean climate, while the south comprises semi-arid Sahara desert.

Population: 32.5 million.

Religion: Pretty much totally Islamic (about 98%).

Ethnic make-up: 99% Arab, Berber or mixed Arab-Berber.

Life expectancy: 73 male, 79 female.

External influences: Following the death of Mohammed in the 7th century, Muslim Arabs invaded and converted the native Berbers to Islam, but the Berbers fought back and it wasn't until the 16th century that they finally succumbed to Arab rule, under the Alaouite family who are still the ruling family today. Came under French Protectorate in the 20th century (with a bit of Spanish interest in the north), leading to a mass influx from France, until 1956 when full independence was granted.

The essentials of their cooking: None can be more traditional than the old tagine. Also a big salad culture, surprisingly often of the cooked and cold, not raw variety. Unleavened bread and pastries, too.

Food they export: Tomatoes, citrus fruits, olives, string beans, other fruit, cheese, melons.

Top 5 favourite ingredients: Olives (and their oil), citrus (including preserved lemons), mint, lamb, grains (couscous and bulgar).

Most famous dish: That tagine again.

What they drink: Lots of sweet mint tea. They also produce a certain amount of wine (most memorable brand being the Cellars of Meknes, a name straight out of Hammer House of Horror).

Best thing I ate: We looked in at the first female co-operative in the country, which produced argan nut oil. The operation was simple, but the oil that ran free from the antiquated nut press was deliciously complex.

Most breathtaking moment: On the edge of the Sahara, in complete darkness due to a power cut, I looked up and NEVER have I seen so many stars. It actually made me catch my breath in wonderment.

Don't ask for...: Kif, the local hashish – it's around but they don't like to talk about it.

lemon wood
pastry
slicer

Part of Morocco's intense charm is that it is a relatively straightforward land, compared to our over-filled Western existence. In our kitchens we tend to have gadgets that purr into action at the flick of a switch, whereas the Moroccan kitchens that I've peeked into over the years are refreshingly lacking in Modern Kit. And yet here is a bit of kit that I'd never seen before: its sole job is to cut cakes and pastry, most especially filo – their favourite around these parts.

Anyone who's been to the main souk in Marrakech knows that it's a bit of a bunfight, to put it mildly, and that tourists are fair game for the local salesmen. But in truth there was nowhere better to start my mission, though I wasn't surprised when my question was met with either shaking heads or pointing at ornamental daggers. Eventually it was a man who sold antique Moorish jewellery who nodded, and with trepidation and excitement I followed him far from the main drag, down smaller and smaller alleys, until we got to a very dim area. In this part of the souk there were workshops rather than stalls: a man mending motorbikes, another with beautiful handmade djellabas and my knife man: these guys clearly were tradesmen, not hawkers.

He sat on a thick carpet in a tiny area surrounded by his tools, pieces of wood, plenty of shavings and a few of the resulting wooden knives and spoons. It was more like a closet than a workspace but he seemed very comfortable in it.

While I was there a man swooshed by carrying a battered metal tray high over everyone's heads as he made his way through the narrow passages. He poured dramatically but without ceremony from an enamel teapot into small glasses, and gave some to the man fixing motorbikes, as well as the knife man and the jewellery seller. Working men in Morocco, even builders, drink loose-leaf green tea full of fragrant herbs: the only thing in common with our builder's tea is lots of sugar.

The knife man spoke no English at all, just smiled a lot and got his old friend the jewellery guy to translate for me. They had both worked at the souk all their lives and knew everyone - it clearly was more than just a place to work. The whole experience was so different from the main part of the souk, which belongs to the stall hawkers, and I felt very privileged and lucky to be there: neither of them was at all bothered whether I bought or not - just gently amused.

This knife was made by a real craftsman to tackle the serious business of pastry and cakes, not just clutter to rip off the tourists. It might not be the most complicated knife to make, but over the years I've come to find it useful, beautiful and representative of that most basic of pleasures: goodwill.

We all know that more than any other skill in the kitchen, pastry is an affair of the heart. With its cushioned, soft-sounding cutting and rounded curves, this simple tool, shaped from lemonwood, is just the most pleasing gadget that you'll ever wrap your fingers around.

Moroccan Recipes

ﻓﻄﻮﺭ ﻓﻲ ﺍﻟﺼﻮﻳﺮﺓ

Breakfast in Essaouira

ﺳﻠﻄﺔ ﺑﻴﺾ ﻭﺧﺮﺷﻮﻑ

Egg & Artichoke Salad

ﺳﺮﺩﻳﻦ ﻣﺤﺸﻲ

Stuffed Sardines

ﻗﺮﻉ ﻣﺮﻳﺶ ﻣﻄﻬﻮ ﻣﻊ ﺍﻟﻜﻤﻮﻥ

Roast Pumpkin with Cumin

ﺑﺎﻗﻼﻳﻦ ﻣﺤﻮﻱ ﻣﻊ ﺍﻟﻜﻤﻮﻥ

Broad Beans Braised in their Pods

ﻛﺘﻒ ﻣﻦ ﻟﺤﻢ ﺍﻟﺨﺮﻭﻑ ﺍﻟﻤﻄﺒﻮﺥ ﺑﺒﻄﺀ

Slow-Cooked Lamb,
Chilli Stock & Melted Onions

ﺑﺮﺗﻘﺎﻝ ﻓﻲ ﻃﻨﺠﺔ

Oranges in Tangiers

MOROCCO #1

JARDINS MAJORELLE
MUSÉE D'ART ISLAMIQUE
MARRAKECH

250 ml

Huile Argan traditionnelle
TAMAZIRT

GLOBAL FOOD COMPANY SARL

Lalla Mira sarl
14, Rue d'Algérie - 44100
ESSAOUIRA - MAROC
Tel. +(212) (0) 44 47 50 46
+(212) (0) 44 47 58 50

Breakfast in Essaouira

Makes enough for about 20ish little pancakes. The batter is knocked up in a couple of minutes, then from when it's rested it takes about 30 minutes to cook all the pancakes and pull the rest together.

200g/7oz fine semolina

60g/2½oz plain flour

½ teaspoon salt

150ml/¼ pint milk

10g/3½ teaspoons dried yeast

---

1 large egg, beaten

---

a bit of light oil (like sunflower) for greasing the pan

To serve

---

argan oil, or any kind of good nut oil - hazelnut is delicious

---

runny honey

---

soft-boiled eggs

---

ground cumin

---

sea salt and pepper

This was our daily rooftop breakfast, overlooking the busy fishermen in the port at a wonderful hotel called Lalla Mira, in the town of Essaouira.

The pancake recipe is taken from Latifa Bennani-Smirès's *La Cuisine Marocaine*, written in French. The texture of the batter consistency translates as 'feeble', where I suppose we would normally say thin, though feeble somehow provides better imagery.

Light, fluffy and airy, there's no doubt that the pancakes are the star, but the real joy is in the combination ... just a bit of this and that which turns out so much greater than the sum of the parts. As far from a full English as the Marrakech souks are from any London street market, but just as easily devoured and a lot better for you!

Sieve the semolina, flour and salt into a big bowl. Mix the milk with 350ml/12fl oz of hot water and whisk in the yeast and the egg. Add the liquid gradually to the dry ingredients, whisking all the time, and carry on going for another 5 minutes to aerate. Then leave somewhere warm for about 2 hours (or overnight).

Heat a griddle or frying pan on a medium heat and grease it lightly. Stir the batter and drop small ladlefuls (about 2 tablespoons) on to the pan to make little pancakes about 6cm/2½ inches in diameter. Cook for a minute or two - they are ready when little bubbles burst on the top. Turn them over and cook for about 20 seconds on the other side.

Serve them with argan oil, honey, eggs, cumin, salt and pepper.

Egg & Artichoke Salad

Serves 4 as a starter.
20 minute job

---

2 cobs of sweetcorn

---

4 eggs

150g/5oz peas (frozen are fine)

---

1 x 300g/10oz jar of artichoke hearts
(packed in oil rather than water),
drained

---

generous handful of mint leaves,
roughly torn

---

1 Little Gem lettuce, chopped into
large pieces

---

juice of ½ a lemon

---

2 tablespoons extra virgin olive oil

---

a big pinch of turmeric

---

salt and pepper

Marrakech is a magical, busy, crazy city. From morning till midnight it's busting full of noise: cars, people, calls to prayer and hawkers all clamouring together to make an exciting din. Not far from the centre sits one of my favourite hotels in the world. From the moment you go through the gates, La Mamounia is like stepping into an Agatha Christie novel; an old school oasis of calm in a sweaty foreign land. Its gardens are also my second favourite in the city, after the stunning *Jardins Majorelle*, designed by Yves Saint Laurent.

I first stayed there in my twenties when my dad bought me and my girlfriend a couple of nights for a birthday present. Coming right at the end of a particularly grungy few weeks of travelling, we thought it was the Best Thing Ever, and the beds were more comfort than we'd known since leaving home. Needless to say we slept so well we missed our flight home and literally had to beg our way back to Britain.

I went back in my thirties (and it still was pretty much the Best Thing Ever) and had this simple and surprisingly delicious salad by the pool.

Shuck the corn from the cobs using a sharp knife (hold the cob vertically on a surface and run the knife down each side to remove the kernels). Lower the eggs into boiling water and cook for 6 minutes; then, when time's up, chuck the peas and corn into the water, too. Cover the pan, bring back to the boil, then drain and run everything under cold water until the peas and corn are cold.

Cut the artichoke hearts into wedges, put them into a big bowl and mix with the mint, corn, peas and lettuce. Squeeze over the lemon juice, season well with salt and pepper, then pour on the oil and toss well.

Spoon the salad into a serving dish, then cut the peeled eggs lengthwise and put them around the edge. Sprinkle the eggs with salt and turmeric.

LA MAMOUNIA

Bienvenue - Welcome - مرحبا

الإسم : Nom : MM SMITHER/MCEVEDY

Name

الـغـرفـة : Chambre N° : 220

Room Number

Stuffed Sardines

Serves 6 and takes 15 minutes
to make and the same again
to cook

75g/3oz mixed herbs, picked and
chopped (prepared weight)

---

zest of 2 lemons, plus more lemons
for wedging

---

a small bunch of spring onions,
finely chopped

---

2 cloves of garlic, finely chopped

---

around 5 tablespoons extra virgin
olive oil

---

12 medium sardines, butterflied,
head off, and with the big bones
trimmed off the fillets

---

about 500ml/17fl oz light oil, for
shallow-frying

---

a big handful of coarse semolina,
for coating

---

salt and pepper

Here in Britain we are so close to the Med, yet when it comes to sardines we are a world away. Instinctively most would think tins, whereas grilling sardines is the single most evocative smell of the Mediterranean I know. We tend to associate them more with the countries on the north side, but fishies have a tendency of getting around, and this recipe from the south side bears more than a passing resemblance to its Italian neighbours.

You can use whichever soft herbs you have around: tarragon, basil, chives, dill, parsley, etc., though I find mint, parsley and coriander is a winner, especially when served with a lemony-dressed fennel salad.

Ask the fishmonger to do the sardine prep work for you.

Mix together the herbs, lemon zest, spring onions, garlic and oil to make a paste, and season it well.

Make sandwiches with the fish: lay half the sardines skin-side down and share the herb mixture between them, spreading it along the fillets with the back of a spoon. Then place the other sardines on top, skin-side up, so you have shiny sardine sandwiches.

Preheat the oven to 160°C/325°F/gas mark 3. Heat the oil in the widest frying pan you have until it's good and hot but not smoking. Put the semolina on a plate and touch both sides of each sandwich in it before lowering it gently into the oil (and if the fish doesn't fizzle when you put it in, the oil isn't hot enough).

Fry the sardines in batches, turning carefully after about 2-3 minutes and cooking for a slightly shorter time on the second side until they are golden brown all over. Drain them briefly on kitchen paper before putting them into the oven to keep warm while you cook the rest.

Serve with a big piece of lemon and a little lightly dressed salad - shaved fennel would be nice, but watercress or baby spinach would be perfect too ... and less faff.

Roast Pumpkin with Cumin

Serves 4 as a side dish, and takes about 35 minutes in the oven

---

1kg/2lb pumpkin

3 tablespoons extra virgin olive oil

1 teaspoon cumin seeds

1 tablespoon honey

a handful of pumpkin seeds

a handful of flaked almonds

salt

The trouble with pumpkins is that they're so bloody huge, but it feels wrong to let an autumn go by without buying at least one of what is my favourite season's biggest mascot. Soup, pie, risotto and then what? Well, this stunning bit on the side is a doddle and very, very tasty.

Having said all that, you can actually make this with any kind of squash.

I remember this being the best dish served at a little restaurant in a town up in the mountains called Chefchaouen. It was after dark, a time when Arabic towns always seem to come alive, with twinkly lights, the lyrical calling from the minarets and the smells of home fires mixing with local *kif* floating atmospherically in through the window. Something for all the senses.

Preheat the oven to 200°C/400°F/gas mark 6.

Peel and deseed the pumpkin, then cut it into medium-sized chunks. Spread the pieces over a baking tray, pour over the oil, sprinkle on the cumin seeds and season with salt. Give all the pieces a good roll around with your hands to coat.

Put into the oven for 20 minutes, then turn the pieces over, drizzle with honey, and sprinkle with the pumpkin seeds and flaked almonds. Put it back into the oven for another 10-15 minutes, keeping an eye on things and turning the pieces if necessary so that they are nicely browned round the edges but don't go through caramelized to burnt.

Transfer to a serving dish, pouring any remaining oil in the bottom of the pan on top.

Broad Beans Braised in their Pods

Serves 4-6 as a side dish.
A 10 minute make then
30 minutes cooking

400g/13oz broad beans in their pods

100ml/3½fl oz extra virgin olive oil

2 cloves of garlic, peeled and finely sliced

1 large onion, halved and thinly sliced

1 whole chilli, dried or fresh

1 x 400g tin of tomatoes

a small handful of mint, finely chopped

a squeeze of lemon juice

salt and pepper

This is a fabulous standard in Morocco, though you need to do it with youngish broad beans at the beginning of the season (i.e. June/July), as the pods are too tough to stew down to the desirable softness with old ones.

It feels kind of like cheating (in a good way) to bypass first the podding, then all that shelling usually done with broadies.

Rinse the beans, trim the tops and slice the pods diagonally into oblique oblongs about 5cm/2 inches long.

Heat the oil in a wide pan. Sauté the beans along with the garlic, onion and chilli for a few minutes, then cover and cook on a medium heat for about 5 minutes. Stir in the tomatoes, mix well and season enthusiastically. Pour in 500ml/17fl oz of water, turn up the heat, put on a lid and bring to the boil. Once boiling, turn down the heat and simmer for 15 minutes.

Take off the lid and let it continue bubbling down for another 15 minutes, allowing the liquid to reduce a bit.

Turn off the heat and let the beans sit for a few minutes before stirring in the mint and lemon juice and having a final taste for seasoning.

Serve warm, not piping hot.

Slow-Cooked Lamb, Chilli Stock & Melted Onions

Serves 4-6. Takes 15 minutes prep, then 2 to 2 hours 30 minutes cooking time

a shoulder of lamb, anywhere between 1.2-2kg/2½-4lbs

2 carrots, peeled and chopped

a few big slices of cabbage

a couple of potatoes, peeled and cut into large wedges

a good handful of French beans

2 sticks of celery, cut into large pieces

60ml/2½fl oz extra virgin olive oil, plus a good glug for the couscous

5 onions, peeled and sliced

250g/8oz couscous

a handful of parsley, chopped

a handful of mint, chopped

juice of ½ a lemon

For the stock

1.5 litres/2½ pints light chicken stock (as in half strength)

3 chillies

3 bay leaves

a big pinch of saffron

4 cloves of garlic, smashed and peeled

1 tablespoon coriander seeds

½ teaspoon cumin seeds

1 tablespoon honey

1 teaspoon ras el hanout (optional)

We had this in the fantastically Arabian Nights-ish restaurant in the medina in Marrakech called Yacout. It follows the principle of a tagine (everything goes in raw with a stock and slow-cooks together), but has the advantage of not requiring an actual tagine to make it.

Preheat the oven to 180°C/350°F/gas mark 4.

If your shoulder is on the larger side then take a minute to trim some of the fat off it - if it comes from a young lamb this won't be necessary.

Heat the stock with the chillies, bay leaves, saffron, garlic, coriander, cumin, honey and ras el hanout if you have it.

Put the meat, skin-side up, into a roasting tray. Surround it with the carrots, cabbage, potatoes, beans and celery and season with a few pinches of salt.

When the stock is boiling, pour it over the lamb, cover the dish with foil, sealing well around the edges, and put it into the oven. After an hour, turn over the meat and shuffle the vegetables about gently, then cover it again and put it back for another 1 to 1 hour 30 minutes (if it's a big leg, go for the longer time and give it one more turn after an hour).

Half an hour before the meat will be ready, heat the oil for the onions in a large, heavy-based pan on a medium heat. Tip in the onions and cook, stirring, for 10-15 minutes with a lid on the pan. When they've collapsed and picked up a bit of colour, take off the lid and turn the heat down. Keep cooking, stirring regularly, for about another 15 minutes, until the onions are sticky, brown and caramelized. Season.

When the lamb is tender, take it out and turn it skin-side up again to rest.

Tip the couscous into a big bowl, pour on the oil, and gently rub the grains through your hands for a minute so they are all coated. Pour/ladle enough hot stock from the baking tray to cover the couscous, plus about 2cm/¾ inch more, then cover tightly with clingfilm and leave to soak for about 5 minutes. Fork through to release the steam and cool it down, stirring in the herbs and lemon juice once it's only slightly warm, not hot.

Pile the couscous in the middle of a suitably dramatic serving dish with the vegetables around, the lamb on top and the onions sitting pretty. Serve with any remaining hot stock in a small saucepan on the side, with the chillies floating.

Oranges in Tangiers

Serves 4, and takes 30 minutes
start to finish

6 tablespoons honey
100g/3½oz bulgar wheat
1 tablespoon orange blossom water
4-6 oranges, depending on size
100g/3½oz pistachios, shelled
a pinch of salt (optional)

On a holiday in Southern Spain, we'd nipped across to Tangiers on the ferry and were there in time for lunch. While I knew that oranges were an important North African export, I'd never thought about or seen grains used before in a sweet situation, and was quite struck. Since then, having the basic ingredients in the house for this faux-sophisticated dessert has got me out of many a pudding hole.

Melt half the honey in 150ml/¼ pint of boiling water. Put the bulgar in a small pan, pour over the honey water and stir in the orange blossom water. Cover with a lid and let simmer very gently for about 10 minutes until all the liquid has been absorbed.

Prepare the oranges by cutting the peel away with a knife, then slicing in between the white dividers and letting the segments fall freely into a bowl. Squeeze what's left of the pillaged orange into the bowl, too. Either with a food processor, knife or the old pestle & mortar, roughly chop the pistachios with a pinch of salt (unless they are already salted).

Stir the rest of the honey into the nuts along with 1 tablespoon of water. Put a pastry ring (about 8cm/3¼ inches across) in the centre of each of 4 dessert plates. Divide the bulgar between them, spoon a layer of the nut mixture on top, then take off the rings to leave low, perfect cylinders. Lay the orange segments around the edge, and drink the juice for a job well done.

Undoubtedly Italy has influenced my cooking, my cultural interests and the link between the two more than any other country. With my father's nigh-on obsession with the Romans, unsurprisingly it was the destination he chose for his daughters' first trip abroad. As a seven-year-old I remember laughing myself off my little chair when my dad told me that the long dry sticks of *grissini* were a kind of bread, and of course the *gelati* also made a big impression.

Over the next decade we went there regularly, knocking off the most important Roman sites and other cultural unmissables, resulting in me knowing considerably more about Italy's history through their *duomos*, *chiesas*, *scoulas*, *gallerias* and *museos* than I did about my own native land. And though, like any reasonable child, I regularly went on strike by about midday, having that morning already stomped round a mausoleum, a baptistery, some Very Old Stones and a few tatty frescoes, somewhere in there a seed was sown.

Italy is a country saturated with its own history, so much so that it seems barely able to function properly in modern times. Each era is rich with relics, and at almost every point in its past, as well as every geographical point, there are proper treasures to be seen. The busy, boisterous streets of Naples, and a trip up the volcano; my first visit to Venice, misty and magical in the chilly January air; a tour of the Duchies of the north-east - some have stayed in my mind for their food, like Parma (ham), Modena (vinegar) and Cremona (mustard fruits), others for their palazzos (Ferrara) and frescoes (Mantua). It seemed appropriate that Sicily waited until I was old enough to

behave badly, which I did, driving round the whole island with a bottle of limoncello in the glove box (one crash a week). I loved the roughness of the south compared with the more formal north, but the unifying factor of the whole country is passion. Music, art, religion, fashion, politics, history, and, of course, food.

I really have found it pretty hard to eat badly in Italy, from full-blown extravaganzas to street snacks, though it has to be said that given the slightest excuse they won't just have a quick bite, they have to make a meal out of it. No where else does five courses seem the norm: they just make it so easy with their antipasti, pasta, primi piatti, secondi piatti and dolce, and that's without the unmissable formaggio.

Of course any country that takes the whole business of eating, not just the food itself but the time and trouble given to it, quite so respectfully was always going to be a spiritual home for someone like me. They shop largely in markets for the fresh stuff, cook in a relaxed way with love and passion, using the recipes of their grandparents, and sit down to eat as a family for hours and hours. Whereas British food culture at the moment wants us to get all our ingredients in a chainstore supermarket, then be able to produce supper in thirty minutes or less and wolf it down in front of the telly. Says it all really.

The last time I went to Italy completes the circle: it seemed only right, given his love of the Romans, that he spend his afterlife mixing with them too, so the three sisters all went over to Rome and, in an act that our dad would have thought ludicrously sentimental, found a particularly pretty piece of masonry in the Forum and furtively tipped out his ashes.

Italy

Fact File

Geographical summary: Peninsula extending from southern Europe into the Mediterranean Sea, and including islands of Sicily and Sardinia. Alps in the north and Apennines form a rocky spine. Three active volcanoes: Vesuvius, Stromboli and Etna.

Population: 60.1 million

Religion: 83% Roman Catholic; remainder Jewish and Protestant and a growing Muslim immigrant community, an estimated 1.2 million.

Ethnic make-up: Mostly Italian. Also around 4 million legal immigrant foreigners and up to 1 million illegal immigrants, mostly from Romania, Albania and Morocco.

Life expectancy: 79 male, 85 female.

External influences: The Romans provided a solid backdrop to their recent history, though there were local skirmishes with the French and Spanish, mainly in the 18th century, and Austria in the 19th; but these were all regional, as Italy was not unified until the Risorgimento of 1870.

Essentials of their cooking: The grill is good, but they're keen on *al forno* (oven-baked), too. Pasta gets boiled quickly, risottos are loved slowly. Puddings and ice creams also essential. Overall it's simple cooking at its best.

Food they export: Wine, pasta, cheese, olive oil, pastry, chocolate, peeled tomatoes, roasted coffee.

Top 5 favourite ingredients: Pasta, tomatoes (fresh and tinned), olive oil, mozzarella, herbs (especially basil, but they're big on all their *erbe*).

Most famous dish: Spag bol.

What to drink: Lots of *vino locale*, light lagers like Peroni, *aqua con gaz*, grappa and limoncello.

Best thing I ate: The only time a plate of food has ever made me well-up was in Milan: a white truffle tagliatelle that was so perfect I couldn't help but shed a tear. Pathetic but true.

Most breathtaking moment: Italy is full of jaw-dropping beauty, but the first time I saw the temples of Paestum will always be up there for me.

Don't ask for…: Deep-pan pizza.

G. Lorenzi's in Milan is a veritable institution to sharpness. For over a hundred years the family has been one of the finest names in the country for cutlery, scissors, chef's knives and infact anything that requires a bit of an edge. The founding father, Giovanni, was German-trained and then came back to the motherland to set up on his own early in the 20th century. It's safe to say he has out-obsessed me as he collected over 3,700 razors, now proudly housed in their museum, if the urge takes you.

I'd seen ceramic knives before but never taken the plunge, thinking myself too much of a ruffian in the kitchen not to break it. But somehow in this city that is more synonymous with style than any other, it felt like the right time. It must, however, be noted that ceramic blades are not just style over substance - infact their 'substance', if you like, is quite compelling, especially once you've got over the fear.

First off they're bloody sharp, keeping their edge much better than steel knives, and with that comes an almost surgical precision. They're easier to keep clean and hygienic as the ceramic doesn't absorb odours as much: I've done the garlic test on that. The strength of the blade is second only to diamonds, according to their blurb, though that doesn't stop my heart leaping whenever I drop it. It is also the only straight edged knife that I use to slice tomatoes.

But for all that, it is beautiful beyond compare with its dark wood handle, purity of blade and perfectly balanced holster: it's not without reason that this is the shop where Armani buys his knives.

Lorenzi's Ceramica

Italian Recipes

Zuppa di Farro e Lenticchie
Farro & Lentil Soup

Sandwich Arrotolate

Warm Chicken Liver Crostini

Carciofi con Polenta
Artichokes with Polenta

Lobster Spaghettini

Pappardelle con Coniglio / sulla Lepre
with Rabbit/Hare

Lombo di Maiale alla Spiedo
Pork & Rosemary Kebabs

Amor de Pera
Custardy Pear Tart

Zuppa di Farro e Lenticchie
Farro & Lentil Soup

For about 6, but my, is it filling. 30 minutes to make and the same again to cook

---

90g/3¼oz smoked back bacon

3 tablespoons extra virgin olive oil

250g/8oz red onions, diced small

2 sticks of celery, preferably with leaves

2-3 sprigs of rosemary, leaves picked and chopped

2 cloves of garlic, chopped

a pinch of dried chilli flakes

175g/6oz small brown lentils, or Puy lentils (not bigger brown ones)

100g/3½oz farro or pearl barley

1 litre/1¾ pints chicken stock

salt and pepper

Farro is an ancient grain in the same family as spelt, so wheat-free folk love it. I'd never had farro in a soup before and it was a total revelation, making the creamiest lentil soup I'd ever tasted - and it helped the digestion, too.

Apart from how totally tasty it was, the other most memorable thing about this soup (which we had in the medieval walled city of Lucca) was that I really wouldn't have defined it as a soup - you could totally stand your spoon up in it, not that that detracted from it in any way.

Italian celery always has leaves, and they really do add to the flavour of a dish like this. Generally celery here has a few little ones in the middle, so I encourage you to go on and dig into your heart - you never know what you'll find in there if you don't look.

Cut the rind off the bacon, and keep it. Chop the rashers into 1cm/ ½ inch dice.

Heat the oil in a wide saucepan, then chuck in the onions and bacon, along with its rind. Put the lid on and cook over a medium heat, stirring occasionally, while you cut the celery sticks lengthwise into 3 or 4 long strips, then into 1cm/½ inch dice. Rough-chop any celery leaves and stir all this into the pan, along with the rosemary, garlic, chilli and a couple of pinches of salt.

Give the lentils a quick rinse, then add them too, as well as the farro. Once the lentils have been in there for a couple of minutes, pour on the chicken stock, give a quick stir, and put the lid on askew.

Keeping the heat medium, bring up to a steady simmer and hold it there - no rapid boiling here, please.

After 20-30 minutes your lentils and farro should both be cooked, but still with a touch of bite. Fish out the bacon rind and chuck it before ladling half the soup into the blender. Whiz for a minute, then tip it back into the pan.

Do most of your seasoning now - salt to taste and a good crack of pepper - then give it a 5-minute rest, lid on, before taking it to the table and finishing each bowl with a pleasant pool of best extra virgin.

Sandwich Arrotolate

Takes less than 30 minutes to make about 35 small rolled sarnies

---

1 large, square white sandwich loaf, unsliced and very fresh

Dijon mustard

---

sliced mortadella

---

fontina, thinly sliced

---

rocket

---

extra virgin olive oil

---

salt and pepper

Trust the Italians to make even a sandwich beautiful - like this it can be so much more than necessary lunchtime fuel: think canapé or super-snack.

The ingredients here are what we had in a café in Venice, but put in whatever you like, though they need to be flat or it won't roll properly. After extensive experimentation, my tip is you'd do well to follow this format: a spreader (like mustard, tapenade or pesto) + some kind of protein (bresaola, mortadella, Parma ham, taleggio, fontina or goats' cheese) + some greenery (rocket, basil or lamb's lettuce).

Cut the crusts off all sides of the loaf then slice it the opposite way from usual, so that you have 5ish giant slices of bread. Spread the bread with mustard, then layer with slices of mortadella, cheese and rocket. Season and drizzle with olive oil.

With the short side facing you, roll the bread up away from you and position it with the seam downwards. Let it sit for a few minutes, to settle, and give it a bit of a press down to encourage it. Slice carefully into rounds, using your best serrated knife.

Warm Chicken Liver Crostini

Serves 6, and takes 15 minutes prep followed by a 5-minute cook

---

250g/8oz chicken livers

50g/2oz streaky bacon, as fatty as possible, cubed small

---

2 cloves of garlic, finely chopped

---

a large sprig of rosemary, finely chopped

---

3 tablespoons Marsala, sherry or sweet wine

---

2 tablespoons butter, softened

---

some thin crackers or toast

---

splash of extra virgin olive oil

---

salt and pepper

Clean the livers by removing the stringy bit in the middle of each one and season them with salt and pepper.

Put a large frying pan on a high heat. Toss in the cubed bacon then turn the heat down so that it browns nicely in 5-ish minutes. When the pieces are crunchy, use a spoon to fish them out of the pan and set aside.

Turn the heat up again and when hot, sear the livers in the pan so that they aren't touching. After a minute, turn them over and when the other side has browned for a minute, take them out and put them with the bacon.

Keeping the heat high, add the garlic and rosemary to the pan and stir briskly. Allow the garlic to get a nice light brown colour (a minute or so), then tip the meats back in. Pour on the booze and gently shake to keep the livers moving for another minute or two, until the liquid has pretty much evaporated away, then throw in the butter and let it melt.

Turn the heat off, tip everything into a food processor and purée, adding a few tablespoons of warm water or a splash more booze to help it reach a creamy consistency. Serve with a drizzle of EVOO.

Carciofi con Polenta
Artichokes with Polenta

Serves 4 as a starter, and takes
1 hour of very satisfying work

---

2 lemons

---

4 globe artichokes, decent size but
not whoppers

200ml/7fl oz milk

100g/3½oz coarse polenta (not
quick cook - look for the word
'bramata')

40g/1½oz Parmesan, coarsely
grated, plus a bit more to serve

90ml/3¼fl oz extra virgin olive oil,
plus more to serve

---

6 cloves of garlic, smashed with the
flat of a knife and peeled

---

a good handful of sage leaves

---

salt and pepper

When I was about twenty-two we went to Verona, and in the Piazza dell' Erbe there was a lady sitting next to her stall of artichokes, stripping them down to the heart for customers who couldn't be bothered to do it themselves. As a young chef who had already spent a fair amount of hours prepping boxes of artis like this in various restaurants, I marvelled not only at her speed, but really just at her presence. You never see anything like that back home.

Anyway, the real delight was that I was passing through Verona about ten years later and I just had to go and see ... and it was as if I was looking at a painting, because there she was, in exactly the same pose, still dropping hearts into a bucket of lemon water.

This is actually a short make: because of our lack of lady in a market square, half the method is given over to how to prep an artichoke, which incidentally takes way longer to write than to do.

Cut one of the lemons in half and rub it all over your hands: not a masochistic moment but to stop the incredible bitterness in artichokes getting into your skin (and if you think I'm making a fuss you clearly haven't attacked many artichokes - try licking your finger after prepping one: triple 'gusting!'). Once your hands are well coated, squeeze the lemon halves some more over a big bowl of water then drop them in.

Starting from the base, strip the leaves from the artichokes by pulling them back towards the stalk and tearing them off. When the pale waist is exposed, cut through it (easiest done with a serrated knife) and chuck the top.

Now switch to a small sharp knife: cut the stalk at about 6cm/2½ inches, and trim away the tough exterior to reveal the edible core of the stem - the outside of the stalk is too tough to eat. Keeping the same knife, shave around the base of the artichoke, removing the stubs of the leaves, then trimming all around the top edge. You should now be looking at a naked artichoke - something about quarter the size of what you bought.

Dig in with a teaspoon where you see the hairy bit (the appropriately named choke) and firmly scoop and scrape it all out to reveal the heart underneath. That's the end of the lesson; just remember, as you work, to put each trimmed artichoke into the bowl of lemon water to stop discoloration.

Now you're ready to start the recipe proper: heat the milk in a pan with 200ml/7fl oz of water. When it is steaming but not boiling, pour in the polenta in a steady stream, whisking all the time. Turn the heat down very low and season. Cook, stirring now and then with a wooden spoon, until thick and the grains are cooked: proper polenta (as opposed to the instant stuff) will always have a fabulous, sexy texture to it - softly granular, though not with any bite. Best thing to do is to check the side of the pack for the cooking time. When you're happy you're there, turn the heat off, stir in the Parmesan and taste for seasoning - quite a lot of both required, then stick a lid on it.

Whilst the polenta is cooking, heat the oil in a large pan, add the garlic and allow to sizzle gently for a few minutes. Dry the artichokes and put them into the pan, heads facing downwards, stalks up in the air. Keep cooking on a medium heat, covered, for 5-10 minutes, until they are dark golden brown on the bottom, then turn them on to their sides and put the lid back on. Roll them once or twice so they cook evenly on their sides until golden and tender - about 6-10 minutes depending on size of artichokes (check them by inserting a sharp knife into the base and if it goes in easily they're done). Then drop in the sage leaves and gently encourage them to fry evenly to the point at which they are beautifully dark green and glassy looking: avoid browning.

Spoon or pipe the polenta on to plates (it may require a splash of hot water and a brief whisk to restore its creamy texture) and put an artichoke heart, some garlic and a few sage leaves on each one. Finish each plate with more olive oil, a squeeze of lemon, a bit more grated Parmesan and a sprinkle of sea salt.

Lobster Spaghettini

Serves 2. Clearly this dish is a bit of a labour of love - perfect for Valentine's Day - so it would be churlish to think it's a quick cook. Set aside an hour and a half and that way you won't get stressed near the end and be drunk when your date arrives

1 live lobster (weighing about 600g/1lb 2oz)

a knob of butter

extra virgin olive oil

150g/5oz dried spaghettini

75ml/3fl oz double cream

a small handful of tarragon, finely chopped

a large handful of flat-leaf parsley, finely chopped

a small squeeze of lemon

salt and pepper

For the stock

200g/7oz shell-on North Atlantic prawns, raw or cooked

a splash of sunflower oil or other light oil

½ an onion, cut in half again

a few cloves of garlic, unpeeled

3 tomatoes

mixed stock vegetables (carrots, celery, fennel, mushrooms, parsley, bay leaves etc.), roughly chopped

The best start to a New Year I've ever had: 1 January, sitting in the Campo Santo Stefano in Venice eating this dish in the sunshine. I don't think I've ever felt so set up for the year to come.

You really should buy your lobster alive for this dish, and just so you know, the RSPCA recommends that you put it into the freezer for 2 hours before you cook it - just make sure you don't freeze it completely.

To make the stock, first whiz the prawns in a food processor for a couple of moments to break them up a bit. Fry them in oil over a high heat for a few minutes, then add the onion, garlic, tomatoes and the mixed stock vegetables. Stir together until the vegetables have warmed up, then cover with water - about 1 litre/1¾ pints. Put a lid on the pan, bring to the boil, then turn the heat right down, tilt the lid so the pan is only half covered, and let it gently bubble for 30 minutes whilst you amuse yourself elsewhere.

Once it's cooked, drain the stock into a bowl, and really push down on the solids using the back of a ladle so that all the goodness is squeezed out. Pour the liquid back into the pan and boil until reduced by about two-thirds, giving it a good skim along the way.

Meanwhile, bring a large pot of water to a rapid boil. Put in the chilled, knocked-out lobster and boil it for 10 minutes. Fish it out, keeping the water, and leave the lobster to cool.

Preheat the oven to 180°C/350°F/gas mark 4. Bring the pan of water you used to cook the lobster back to the boil, with a big pinch of salt and a dash of olive oil; keep the lid on. Boil the spaghettini in the lobster water until just *al dente*, then drain and cover. As the pasta is cooking, lay the lobster on its back and use a long sharp knife to split it into two lengthwise. Crack the claws with the back of the knife, put on to a baking tray and spread the butter on the lobster flesh. Put the empty pasta pan straight back on the heat and when it is really hot pour in the prawn stock (helps double-time reducing). Bring to a rapid simmer, add the cream and seasoning, and let it bubble until it is a sauce-like consistency.

While the sauce is reducing, cover the lobster with foil and reheat in the oven (10 minutes). When you are ready to serve, stir the cooked pasta, tarragon, parsley and seasoning into the sauce. Finish with a squeeze of lemon. Plate the lobster and, like the presentation I had in Venice, use tongs to drape the pasta over and around the lobster's body.

Pappardelle con Coniglio/sulla Lepre
with Rabbit/Hare

Starter for 6, Mains for 4.
Takes 2-3 hours all in,
but most of that work is
done by the rabbit not you

---

1 rabbit or hare, weighing about
500-700g/1-1½lb, jointed (you can
ask the butcher to do this) with the
saddle and ribs split: you should have
a total of 6 pieces, 4 of them legs

---

4 tablespoons extra virgin olive oil,
plus a dash for the pasta

---

1 large carrot (or 2 small ones),
quartered lengthwise and then sliced

---

6 small shallots, peeled and whole

---

3 sticks of celery, diced, and leaves
chopped if you have them, too

---

3 sprigs of rosemary, leaves picked
and chopped

---

2 bay leaves

---

3 cloves of garlic, chopped

---

1 tablespoon peppercorns

---

a third of a bottle of red wine
(about 250ml/8fl oz)

500ml/17fl oz chicken stock

---

a small glass of Marsala/Madeira

30g/1¼oz butter

---

a small bunch of grapes (about
200g/7000z)

125g/4oz pine nuts, lightly toasted

---

small handful of flat-leaf parsley

500g/1lb dried pappardelle

---

salt and pepper

This is real old-school Tuscan cooking. We had it at a fantastic restaurant called Da Delfina that Rose Gray recommended ... high praise indeed.

They used wild rabbit, but you can also use a hare or a farmed rabbit. The hare will be the leanest and gamiest; the farmed rabbit considerably less, and the wild bunny somewhere between the two. If you can work a day in advance, the flavour of the meat is really enhanced by sitting in its juices overnight after cooking and before removing the meat from the bones.

Preheat the oven to 170°C/340°F/gas mark 3½.

If you have them, take the heart, liver and kidneys out of the rabbit (keeping them for later), check it for fur, rinse under cold water and pat dry. Heat half the oil in a large shallow pan that can go into the oven and season the meat liberally with salt and pepper. Once it's properly hot, lower the pieces of meat into the oil and brown well on all sides, then take out and put aside. Add the rest of the oil to the pan, drop the heat down a bit and follow with the carrot, shallots and celery. Stir well and put a lid on. Cook for 5 minutes, giving it the odd stir, then add the rosemary, bay leaves, garlic and peppercorns and stir again.

Nestle the meat in the vegetables along with any meat juices, then add the wine, bring to the boil and let it simmer for a minute before pouring on the stock, which should pretty much cover the meat. Bring back to the boil, add salt, cover and put it into the oven for 1 hour 30 minutes, until the meat is very tender. Cool with the lid on until handleable.

Shred the meat discarding all the bones, stir it back into the sauce and put the pan on a medium heat with a lid on.

Trim and roughly chop any organs you have kept (heart, liver, kidneys) and add to the pan, along with any blood (if you like). Stir in the Marsala, half the pine nuts, the butter and grapes and let it bubble gently without a lid for 8ish minutes until the grapes are softened and their colour muted, then turn the heat off and put the lid back on. Roughly chop the parsley and mix with the pine nuts you kept back.

Cook the pasta in boiling salted water until *al dente*, then drain and put it into the empty pan with a dash of olive oil. Add the sauce, fold gently and taste for seasoning before finishing with the parsley and pine nuts.

Lombo di Maiale alla Spiede
Pork & Rosemary Kebabs

Serves 4, and takes 30 minutes at the beginning, then 1 hour to marinate and 20 minutes to finish it off

---

4 long, woody stems of rosemary (about 30cm/12 inches each)

2 pork tenderloins, each weighing around 400g/13oz (trimmed weight)

a big splash of extra virgin olive oil

4 cloves of garlic, finely chopped

250g/8oz melted piggy fat from *lardo*, fatty pancetta or good old-fashioned lard (though if you manage to find *lardo* then you'll need to start with around 400g/13oz and roughly dice it before melting) or you can go for a combination of pork fat and EVOO

1 ciabatta about 275g/9oz

salt and pepper

God bless the peasant farmers that came up with this, a supper of pig and fat and salt and sticks that reeks of rustic. We had it in a little local restaurant up in the hills around Florence, not far from the quarry where Michelangelo cut his teeth, not to mention some fine marble.

This dish isn't the healthiest thing you'll ever eat but it may well be one of the yummiest. The authentic fat to use is a block of *lardo di Colonnata*, a salted pork fat cured with rosemary, which if you ever come across it is a must-buy. A kilo block of *lardo* is one of the more treacherous illegal imports I've brought home, but it goes a long way and made me happy for a couple of months. Probably the best substitute is a piece of fatty pancetta, heated in a frying pan so that the fat melts, topped up to the amount needed with olive oil. Or even a block of lard, but I'd add a bit of extra virgin olive oil in there for added flavour, as this dish is all about flavourful fat.

Strip the leaves from the rosemary stems, leaving just a bushy tip on each one, and finely chop the leaves.

Cut the tenderloins into slices about 3cm/1¼ inches thick (to make about 16 pieces) and marinate them in the extra virgin, half the garlic and half the chopped rosemary for about an hour or so.

Once the meat has had as much marinating time as you can afford it, preheat the oven to 200°C/400°F/gas mark 6. Heat the pork fat in a small pan and gently fry the rest of the garlic and rosemary leaves with a good seasoning of salt (though you won't need any salt if using *lardo*), and season the tenderloin pieces, too.

Cut the ciabatta into chunks about the same size as the pieces of pork - you'll need 20 pieces. Dip the pieces of bread into the melted fat, pressing each one down so that they really soak it up, and thread the bread and meat alternately on to the rosemary sticks: 5 bread pieces and 4 pork pieces per stick, each one starting and finishing with a piece of bread.

Line them all up on a baking tray, spoon over any leftover fat and put into the oven for 12-15 minutes. Leave to rest for a couple of minutes, then carefully lift the sticks on to a suitably gorgeous serving dish and pour over any juices. Serve with wedges of lemon and a plain tomato salad (as in no dressing or seasoning - there's enough going on already!)

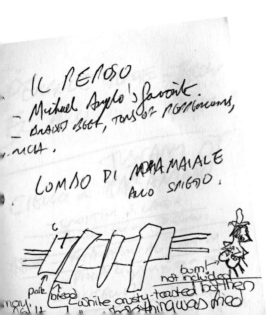

Amor de Pera
Custardy Pear Tart

Makes 8 good slices, and takes
1 hour 30 minutes on and off to
make this stunner, then 1 hour+
chilling time

This is from Do Forni, a Venetian restaurant where we were escorted through the dining room, and out the other side into another *calle*, then in the door opposite to get to a second dining room - good use of space in this higgledy-piggledy city. We had a cracking evening of *brodo di nonna*, *lo stinco*, and lots of Amarone, and polished it all off with this fine pud: this tart may look a bit showy and French but the name, not to mention the taste, is pure Italian Romantic: a dessert to make you swoon.

Make the pastry by combining the flour and sugar in a food processor for a minute, then blend in the butter quickly piece by piece. Briefly mix in the egg yolks and turn the machine off immediately - the whole process should take 3 minutes. Wrap in clingfilm and rest in the fridge for 30 minutes.

For the pastry

250g/8oz plain flour

75g/3oz icing sugar

125g/4oz cold unsalted butter, cubed

3 egg yolks

Now to the pears: heat the sugar in a wide, shallow pan with 500ml/17fl oz of water, the scraped vanilla pod and the Amaretto. Halve the pears and scoop out the cores with a teaspoon, leaving the stalks on. When the sugar has dissolved, lay in the pear halves (making sure they are all in the liquid, otherwise change pans) and poach at a steady simmer, covered, for about 10-15 minutes, until cooked through but not soft.

For the pears

125g/4oz sugar

1 vanilla pod, split lengthwise and
scraped

60ml/2½fl oz Amaretto

6-ish firm dessert pears (Comice or
Conference), peeled

To make the crème pâtissière, first heat the milk. Separately whisk the yolks in a mixing bowl with the sugar until pale, then beat in the cornflour. Once boiling, whisk the milk on to the egg mixture, then pour into a clean pan over a gentle heat. Bring to a boil and let it bubble for a minute, whisking all the time, then take off the heat and cool completely with a piece of clingfilm laid directly on the surface.

Preheat the oven to 180°C/350°F/gas mark 4. Roll/grate (on the big holes) and press the pastry into a fluted tart case with a push up base 28 x 4cm/11 x 1½ inches, then put it into the freezer for 10 minutes. Once it's firm to the touch, put it into the oven and bake blind for about 15-20 minutes until lightly golden, then let it cool for a few minutes.

For the crème pâtissière

500ml/17fl oz milk

3 egg yolks

75g/3oz caster sugar

40g/1½oz cornflour

Take the pears out of the poaching liquid and boil the liquid to reduce it by two-thirds. As this is happening, soak the gelatine in cold water for a few minutes. Whisk in the floppy leaves, then leave to cool to room temp.

To top it off

2 leaves gelatine (about 6g/¼oz)

a handful of flaked almonds, toasted

Final leg: pour the crème pâtissière into the pastry case and level the surface. Arrange the pears on top and sprinkle with toasted almonds. Spoon over the liquid to glaze, and chill for at least an hour to set.

Japan

Spiritual, aesthetic and freaky in equal parts: nothing was straightforward, all of it fun. From breakfast, consisting of an average of sixteen largely unidentifiable, beautifully presented little dishes, right through to bedtime on a tatami mat, it was one long weird and wonderful adventure.

We started in Tokyo, spinning with jetlag and overexcitement that we just about managed to contain by dawn, and from there on in the pace just quickened. We headed out of town past Mt Fuji and started our tour of the islands. Immediately we hit things I wasn't expecting, snow being the first, as it had been warm in the capital, and mountains - I hadn't really taken on board that really Japan is one long mountain range popping out of the sea.

The surprises and novelty never wore off for the whole trip, but within it there was harmony and balance, which is important to their culture. The madness of the cities, Tokyo in particular, was balanced from within by the serenity of their famous gardens (except in Kanazawa, where we managed to have a massive row about a crane). I don't think I've ever been as excited at 5 a.m. as I was in the Tsukiji fish market in Tokyo, but the yin to that yang was the time spent staying in a monastery in Koyasan, thought to be the birthplace of Buddhism in Japan and also one of the most sacred places for Shinto - a religion that makes sense surrounded by such natural beauty ... and we grew very fond of their fat little figures with red bibs on.

All old Japan is elegant: the art, writing and architecture, whereas new Japan grabs your attention with its crazy packaging and flashing lights. The bullet trains are the fastest thing on land, but kabuki theatre must be the slowest - eight hours later and I had no greater wisdom, just a badly cricked neck.

We were chasing the arrival of the cherry blossom (*hanami*) all around the islands, which to the Japanese is kind of like Springwatch crossed with the Grand National. Mostly we were just a week or so too early, but every now and then we got lucky and on those occasions I've never seen trees erupt with such vigour. But within the chase there was time for reflection: at the many multi-storied horned temples, or the Philosopher's Walk in ancient Kyoto or 'relaxing' in the famous steaming sulphur pools of Kyushu, which were so stupidly hot it throbbed under my fingernails.

Then back to Tokyo, where you'd get in a cab in a gridlocked street, show the driver a card with your address on it and half an hour later he'd ask to see it again as if for the first time. And my final word is if you ever get the chance to spend just one night at the Park Hyatt, it's worth having beans and rice for a month when you're back.

FACT FILE

Geographical summary: Very mountainous archipelago made up of four main islands, Hokkaido, Honshu, Shikoku and Kyushu, and around 4,000 smaller ones. Cold and snowy in the north to subtropical climate of Okinawa in the south.

Population: 128 million.

Religion: Shintoism and Buddhism, combined by many people.

Ethnic make-up: 98.3% Japanese; 1.7 % other (mostly Chinese or ethnic Korean).

Life expectancy: 79 male, 86 female

External influences: Rarely invaded – no one else has left their mark.

The essentials of their cooking: First, it must be beautiful. All culinary base techniques are covered: steaming, steeping, grilling, braising, frying, and most famously raw.

Food they export: Pastry, drinks, flour, rice fermented beverages, apples.

Top 5 favourite ingredients: Seaweed, fish (especially the much revered tuna), bean curd (miso, tofu), vinegar, rice.

Most famous dish: Sushi.

What to drink: Sake (cold with cold food and warm permitted, but not encouraged, with hot). Kirin, Asahi and Sapporo beer. Coffee in cans that come hot out of the vending machine!

Best thing I ate: In a sushi bar in Tokyo that specialized in food from the Edo period (17th to 19th century), I ate twitching prawn (well, we called it that anyway). Plucked from the tank, beheaded and peeled in a flash, then slapped on a lozenge of rice with a faint swoosh of wasabi. You can guess what it was still doing when I put it in my mouth...

Most breathtaking moment: Not sure it was the most breathtaking, but visiting Hiroshima was certainly the most poignant. They weren't sure anything would ever grow again, and yet a vibrant city now stands there under the constant visual presence of the A-bomb dome, the only building still standing after the attack.

Don't ask for...: A business card by casually holding out your hand or they'll whip it off with a samurai sword. They're a merciless lot and etiquette is everything here: to show respect you must receive it with both hands.

Unagi-Saki

Japan is without doubt the easiest country in which to buy a knife of interest and personality ... the hard part is not coming back with a suitcase full. For me, I was being pretty restrained and had acquired only a couple of blades by the time we hit Kyoto, about halfway through our trip, but then I got well and truly smacked with the full force of centuries of Japanese knife artistry.

Aritsugu is a 400-year-old family business, and they're rightly proud to have been making knives for the Imperial family since the late Middle Ages. The words 'kid' and 'toyshop' don't even touch the sides: the feelings I had as I walked through the door were more akin to a junkie in a field of poppies: wide-eyed, heart palpitating, slightly sweaty hands - my stomach seized up in the presence of such beauty ... and so much of it.

The shop is not large but it's well laid out, with knives on the left side, other cooking utensils on the right and a little workshop for sharpening and engraving at the back: I must have walked the length of it thirty times as I started to hone down my choice. In Japanese cuisine almost every job has a specific knife for it, which makes for hundreds of beautiful knives with, to our gauche, Western eye, only small variations.

Back home you can now get very good Japanese knives, and then there's the internet too, so eventually I went for a knife the like of which I'd never known, seen or heard tell of before. It's the blade in my collection that I'm more proud of than any other, for its extraordinary shape, well-thought-out lines, simple aesthetics and killer edge. It's the only knife I have where I find I get better accuracy from it holding it like a pen with the butt up, rather than across the palm of my hand, and its purpose, so I was told, is specifically for cleaning eel.

I'm very proud to introduce you to the heart-throb of my collection - the single-edged, Kanto-style Unagi-Saki. Elegant and brutal. So Japanese.

伊藤若冲

乗興舟

Imperial River Voyage

京都国立博物館
KYOTO NATIONAL MUSEUM

japanese
recipes

エビの茶碗蒸し
Brown Shrimp
Coddle

「ライジング・サン」サラダ
Rising Sun
Salad

サーモンの生姜焼き
Confit Salmon
& Ginger Juice

茄子の甘酢煮込み
Sesame Sweet &
Sour Aubergines

牛(肉)の味噌炒め
Seared Beef,
Shaved Onion
& Miso

鯛めし
Steamed Bream
& Rice

Brown Shrimp Coddle

Serves 4, and takes 15 minutes
prep and around 40 minutes
in the oven

---

5 radishes, cut into fine matchsticks

50g/2oz edamame, podded weight

10g/½oz dried hijiki seaweed
(optional but authentic), soaked in
boiling water for 5 minutes

100g/3½oz brown shrimps

---

6 or 7 eggs, depending on size

---

2 tablespoons fish sauce

125ml/4fl oz warm water

Eggs and the sea have a secure and happy partnership (think smoked salmon and scrambled eggs), so hold on to that thought as you embark on this journey to another land.

On the one hand it's just a set egg custard with a few bits in it, and on the other it's like nothing I've ever eaten before. It is, however, weirdly addictive, and now whenever I turn Japanese I always ask the restaurant if they do it; and what's even stranger is that even if it's not on the menu they usually oblige. Just for the record, it should really be a single gingko bean in it, not a handful of edamame, but I've taken a bit of artistic liberty on the grounds of sourcing.

My sister Floss, who likes a bit of comfort food, has declared this to be the ultimate in soothing eats.

Preheat the oven to 150°C/300°F/gas mark 2.

Mix together the radishes, edamame, seaweed and shrimps and divide the mixture between 4 large ramekins/coddlers/tumbler-like glasses/something similar.

In a jug beat the eggs with the fish sauce and water, then pour on top of the other ingredients, taking care to make sure that all the levels are pretty much equal.

Stand the containers in an ovenproof dish which needs to be roughly the same depth or deeper than they are, and, if you're using glass, pour a couple of centimetres/an inch of cold water into the bottom of the dish before topping up with boiling water to the same level as the egg mix in the glasses. Cover with a lid or foil and cook in the oven for 35-40 minutes depending on the exact dimensions of your vessels, until just about set - it's OK if they're still a little wobbly in the middle.

Take out of the water and cool for just a minute, before serving on little side plates with teaspoons and a slight air of expectation.

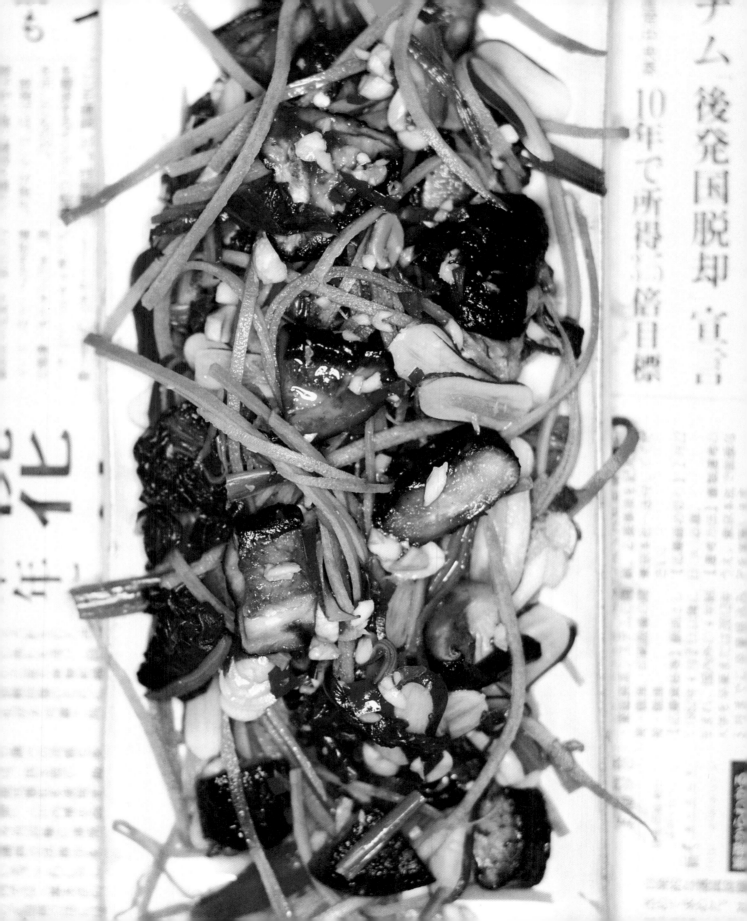

Rising Sun Salad

Serves 2 and takes less than 30 minutes

2 tablespoons sesame oil

a handful of shiitake mushrooms, cut into big pieces

2 tablespoons sake

1 tablespoon mirin

175g/6oz spinach (with stalks is best), sliced into ribbons of about 2cm/¾ inch

2 carrots, peeled and cut into thin matchsticks (or grated if you're feeling lazy)

a bunch of radishes, sliced

For the dressing
1 chilli, roughly chopped

a handful of plain salted peanuts

1 tablespoon soy sauce

1 tablespoon rice wine vinegar

2 tablespoons mirin

I defy anyone landing in Tokyo for the first time not to be completely dumbstruck. And jetlagged. We landed late at night, and by the time we'd got up to our hotel room on the zillionth floor and ogled the amazing view for a good while, dawn was breaking and we ordered room service.

As the sun rose, we had this simple salad with a bottle of sake, and I'll never forget it as the first thing we ate in this very foreign land.

Heat the oil in a pan and fry the mushrooms for a couple of minutes. Add the sake and mirin and cook on a medium heat for a few more minutes until the liquid bubbles away. Turn the heat off and let the mushrooms cool down.

Put a saucepan on the heat, wash the spinach and when the pan is hot throw it in, give it a brief stir and put a lid on. As soon as it's wilted - about a minute - lift it out and spread on a plate to cool. Chuck the carrots and radishes in your serving bowl, give the spinach a quick but firm squeeze to get out some of the excess water then add it too, as well as the mushrooms.

To make the dressing, use a pestle and mortar (or a knife) to roughly crush and combine the chilli and peanuts. Stir in the other ingredients, then spoon over the salad.

Confit Salmon in Ginger Juice

Serves 4 as an elegant starter, and takes less than 30 minutes

---

around 600ml/1 pint rapeseed/light olive oil/grapeseed oil (or enough to submerge your salmon pieces)

300g/10oz piece of salmon, from the head end, skin on and pinboned

---

150g/5oz ginger, washed and peel left on

---

2 tablespoons sake

---

2 tablespoons mirin

---

1 tablespoon light soy sauce

---

a small handful of alfalfa sprouts

½ punnet of mustard cress

50g/2oz salmon eggs

Purity is an important part of Japanese culture, and the cleanliness of this dish reflects that. We eat porridge for breakfast and they eat salmon, ginger and salty soy: ours is for the energy levels, but this, first thing in the morning, definitely feels like brain food. In our lives it probably sits better as an evening starter, by which time the day part for brains has largely passed us by. *Sigh*. Still tastes damn good, though.

Warm the oil in a shallow pan/small frying pan (about 20cm/8 inches across) over a medium heat: you're looking for the point at which a corner of bread fizzles with small bubbles but nothing explosive happens when you drop it in. From there turn the oil down a bit and wait a couple of minutes so that the temperature stabilizes (for those with thermometers, it'll be around 110°C/230°F).

Halve the salmon along both axes to make 4 squarish blocks, then slide them into the oil, skin-side down. They should sink and bubble gently but you don't want them to colour at all. Cook for 3 minutes, then gently lift them out and drain on kitchen paper.

Using the big holes, grate the ginger into a bowl. Pick up half of it, squeeze the fibres over a little bowl to extract the juice, and once you've squeezed the life out of it do the same with the other half - it should produce 3-4 tablespoons of juice (you can keep the squeezed solids to make tea/toddies). Mix the ginger juice with the sake, mirin and soy.

When the salmon has cooled to room temperature, peel off the skin. Spoon the sauce on to 4 plates, and put a piece of fish on each. Mix together the alfalfa and mustard cress, and put a small pile on to each of the fish pieces. Share the salmon eggs between the 4 plates and serve the whole thing at room temperature.

Sesame Sweet & Sour Aubergines

Serves 4 as a main or 6 as a side dish. Takes about 30 minutes on and off to get them in the oven, then 1 hour 30 minutes cooking time

---

1kg/2lb aubergines, sliced into pieces about 5cm/2 inches thick

---

30g/1oz sesame seeds

50g/2oz ginger, washed but unpeeled and diced quite small

100ml/3½fl oz toasted sesame oil

160ml/¼ pint mirin

250ml/8fl oz rice wine vinegar

160ml/¼ pint light soy sauce

---

4 tablespoons honey

---

salt and pepper

I found breakfast in Japan a totally hilarious experience: from snotty seaweed to astringently pickled plums that made your eyes water, this is one nation that has mastered the art of getting going in the morning. This dish was part of another multi-dish breakfast feast, including one that went down in my diary as 'Dr Who Chicken meets Swamp People'. No ... I've no idea either.

This is super-special either warm or at room temperature, but hold on to your hats as it's pretty intense, so serve with simply grilled meat/fish and some very plain rice.

Preheat the oven to 180°C/350°F/gas mark 4. Spread about 3 big pinches of salt (preferably sea salt) over the base of a baking dish about 40 x 30cm/16 x 12 inches that will hold the aubergine slices quite tightly.

Score a shallow cross-hatch on each face of the aubergine slices and lay them flat in one layer on the salt. Sprinkle over another couple of pinches of salt and leave them for about 20 minutes.

Lightly toast the sesame seeds in the oven for a few minutes.

Put the ginger, oil, mirin, vinegar, soy and honey into a saucepan and bring to a simmer. Turn off the heat, and when the sesame seeds come out of the oven add those to the pan.

Pat the aubergine slices dry with kitchen paper and wipe out the baking dish. Pour in the contents of the pan and sit the aubergine slices in it, flat, so that the liquid comes about half to two-thirds of the way up them. Cover the dish with foil, sealing the edges as much as possible so that the aubergines will steam a bit, and put it into the oven. After 30 minutes throw away the foil, turn them over and put them back in the oven for another hour, turning again halfway through.

Seared Beef, Shaved Onion & Miso

**Serves 2, and it can all be done
in 15 minutes**

2 tablespoons light oil

1 white onion, sliced as thinly as
possible (ideally on a mandolin
or the thin slicing attachment
of a food processor)

2 rib-eye steaks, as good a quality
as you can afford, weighing around
225g/7½oz each

75ml/3fl oz sake

2 tablespoons miso paste (either
from a tub or sachets for miso
soup), dissolved in about 60ml/
2½fl oz water

salt

We'd got on a train in sunny Tokyo, fallen asleep and woken up a few
hours later stunned by the deep snow outside. Our destination was
Takayama, the mountainous home of the famed Hida beef: every bit
as serious as the Wagyu cows, who live in Kobe, just a different breed
in a different prefecture.

As with their more famous countrymen, Hida beef is a fat-marbled, melt-
in-the-mouth sexy sexy sexy extravaganza: we were served this as dish
six of a twelve-course supper (not unusual at all in Japan), and to be honest
I would have swapped all the other eleven for another one of these.

Best beef of my life.

Get the steaks out of the fridge well in advance so that they are at room
temperature the whole way through before you start cooking.

Heat the oil over a high flame in a heavy frying pan or skillet big
enough to hold both your steaks. When it is really hot, drop in the
onion and cook with a lid for a couple of minutes, giving them the odd
stir. Take the lid off and cook for a couple more minutes, so that they
colour lightly, then spoon the onions out of the pan and into a bowl.
Give the pan a quick wipe out with dry kitchen paper then put it back
on the high heat.

Season the steaks with salt lightly on both sides and wait for the dry pan
to get searingly hot. Cook the steaks for 1 minute on each side to pick
up a bit of colour, then pour in the sake followed a few seconds later by
the diluted miso. After about a minute, turn the steaks over again, and
cook for about another minute before taking them out of the pan and
turning off the heat. Let the meat rest for a couple of minutes while you
finish the sauce, letting it down with a tablespoon of water or so if it's
got very reduced, and pouring in any juices from the resting meat.

Slice the steaks, pour over the miso sauce and finish with the onions.

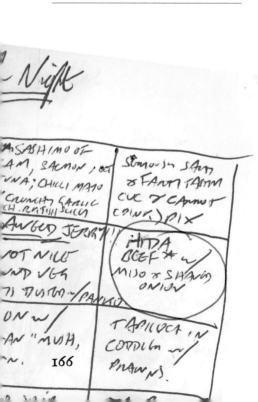

166

Steamed Bream & Rice

Serves 2, and all in all takes about 1 hour, but half of that is waiting for the rice to cook

100g/3½oz brown rice

1 tablespoon sesame oil

a few outer cabbage leaves (such as Savoy, tenderheart/Hispi or Chinese leaves)

2 bream fillets, about 125g/4oz each

2 tablespoons light soy sauce, plus more to taste

2 spring onions, sliced diagonally

a large handful of beansprouts

salt

You can do this in any kind of makeshift steamer (a colander comes to mind) but there's something innately pleasing about doing it either in one large or in individual steamer baskets. This is especially true because of the way it was served to us: a kimono-clad beauty glided over, humbly bearing the baskets; she then presented them to us for a prettiness inspection, but instead of putting them down she nimbly mashed it all up at our table, then placed it in front of us in little bowls. I'm not sure why, but watching this lovely lady labour a little made me enjoy it even more.

Over a low heat, fry the rice in the oil so that it sizzles gently for a minute before pouring on about 300ml/½ pint of cold water (though if your pan is very wide you might need a bit more to get enough depth - the rice should come about halfway up the water).

Turn the heat up to high, and when the water comes up to the boil, put on a lid and turn the heat down very low. The rice should take about 25-35 minutes to cook - it's ready when you can see steam chimneys and no water is left at the bottom ... but taste it to check. When it's ready, turn the heat off, leave the lid on and let it sit for about 5 minutes.

Once the rice is working, cut out the tough central stem from the cabbage leaves and use them to line the steamer basket(s). Season the flesh side of the fish with a little salt. Fill the cabbage-leaf case(s) with cooked rice dressed with half the soy, and lay the fillets on top, skin-side up.

Cook above a pot of steadily simmering water for about 8-10 minutes, or until the fish flesh is white.

This next step is up to you: you can either serve it just like this, or to be proper about it you can take the dish apart and mix everything together: peel the skin off the fish and put the flesh into a mixing bowl, then roughly chop the cabbage leaves and mix it all up, sprinkling in the remaining soy, adding more to taste if necessary.

Serve scattered with spring onions and a pile of beansprouts.

Surprisingly little is known over here about this group of 7,000 islands in the South China Sea; prior to my trip, I think my sole point of reference was the envelopes, which despite frequent questioning, no one in Manila could shed any light on. And to be honest I still can't claim to be an expert, as although I got a good overview of the country researching for the piece I was writing, I flattened myself with some fairly major bug, from a mushroom burger of all things. Yes, this is the sad lot of the intrepid foodie traveller, and yet I never learn, and still eat all the weird shit that comes my way.

But enough of the bad times and on to what I did actually glean about these innately friendly, chilled-out people, who instantly won my heart when I was told that they eat five times a day: the usual three main meals, but with the added bonus of mid-morning and mid-afternoon *merienda* - like elevenses and teatime, but a bit more compulsory.

Of those thousands of islands you can then group them into provinces, and, a bit like Italy, this is a country with real regional identity. Broadly speaking it's rich and fertile in the north, Luzon, poor and quite unspoilt in the south, Mindanao, with a lot of small islands and typhoon territory in the middle, the Visayas. As with most visitors (of which it's worth noting that there are surprisingly few), I spent the majority of my stay on the most populated main island of Luzon, and although I could see and feel that I was in Asia, it was really the deep-seated influence of two Western cultures that astounded me.

Of the two, the Spanish came first and stayed a lot longer - about 300 years. Filipinos are overwhelmingly Catholic: Spanish-style churches are everywhere, you constantly seem to be bumping into elaborate street processions involving effigies of saints, and the fact that ten is not an uncommon number of siblings all point to the long arm of the Vatican. The Iberian influence also extends to their food: there's a national favourite called tapa, empanadas are a common street snack, and paella is a regular on menus.

And then, more recently but just as powerfully, the Americans came in search of colonies at the turn of the 19th century and didn't really properly get out until the end of World War II. I saw as many burgers and hotdogs on the streets of Manila as you would in Manhattan, Coke was the drink of choice for those with enough money, most people dressed in US-style clothes, and they don't half love a mall: three of the five largest malls in the world are in the Philippines. For some reason, I was comfortable with the way that the Spaniards had rubbed off on the native population, but the Yanks seem to have stamped on it rather than blended with it (though I admit it could equally have been the Filipinos embracing this new superpower).

Having said all that, it was the first democracy in Asia, and apart from in the busy capital, there was a tangible relaxedness in the people. It was immediately refreshing how both of these influences diminished in direct proportion to how far they were from Manila. I loved the thriving markets in the heart of each town, and their kind, easy-come-easy-go nature, but it has to be said that just like those envelopes, the real Philippines remains a bit of a mystery to me.

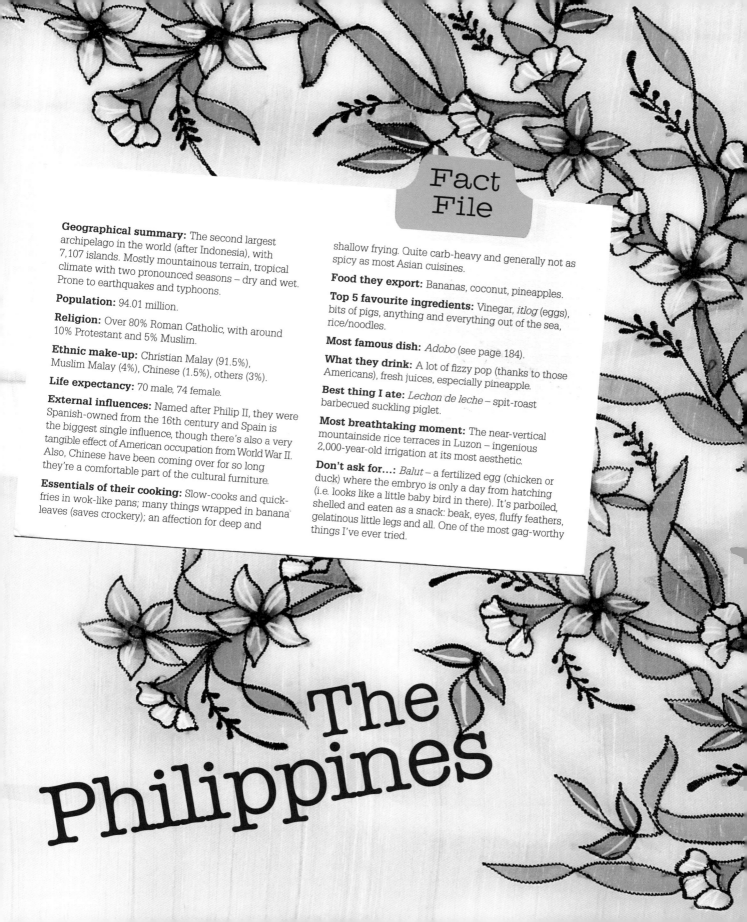

Fact File

Geographical summary: The second largest archipelago in the world (after Indonesia), with 7,107 islands. Mostly mountainous terrain, tropical climate with two pronounced seasons – dry and wet. Prone to earthquakes and typhoons.

Population: 94.01 million.

Religion: Over 80% Roman Catholic, with around 10% Protestant and 5% Muslim.

Ethnic make-up: Christian Malay (91.5%), Muslim Malay (4%), Chinese (1.5%), others (3%).

Life expectancy: 70 male, 74 female.

External influences: Named after Philip II, they were Spanish-owned from the 16th century and Spain is the biggest single influence, though there's also a very tangible effect of American occupation from World War II. Also, Chinese have been coming over for so long they're a comfortable part of the cultural furniture.

Essentials of their cooking: Slow-cooks and quick-fries in wok-like pans; many things wrapped in banana leaves (saves crockery); an affection for deep and shallow frying. Quite carb-heavy and generally not as spicy as most Asian cuisines.

Food they export: Bananas, coconut, pineapples.

Top 5 favourite ingredients: Vinegar, *itlog* (eggs), bits of pigs, anything and everything out of the sea, rice/noodles.

Most famous dish: *Adobo* (see page 184).

What they drink: A lot of fizzy pop (thanks to those Americans), fresh juices, especially pineapple.

Best thing I ate: *Lechon de leche* – spit-roast barbecued suckling piglet.

Most breathtaking moment: The near-vertical mountainside rice terraces in Luzon – ingenious 2,000-year-old irrigation at its most aesthetic.

Don't ask for…: *Balut* – a fertilized egg (chicken or duck) where the embryo is only a day from hatching (i.e. looks like a little baby bird in there). It's parboiled, shelled and eaten as a snack: beak, eyes, fluffy feathers, gelatinous little legs and all. One of the most gag-worthy things I've ever tried.

The Philippines

Balisong

KUTCILIYO

What we have here are two very different styles of knifery: first is a regular kitchen knife, or *kutciliyo* as they call them. What attracted it to me predominantly was its shape, so reflective of the magpie aspect of Filipino culture that I'd seen: part cleaver, with the Chinese influence so strong in the food over here, but not committedly so - it still has a character all of its own. Some might say that the handle was crudely shaped for ergonometry, but I like those irregular strokes, so obviously made by a man, not a factory line. The metal from the blade continues in a thinner piece right through to the butt (known in the industry as full tang), where there's a protruding diamond-shaped rivet, instead of the more common side rivets in the handle. Above all it has perfect balance and weight - probably the best suited to my liking in all my collection.

The second knife is a lesson in 'rules are there to be broken' ... even if you made them yourself. Really, the deal was kitchen knives only: knives are a contentious enough issue without bringing in hunting or fighting, and I really wanted my collection, and this book, to be about reclaiming the knife from the streets and putting it back in the kitchen. But this *balisong*, or

butterfly knife as they're sometimes known, was so beautiful a piece of craftsmanship, not to mention an integral part of Filipino heritage, that it would have been churlish not to include it. Although nowadays they are widely associated with many Asian martial arts, they originated in the province of Batangas. They fold up to look like sticks, legend has it, to fool their erstwhile Spanish overlords into thinking the natives were unarmed. Balisong come in all sizes from ten centimetres to over half a metre, and don't usually have wavy blades - I just thought it looked less threatening. It is said that all inhabitants of the Batangas province carry one wherever they go.

I need a knife, I said to my guide, and the Philippines is one place where they don't blink twice at such a request. A little later in the day, driving from the centre of Taal to a little restaurant on the outskirts of town, we abruptly stopped at what was more than a stall and not quite a shop, but perfect for me with its array of kitchen knives (of the homemade kind), scissors and, of course, all shapes and sizes of *balisong*. Nice lady owner too, with one hell of a cool name: Liza Balisong.

ISANG
MUSHROOMBURGER
BUSOG KA NA!

GUAVA
SYRUP

LUZON · VISAYAS · MINDANAO

PHILIPPINES

Filipino Recipes

Achara
Sweet Pickled Veg Condiment

Clam & Ginger Broth

Empanaditas
Little Porky Flaky Pastries

Pancit Guisado
Traditional Noodles

Pork Adobo

Maria Clara's Secrets
Coconut rice, Muscavado Crunchies,
Mango & Ice Cream

Banana Turon

Peanut Brittle

PHILIPPINES AT ITS BEST

BEFRIENDING PHILIPPINE CUISINE...

DISHES

VEGETABLES
petsay :: bokchoy
repolyo :: cabbage
pipino :: cucumber
talong :: eggplant

MEAT & POULTRY
karne :: meat
manok :: chicken
karne ng baka :: beef
karne ng baboy :: pork
kambing :: goat

DRINKS
tubig :: water
kape :: coffee
tsa :: tea
salabat :: ginger tea
tsokolate :: chocolate
alak :: liquor

Achara
Sweet Pickled Veg Condiment

Fills a 1 litre/1¾ pint kilner jar, and requires overnight salting, then 10 minutes to make and a week to do its thing in the fridge

---

400g/13oz green papaya (about a half), peeled and grated or cut into matchsticks

---

1 tablespoon salt

---

1 medium carrot, julienned or cut in matchsticks

---

1 white onion, grated and squeezed

---

1 red pepper, cut into thin strips

---

1 green pepper, cut into thin strips

For the syrup

150g/5oz caster sugar

175ml/6fl oz white wine vinegar

1cm/½ inch piece of ginger, cut into thin matchsticks

2 cloves of garlic, sliced thinly

a lot of pepper

Filipino gift to the universal world of pickles - they mostly eat this with meat or fish (grilled or fried), but really it enhances pretty much every meal. A jar lasts for months and keeps getting better, and I've found it to also be a great standby nibble/canapé on a slice of cucumber or a piece of pepper.

Memorably my favourite condiment of 2007 - we constantly have a jar on the go and I tend to have a cheeky dip-in when visiting the fridge.

Find green papaya in the ethnic produce section of your supermarket, or in Asian shops.

In a large bowl, mix the green papaya with the salt. Cover with clingfilm and stick it in the fridge overnight.

Knock up the syrup by boiling all the ingredients together and letting it simmer for 5 minutes, then leave to cool overnight as well.

The next day, rinse the papaya, tip the pieces into a towel and wring it hard to squeeze out the water. Give the bowl a brief rinse and dry, and mix all the vegetables in it together thoroughly, then pour on the syrup. Stir, roll and coat, then transfer to a large sterilized jar; get rid of any bubbles by pushing the vegetables down below the level of the liquid with the back of a spoon.

Put it into the fridge and turn briefly upside down every day for 1 week to get it ready.

Clam and Ginger Broth

Serves 2 in around 15 minutes

a splash of toasted sesame oil

500g/1lb clams

a nugget of ginger, cut into fine matchsticks

a few slices of bird's-eye chilli (optional)

100g/3½oz mushrooms, sliced thinly (nice with oyster mushrooms, in which case trim and tear rather than slice)

a splash of fish sauce

½ a bunch of watercress, roughly chopped

Though it was easy eating, I found quite a lot of food in the Philippines quite heavy and greasy, so when I was served this in a little restaurant just off the beach in Manila, less than half a mile from where the clams were landed, I instantly felt like I'd relocated my pulse.

Put the clams in a colander or sieve and run under cold water for a minute or two. Heat the sesame oil in a saucepan over a medium-high heat and when the oil is hot, add the clams, ginger and chilli, if you fancy it, then cover with a lid and give the pan a good shake. After just a minute pour in 500ml/17fl oz of cold water, turn the heat to maximum and put the lid back on. Bring to the boil, then turn down to a simmer.

By now the clams will have opened (and throw out any that haven't); take them out with a slotted spoon and divide them between 2 warmed bowls. Skim any scum off the surface, toss the mushrooms into the pan, add the fish sauce and the watercress, then stir and taste. When the mushrooms have been in for about 3 minutes, ladle the broth over the clams and eat immediately.

Empanaditas
Little Porky Flaky Pastries

Makes about 30, and you need to set aside about 1 hour 30 minutes to make these parcels of pleasure

For the pastry

600g/1lb 2oz plain flour, plus more for dusting

1 teaspoon baking powder

2 teaspoons sugar

1 teaspoon salt

375g/12oz cold unsalted butter, cubed

2 eggs, lightly beaten

12–14 tablespoons iced water

For the filling

50g/2oz glass noodles

2 tablespoons light oil (like groundnut)

1 onion, diced

300g/10oz pork mince

4 fat cloves of garlic, minced

2 big pinches of ground cumin

2½ tablespoons rice wine vinegar, plus another good splash

a handful of raisins

1 potato (about 175g/6oz), peeled and cut into rough 2cm/¾ inch dice

275g/9oz squash, peeled, deseeded and cut into rough 2cm/¾ inch dice

a big handful of coriander, finely chopped

peanut or veg oil, for deep-frying

salt and pepper

The best town market I went to in the Philippines was in Taal, which sold a fabulous array of street food snacks and where I met the genius empanaditas man. Not only were these little offspring of the empanada the tastiest I'd ever eaten, with their crisp, flaky pastry and perfectly spiced filling, but he hand-made 1,500 every day! Top party food.

The easiest way to make pastry is in the food processor: add the flour, baking powder, sugar and salt, and pulse it as you drop in the butter very quickly (only a minute total spinning time), but one cube at a time. Mix together the egg and iced water and whizzing quickly again (30 seconds or less) tip them in to make a really soft dough. (You can also make it the old-fashioned way: rub the butter into the dry ingredients and then stir in the liquid.) Wrap the pastry in clingfilm and chill in the fridge for 30 minutes.

Pour boiling water over the noodles and let them soak for 2–3 minutes, then drain and run under the cold tap. Heat the oil in a large frying pan over a medium heat, and fry the onion in it. After a minute, stir in the pork, garlic, cumin and some salt, and cook for a few more minutes, stirring.

Add the vinegar, raisins, potatoes and squash and stir well. Turn the heat up, then pour on 250ml/8fl oz water, pushing down the vegetables so that they're covered. Season with salt and pepper and cover with a lid.

After 10–15 minutes, stir to check all the liquid has reduced away and the veggies are breaking down. Turn off the heat, roughly run a masher over the mixture and transfer to a mixing bowl. Once cooled, stir in the noodles and coriander with another good splash of vinegar and salt to taste.

Once your filling is ready, turn your attention to the dough: because it's so buttery it gets more difficult to handle the longer it is out of the fridge, so leave half of it inside while you roll out the other half on a quite heavily floured surface to a thickness of around 0.5cm/¼ inch.

Cut out wide circles about 10cm/4 inches across, then roll in one direction only, to get ovals. Brush them with water, pile a little filling in the centre, fold it over and seal with your fingers first, and then with the end of a fork.

Deep-fry the empanaditas in batches in a pan of hot oil (the oil should be at least 4cm/1½ inches deep), for around 4–6 minutes, or until deep golden brown, turning halfway through. Rest them on kitchen paper for a minute before piling them up and handing them round.

Pancit Guisado
Traditional Noodles

Serves 4, and takes about
15 minutes to get everything
ready, then is a 10-minute cook

500ml/17fl oz chicken stock

---

3 rashers (50g/2oz) streaky bacon
(unsmoked), sliced

150g/5oz glass noodles

---

2 tablespoons groundnut oil

¼ of a small white cabbage
(300g/10oz), sliced

125g/4oz French beans, cut into
(roughly 3cm/1¼ inch) lengths

---

3 cloves of garlic, chopped

---

1 bird's-eye chilli, sliced (optional)

125g/4oz prawns, peeled (whatever
size you fancy) and de-veined if
necessary

---

1 carrot, grated

---

1 lime, and more to serve

1½ tablespoons soy sauce

Unsurprisingly, given the geography, China is a strong influence on the local cuisine; but this Pinoy version of a chow mein is so much fresher and lighter. Their favourite palate-sharpener over there is a hybrid citrus called kalamansi - like a lime but with thinner skin and a slightly mandarin-ish tone - but for the purpose of our exercise regular lime works just fine.

I had this in the café of the impressive and beautiful Casa Manila in Intramuros, the old capital. Part authentic, part reconstruction of a colonial Spanish house, its restoration had been actioned by Imelda Marcos (still a local heroine, welcomed enthusiastically anywhere she graces with her presence) and was one of the most attractive buildings I saw in this city that was culturally splatted by American bombers and Japanese firepower in World War II.

Once you're up and running it's a damn quick cook, as the heat stays high throughout, so you need to make sure you prep all the ingredients before you start.

Bring the stock to a simmer and drop in the bacon. Put a lid on the pan, bring back to the boil and then take the bacon out again with a slotted spoon.

Put the noodles into a bowl and pour the hot stock over them to rehydrate, turning them now and then so that all the noodles soften.

Heat the oil in a wok or a large, wide pan, then, once it's hot, add the bacon and toss for a few minutes until it starts to brown. Scatter in the cabbage and beans, stirring for another minute before chucking in the garlic and chilli. Give it all a good toss, then add the noodles plus any remaining stock, the prawns and carrot. Put a lid on the pan and keep cooking for about 3 minutes.

Take the lid off and keep stirring until any liquid has pretty much evaporated away, then take off the heat and finish with a good squeeze of lime juice and soy to taste.

Pork Adobo

Serves 4-6, and takes roughly half an hour to get it going then an hour cooking on it's own

---

60ml/2½ml groundnut (peanut) oil

---

10 cloves of garlic, sliced

700g/1lb 6oz pork belly (no bones but skin on), cut into chunks about 5 x 2.5 x 2.5cm/2 x 1 x 1 inches (you can ask your butcher to do this or just go at it yourself)

---

2 red onions, peeled and thickly sliced

---

2 red or green peppers, cut into large bite-sized pieces

---

a good thumb of ginger, trimmed, washed and coarsely grated

½ tablespoon paprika

250ml/8fl oz white wine vinegar

125ml/4fl oz light soy sauce

---

6 bay leaves

---

1 level tablespoon peppercorns

---

salt

Adobo-ing is part of the National Culinary Curriculum in the Philippines, and vinegar is the defining factor of their *adobo*. Not for the faint-hearted though, because as well as being totally delicious, or *masarap* as they say, it's full-on flavour, so eat it with plain rice.

Heat the oil in a large, wide pan (around 25cm/10 inches across and at least 7cm/3 inches deep) over a high heat.

Drop in half the garlic slices, give them a swirl, and after a couple of minutes when they are golden, take them out with a slotted spoon and put on kitchen paper.

Keeping the heat high, add the pork pieces to the pan and let them sizzle for about 10 minutes, until golden brown. When they are starting to stick to the bottom of the pan, chuck in the onions, peppers, ginger and the rest of the garlic (don't worry if your pan is pretty full - it'll all collapse in time). Give it all a bit of a mix, cover, turn down the heat and cook for about 5-7 minutes, giving it the odd stir, until the veg are starting to soften.

Add the paprika and mix well, then pour in the vinegar and soy, along with 500ml/17fl oz of water. Once the liquids are in there, chuck in the bay leaves, peppercorns and a couple of big pinches of salt.

Bring to the boil, then turn the heat down to a steady but busy simmer. Cook and reduce for about 50-60 minutes, stirring from time to time, until the liquid has a thick, coating consistency. Sprinkle with the fried garlic before serving.

Maria Clara's Secrets
Coconut Rice, Muscavado Crunchies, Mango & Ice Cream

Serves 4-6, and takes 30 minutes to knock it up followed by cooling and chilling time

100g/3½oz sticky Thai rice (available in most supermarkets)

1 x 400ml tin of coconut milk

4 tablespoons sugar

40g/1½oz muscovado sugar (I use dark but light is fine)

2 ripe mangoes, sliced

vanilla ice cream

This was pudding in the best restaurant I ate at in Manila, Bistro Remedios, specializing in food from the Pampagna region, an area famed for it's culinary prowess. Of the other six courses that preceded it, the highlights were some tiny little deep-fried crablets (baby crabs), a fantastic fiddlehead fern salad, and rice that was cooked inside a thick bamboo stick in a fire - this last dish apparently a jungle survival technique taught by the locals to American soldiers during World War II.

Maria Clara is the heroine in *Noli Me Tangere* by José Rizal, a romantic swashbuckling novel and probably the most famous book to come out of the Philippines. Why the delightful owner of this special restaurant decided to name his dessert thus is a cultural nuance too far for me, but it's a simple yet different pudding and I'm sure Maria Clara would approve of her secret being shared.

You can prepare the rice the day before if that suits you, which also applies to the magic little sugar crunchies.

In a heavy-based saucepan, mix the rice with 125ml/4fl oz of water, the coconut milk and sugar and stir to a boil over a high heat. As soon as it starts bubbling, turn the heat down so that it is as low as possible and stir frequently for the 15-20 minutes it takes for the rice to cook, to prevent it from sticking. Turn off the heat and leave it to cool (if you're in a hurry you can speed this up by spreading it out on a large plate/tray).

When the rice is cool, lay out a large piece of clingfilm and put the rice on to it in the shape of a log about 5-7cm/2-3 inches in diameter. Roll up the clingfilm, twist the ends and put the log into the fridge for a couple of hours.

Preheat the oven to 200°C/400°F/gas mark 6. Spread the muscovado on a baking tray, breaking up any big lumps into smaller ones. Bake for about 5 minutes catching it just before it starts to melt, then leave to cool for about 10 minutes before lifting off the crystallized pieces of sugar with a palette knife.

Serve the rice in slices with some pieces of mango, a scoop of vanilla ice cream and a scattering of the muscovado crunchies.

Banana Turon

**Serves 4, and takes round
about the 30 minute mark**

For the sauce

100g/3½oz sugar

2 star anise

a fat thumb of ginger, trimmed
but left unpeeled

For the bananas

1 litre/1¾ pints light oil (re-usable
afterwards)

8 spring roll pastry sheets

8 finger bananas (available in most
supermarkets), or 4 large regular ones
chopped in half across the middle

granulated sugar, to serve

In the Philippines you get those short, fat, finger-sized bananas, which
are common to many hot countries and ideal for this dish; a lot of
supermarkets over here now carry them.

Locally they are also known as a cure for a bad tummy (the raw bananas,
that is, not this dish ... deep-fried bananas doesn't sound like a cure for
much other than indulgence).

To make the sauce, put 175ml/6fl oz of water into a saucepan over a low
heat with the sugar and star anise. Roughly grate the ginger and add
it to the water, squeezing the fibres that won't go through the grater
into the pan to extract their juice. Stir once, then heat to bubbling,
disturbing it as little as possible, until it is light golden and slightly
thickened i.e. syrupy - this should take around 15-20 minutes.

Meanwhile heat the oil in a smallish pan - it needs to be big enough to
hold 4 wrapped bananas at once but small enough to give 4cm/2 inches
depth of oil. Use each pastry sheet to wrap up a banana (or half aross
the middle if you're using regular-sized ones): lay it flat, put the banana
across the middle, fold in the sides and roll it up like a pancake. It
should look roughly like a spring roll.

Gently lower them into the hot oil in 2 batches and fry until golden;
they should take about 5 minutes - turn them if they're floating.

Drain briefly on kitchen paper and roll immediately on a plate with
granulated sugar on it. Let them cool for a few minutes whilst you have
a quick look at the syrup: if it's set solid just splash in a little water and
put it back on the heat for a couple of minutes to loosen and warm up
before serving.

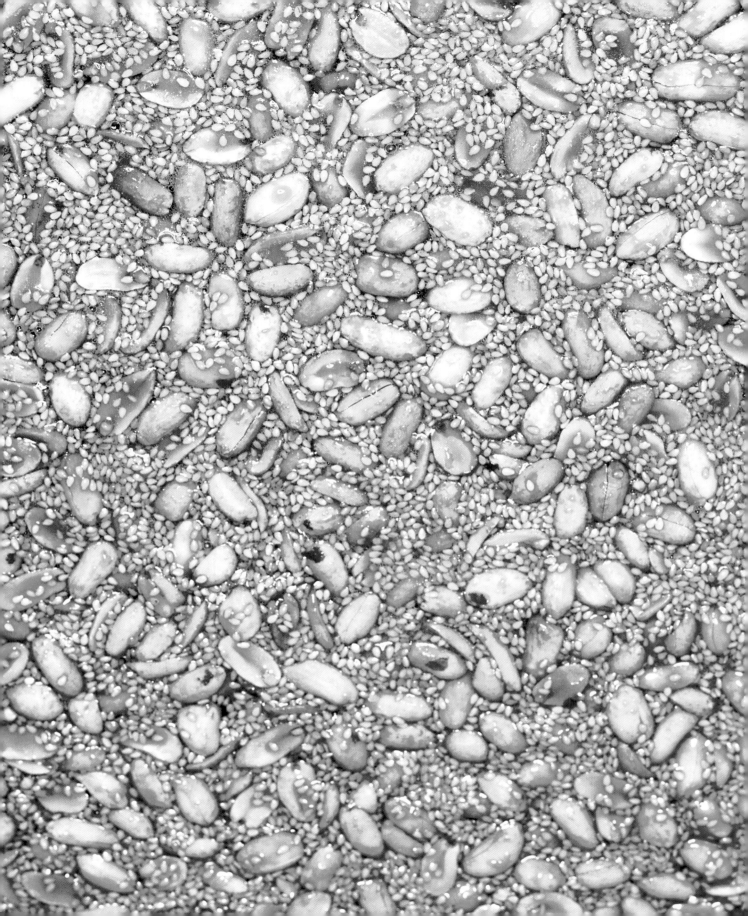

Peanut Brittle

Makes enough for a fair amount of folks to get chewy, and takes about 20 mins + cooling time

500g/1lb sugar

200g/7oz salted peanuts

100g/3½oz sesame seeds

splash of light oil, like sunflower

So there we were on the way to a cockfight, as you do of an afternoon, and our guide decided to take us to a friend's sweetie factory to get a little something to nibble on as we watched the sport.

Said friend, Beth, had her enterprise up a track, under corrugated iron, and it consisted of various big pots of caramel over coals dug into holes in the ground, and several rickety trestle tables laid out with enormous shallow trays. No floor, no walls, no fuss, just a really great product based on the special little peanuts that grow there.

Twenty minutes later I was very glad to have such a crunchy, toothsome distraction as we sat in a room packed with men hollering at each other and two cocks with razor spurs going at it in the middle.

Lay a piece of greaseproof paper on a baking tray and lightly oil it.

Put the sugar into a heavy-bottomed pan and, off the heat, gently pour on 100ml (3½fl ozl) water. Stir briefly with your finger until all the sugar is wet, trying not to get it too far up the sides.

Put the pan on a high heat and resist the urge to stir, though you can give it a very relaxed swirl from time to time. When it starts to bubble and go golden in spots, you really need to keep swirling gently to keep the caramelization even throughout.

When it is a deep, dark, golden brown (about 15 minutes), turn the heat off immediately, tip in the peanuts and sesame seeds, stir briefly to make sure that all the nuts are coated and then pour on to the greased paper, letting it run a bit so it's all spread out in a layer.

Leave it to cool and as soon as you can handle it peel off the greaseproof or else it will leach and stick.

Break up with a knife or hammer and store in an airtight container between layers of new greaseproof.

(By the way, the easiest way to clean the ex-caramel pan is by filling it with water, chucking in the spoon you stirred it with, and letting it simmer on the stove for a few minutes.)

Cuba & The

Strange as it may seem for the climate we live in, the idea of a Caribbean holiday had never really appealed. I'm not very good at sitting still, especially in hot sun, and I tend to like my away time to be one of learning, in a lightweight kind of way. But my mother-in-law had heard about this old sail ship that did some island-hopping: travelling around on a piratical craft with sails billowing in the wind, downing anchor in secluded coves, and storming the beaches in satellite boats suddenly seemed suitably adventurous and appealing.

And, of course, it was and it wasn't like that: the setting was bang on, right down to us mooring in the bay where *Pirates of the Caribbean* was filmed, and the boat, though a little too clean for proper pirates (our quarters had a fake fireplace and a bath, which if you're ever seasick is my top tip to hang out - it's a double water gravity thing), was astounding with its fifty-four sails and three masts: many a star-watching night was spent giggling on the spanker deck. The natural beauty was extremely soul-nourishing: flowers that were crazily attractive to woo the spoilt bees; arboreous islands, mostly volcanic, would peek out of the gentle ocean with their picture-perfect bays that for centuries have been the entry point for gaining the shore.

In Barbados we visited a Jacobean mansion built in 1650, St Nicolas's Abbey, an early sugar plantation that has been making a very special rum for 300 years. On Martinique we saw where Napoleon's Josephine was born, and walked around the eerie remnants of St Pierre, a Pompeii-like town where in 1902 nearly all the 50,000 inhabitants had been killed in seconds from poisonous gases when Mount Pelée blew. Legend has it that the only person to survive was a guy in the town jail ... not quite sure what

the moral is there. But the highlight for me was in Grenada, learning how chocolate is made from big slimy white seeds encased in a hard vermilion fruit. Of course I knew the theory, but the reality that something so utterly divine starts its life so gross-looking was a bit of an eye-opener.

And really, apart from a fair amount of horizon-watching and the odd toe in the weirdly warm water, that was the Caribbean.

Figuring we'd need a bit of 'us' time, we'd arranged to jettison the older folks and fly just the two of us via Jamaica to Havana for the second half of the adventure. Arrival was interesting: you can't buy Cuban currency outside of the island, and when we tried to draw down cash on our cards, they were denied. For once in my life, this wasn't lack of funds but because my English card was now American owned - a big no-no in these parts. After a few frantic calls and sweaty hours we managed to get some cash wired over, and could at last get exploring.

Havana is hugely atmospheric with its grand fenestrated houses, brightly coloured and crumbling to the extent that our hotel warned of walking under the balconies. There were constant reminders about the glory of the revolution: street names, statues and monuments everywhere, literature in bookshops, massive murals of Che, and of course the Museo de la Revolución, with the boat out front that brought over Fidel, Raúl, Che and eighty others from Mexico in 1956 to kick-start the revolution.

The days are full of bustle: street sellers with trucks filled with fruit, constant dodgy-looking construction repair work, big automobiles from the 1950s and '60s cruising around, all looking like a film set against the backdrop of such faded glory.

Caribbean

But through all the vibrancy there was a tangible underlying sadness and it was plainly apparent that times here were really tough: at one point we saw a near stampede down the street towards a lorry that had just rocked up, and when we followed the crowd it turned out to be a truckload of black market loo paper.

We got chatting to the guy who was cleaning the pool at our hotel and turned out he was a nuclear physicist (no joke), but the government had pulled the plug on any financing so he opted for the one trade that he figured was still viable - tourism. But mostly this struck home at night: as soon as dusk had fallen the city became like a stranger. There was no street lighting, so whereas in the day all the massive open doors of the old houses were like invitations to explore other worlds, by night they became places for predators to lurk - crime is high in the city.

Definitely the best thing we found in terms of evening entertainment seemed to support our observations of the many faces of Havana: in fitting contrast with the earnest omnipresence of the communist struggle, our funniest night out was undoubtedly the dazzling Club Tropicana in all its fabulous frivolity.

fact file

GEOGRAPHICAL SUMMARY: Archipelago of about 7,000 islands, islets, reefs and cays extending 2,500 miles in length and 160 miles in width in the Caribbean Sea. Lies south-east of the Gulf of Mexico, between North and South America. Generally tropical climate, but it depends on local variations in mountain altitude, water currents and trade winds. Tropical storms, hurricanes and volcanoes.

POPULATION: Around 42 million (2010 est.).

LARGEST BY POPULATION:
Cuba 11 million (Cuba also the largest by area: 110,859 square kilometres (42,803 square miles)). Smallest by population: Saba 1,500.

RELIGION: Christianity (most notably Catholicism) in its various forms is the dominant religion. There's much variation between the islands, but syncretism, or mixing and matching elements of various religions, is a prominent feature throughout. The best-known syncretic religion is Rastafari, whose influence reaches wider than its native Jamaica.

ETHNIC MAKE-UP: With a few exceptions (like Puerto Rica, Cuba, Dominican Republic), the islands are predominantly black, but mulatto, mestizo, East Indian, Carib Amerindian mixed, European and white are all also listed.

LIFE EXPECTANCY*: 74 male, 79 female.

EXTERNAL INFLUENCES: The Amerindians were doing fine on their own until the Spanish and Portuguese came over looking for gold in the 15th century, and from the end of the 1600s for the next couple of hundred years all the islands got caught up in a European power struggle. English, Dutch, French, Danish and Spanish colonized and enslaved the local population, as well as bringing over hundreds of thousands of slaves from Africa, for the production of sugar. By the 19th century the Americans had started wading in too. Independence movements started around then and gradually the islands all became self-governing, but some not until as late as the1970s and '80s. In the 20th century, when Cuba declared itself for the Communists, the Yanks started getting ever more involved in the area to try to keep the lefties at bay (of pigs).

THE ESSENTIALS OF THEIR COOKING: With obvious differences and national culinary pride on each island, it is still possible to point to some generalities: being islands, the goods of the sea are a mainstay, generally fried or grilled/barbecued, sometimes blackened with spices. And as is often the case with poorer countries, carbs are also vital, from breadfruit to dumplings to cassava to yams. Spices are abundant on many of the islands and play an important part in their taste (with the possible exception of Cuba). Fruit is magnificent, simple salads too, and then there are those Scotch bonnets to watch out for.

FOOD THEY EXPORT: Bananas, rum, sugar, citrus fruit, coffee.

TOP 5 FAVOURITE INGREDIENTS: Fish, allspice, thyme, Scotch bonnets, plantains.

MOST FAMOUS DISH: Hard one, as all the islands have their own dishes they're proud of, but it would probably be jerk chicken.

WHAT TO DRINK: Anything with rum in it (or *ron*, as they call it in Cuba)…or just on its own, Carib and Banks beer, malted drinks, Guinness in bottles, intense coffee.

BEST THING I ATE: Got to love those daiquiris.

MOST BREATHTAKING MOMENT: Sitting in the shade but still feeling the effect of the sun all around in a little restaurant on a Bajan beach, just feet away from a perfectly lapping sea, eating super-fresh fish and salad with a icy beer and suddenly realizing, thirty years too late, the attraction of beach holidays.

DON'T ASK FOR…: Directions to the nearest gay bar.

(Given the nature of their geographical spread and the fact that they are generally all independent nations, there are some pretty broad brushstrokes in the overview.)

*Life expectancy is the mean average taken from sample of twelve islands: Cuba, Bermuda, Aruba, Antigua & Barbuda, Turks & Caicos, Curacao, Cayman Islands, Puerto Rico, the Bahamas, Montserrat, St Lucia and Anguilla.

Grenadine Scrimshaw

If my self-set criteria for the knives I bring back are a) culinary b) typical of the place, then realistically this beautiful bit of scrimshaw from a tiny island called Bequia probably scores 1½. Though not unique to the Caribbean by any stretch, this technique is very much part of the local heritage, and has been for a couple of hundred years, born from bored sailors carving pictures into whales' bones and teeth ... once they'd captured the whale, of course. They generally drew either things they saw (landing a whale, ships, islands) or things they missed (ladies and more ladies).

Nowadays, due to the ban on commercial whaling, it's a dying art: my little penknife is hand-carved not into bone but something altogether more PC, though none the less pretty for it. It's the work of one of the few scrimshanders left, a Yank by birth, Sam McDowell, which makes it one of only two knives in this book I can trace back to its actual maker.

Sam is now a resident of Bequia, really just a few buildings, a post office and a bar huddled around the port cove - real back end of nowhere stuff, but I guess that gives him time to practise his art. As well as being extremely pretty, it's functional: of a proper weight, with two lethal Japanese steel blades that snap closed with a satisfying thunk.

But more than that, it's evocative of the sea that defines this group of islands, and in my experience from showing it to people it has an almost tangible attraction: nobody can ever resist holding it tightly in the palm of their hand, and giving it a squeeze: it's almost like there's a bit of sailor's magic in there.

In penknife terms, these days belong to the age of the fat handyman penknives: practical but so production line, which is why I adore my sailor's scrimshaw and really do carry it with me at all times.*

*Except hand luggage at the airport.

Cuban & Caribbean Recipes

Buljol
Salt Cod With Lime & Thyme

Avocado & Palm Heart Salad

Very Butch Chilli Sauce

St Lucian Bouillon

Rabbit Lasagne

Banana Daiquiri

Blood Orange Margarita

Buljol
Salt Cod with Lime & Thyme

Makes meals for 2 hungry people or 6ish as snacks. Once the cod is soaked it takes about 30 minutes

---

300g/10oz dried salt cod, put into a container under cold running water for 5 minutes, then soaked for several hours, changing the water a couple of times, or overnight*

---

4 tablespoons extra virgin olive oil

---

1 green pepper, diced

2-3 spring onions, diced

---

3 tablespoons picked thyme leaves, roughly chopped

8-12 cherry tomatoes, quartered

---

chilli to taste (ideally Scotch bonnet, but be careful), finely chopped

---

juice of 2-3 limes

---

salt and pepper

*300g/10oz dried salt cod should produce around 400g/13oz once soaked.

Thyme, lime and bloody hot chillies are the Caribbean's Holy Trinity. Apparently this is usually served for breakfast, but we had it for lunch, overlooking the eponymous harbour bridge in Bridgetown, the capital of Barbados.

Who knew that dried fish could taste this fresh? Which is why it's always worth having a block of salt cod in the house, but a couple of tips on storage: firstly it must stay dry, so you can't keep it in the fridge or it will moisten. Secondly, tupperware not a bad idea as it can be quite pungent in its dehydrated form.

Briefly rinse the soaked salt cod and put it into a saucepan, covered with fresh cold water. Bring to the boil and simmer fast for 20 minutes, then drain and rinse under cold water.

Whilst the cod is cooking, prep all the other ingredients into a big mixing bowl.

Once cooled, flake the fish into the bowl too, and mix well. Taste for seasoning and squeeze in more lime juice for added bite. Serve on toast or crackers.

Avocado & Palm Heart Salad

Serves 2 for lunch or 4 as a starter, and takes about 15-20 minutes to put together

This salad couldn't be any more summery if it had a bikini and shades on.

In the Caribbean I had palm hearts for the first time: our guide just hacked down a young palm tree, cut through to its middle and then sliced away for us to taste: sweet, slightly nutty and both crunchy and tender. You can get them jarred or tinned here in good supermarkets and delis, and they still have a special kind of gentle flavour, just lacking the bite of fresh from the tree.

2 green chillies, thinly sliced

1 tin/jar of palm hearts (around 180g), sliced

½ a cucumber, peeled, seeded and thinly sliced

a small handful of mint, finely chopped

1 tablespoon grapeseed or other nice light oil

juice of 1-2 limes

1 papaya, peeled, seeded and sliced

1 avocado, peeled, stoned and sliced

Put the chillies, palm hearts, cucumber and mint into a bowl and add the oil and half the lime juice. Arrange the papaya and avocado slices around a plate, pile the dressed mix in the middle and squeeze more lime juice liberally over the whole thing.

Very Butch Chilli Sauce

Makes 1 jar of tasty, liquid dynamite: takes 20 minutes making and a week of sitting

No trip to this part of the world is complete without a totally mind-blowing chilli accident, due to the fact that their chilli of choice, the Scotch bonnet, is one of the fiercest on the planet.

This recipe is for a very butch sauce, so we're leaving the seeds in, but it's up to you.

5 fat cloves of garlic

10-15 Scotch bonnet chillies, with the stalks discarded

3 tablespoons picked thyme leaves, chopped

1 small red onion, roughly chopped

100ml/3½fl oz cider vinegar

2 bay leaves

1 teaspoon salt

Crush the garlic with the flat side of a knife, and peel. Put all the ingredients except the bay leaves into a blender and blitz really well until smooth.

Pour into a sterilized jar, submerge the bay, and leave for a week in the fridge to sort itself out. Keeps firing for years.

St Lucian Bouillon

Serves 4-6, and once the gammon is cooked (about 4hrs) it's only 30 minutes to the finish line

---

a gammon hock or knuckle (on the bone and preferably smoked), weighing about 1-1.5kg/2-3lbs

1 carrot, topped and tailed

a couple of bay leaves

1 large or 2 small onions, peeled

4 cloves

250g/8oz potatoes, peeled and cut into big chunks

1 sweet potato (about 350g/11½oz), peeled and cut into big chunks

1 plantain, peeled and sliced

a good shake of cayenne

2 pinches of ground allspice

200g/7oz cabbage (Savoy is my fave, but white is fine), with the tough stalk in the leaves sliced out and the rest cut into chunky bite-sized pieces

150g/5oz peas

salt and pepper

For the dumplings

150g/5oz self-raising flour

½ teaspoon baking powder

1 tablespoon butter

Opposite: Very Butch Chilli Sauce (above) with St Lucian Bouillon (below).

Bouillon is the most popular dish of this gorgeous island in the Lesser Antilles, and both cooking and eating it nicely reflect the relaxed nature of life. This hearty one-pot dish is mainly eaten for breakfast and sometimes lunch, though for us it probably sits better for supper.

As a lot of the penetrating flavour comes from the meat, ideally you'll make this with a gammon hock/knuckle, which is cured but raw and therefore still has all its goodness to impart, as opposed to a ham hock/knuckle, which is cured and cooked. Serve with a good dollop of hot sauce - Very Butch Chilli Sauce (see page 203) would be ideal.

Put the gammon into your biggest pot with the carrots, bay leaves and the onions, studded with the cloves, then pour over cold water to cover - anywhere between 2.5-3.5 litres/4-6 pints. Turn the heat up to max, stick a lid on, and when it comes to the boil, turn the heat right down until just bubbling and cook for about 4 hours, until the meat is super tender and falling off the bone.

Use a slotted spoon to lift out the solids except the bay leaves, and put them aside. Measure the stock, top it up with water to make it back up to 2.5 litres/4 pints, then bring it back to a simmer, season, and drop in the potatoes and sweet potato.

Chuck out the studded onions and the carrots - their job is done - and take a couple of minutes to shred the meat into chunky pieces, lobbing any skin, bones and gristle.

Put the meat back into the pot, along with the sliced plantain, cayenne and allspice.

Make the dumplings by mixing together the flour, baking powder and a couple of pinches of salt, then rubbing in the butter. Slowly add enough water to make a stiff dough; it will probably take about 50-100ml/ 2-3½fl oz. Knead for a few minutes and use your hands to roll the dough into a rope of about 3cm/1¼ inches diameter, then cut it into pieces about 3cm/1¼ inches long, making about a dozen dumplings.

When the veggies in the pot are just tender (probably about 15 minutes), drop in the dumplings, pushing them beneath the surface of the simmering liquid, and then follow them with the cabbage. Season well, replace the lid and simmer for 10 minutes before stirring in the peas and cooking for a last couple of minutes.

Turn the heat off and leave to sit for 5 minutes before serving.

Rabbit Lasagne

Serves 8, and worth every minute of 1 hour 30 minutes it takes to make - you get to relax once it's in the oven (35 mins-ish)

---

1 rabbit (weighing about 1.75kg/3½lb), butchered as per the method (ask your butcher)

---

3 tablespoons light oil, such as olive oil, vegetable or sunflower

---

1 large onion, diced

---

2 teaspoons paprika

100g/3½oz mushrooms (chestnut mushrooms are perfect, though button will do), quartered

---

4 cloves of garlic, chopped

---

1 teaspoon dried oregano

---

a couple of bay leaves

300ml/½ pint white wine

---

1 litre/1¾ pints chicken stock

---

6 tablespoons extra virgin olive oil

---

2 large aubergines, cut into 1cm/ ½ inch slices

60g/2½oz butter

75g/3oz flour

200ml/7fl oz double cream

---

1 x 400g tin of chopped tomatoes

---

about 450g/14½oz lasagne (buy one that doesn't need to be pre-cooked)

---

a nugget of Parmesan

---

1 x 200g jar of piquillo peppers, sliced

---

salt and pepper

Eating out in Cuba is divided into two categories: there are the state-owned restaurants (being a communist country), which have a pretty depressing atmosphere and the food's not much better. Or you eat in paladares. The state allows people to supplement their measly income by having a few tables in their front room - by law they are not allowed to seat more than twelve people, but this seems flexible in my experience.

I had this in the most famous paladar in Havana, La Guarida, which was more restauranty than domestic, and although it's a little time-consuming to make it is without doubt the best lasagne I've ever made or eaten.

Separate the meat into three groups: the four legs (to be slow-cooked), the loins and the flappy bit of skinny meat attached to them (to cook later), and the bones (ribcage and backbone both roughly chopped into 2 or 3 pieces). Any excess bits of fat can be discarded, and if it comes with liver and kidneys set them aside for later, too.

Put a wide pan on a high heat. Season the legs with salt and pepper, and carefully lower them into the hot oil. Brown well on both sides, then take them out of the oil and set aside. Brown the bones next, then take them out as well and drop in the onion. Stir for a minute or two until it is starting to brown, then turn the heat down to medium. Add the paprika, mushrooms, garlic, oregano and bay leaves and cook for a few more minutes.

Put all the browned meat and bones back into the pan, along with any juices that have come out of them, and push down the contents of the pan so they are quite compressed. Pour in the wine and let it bubble for a few minutes before adding the stock. Bring back to the boil, then simmer with a lid on for 1 hour.

Meanwhile, preheat the oven to 220°C/425°F/gas mark 7.

Take 2 baking or roasting trays big enough to hold all the aubergine slices and cover the bottom of each tray with the extra virgin olive oil. Lay the aubergine slices in the oil, salt them lightly, then turn them and salt again. Put the trays into the oven for 15 minutes, then turn the slices over.

Put them back in the oven and after another 5 minutes they should be golden brown on both sides. Once they come out turn the oven down to 200°C/400°F/gas mark 6.

When the bubbling rabbit on the hob has been going for 1 hour, lift just the legs out and put them aside to cool. Leave the bones in the pan and turn up the heat to boil for about 5 minutes, then turn the heat off, lift out the bones and chuck them away.

Strain the oniony stock into a jug (should be around 1 litre / 1¾ pints), keeping the onions and mushrooms. Give the pan a quick wipe, put it back on a low heat and melt the butter in it. Stir in the flour and cook for a minute to make a roux, then start adding the rabbit stock in ladlefuls, stirring / whisking after each one until smooth. When you've made about 3 additions you can pour the rest of the liquid in, bring it quickly to the boil, whisking all the time, then turn off the heat and stir in the cream. Season and mix back in the onions and mushrooms.

Pick the meat off the legs and put into a bowl with the chopped tomatoes. Separately slice the raw rabbit loins + attached flappy bit into pieces 1-2cm / ½-¾ inch thick, and add the roughly chopped liver and kidneys if you want.

And now it's time to assemble the dish: start by dividing your pasta into 4 equal piles - this stops you running out. Ladle about a third of the creamy sauce into the bottom of a dish around 30cm/12 inches square by 6cm/2½ inches deep. Spread it around, then cover it with a layer of lasagne. Spread over the rabbity tomato sauce, and top with another layer of lasagne.

Next, add another third of the creamy sauce and nestle all the aubergines in it. Cover with a third layer of lasagne and scatter with the sliced peppers, along with the raw pieces of loin and innards, which will need seasoning. Finish with the remaining lasagne and top with the last of the creamy sauce and some grated Parmesan.

Cook according to the instructions on the lasagne packet - usually about 30-40 minutes until the top is gloriously golden and the pasta soft when you push a knife into it. Serve with the kind of pride usually associated more with lions than rabbits.

Banana Daiquiri

Serves 2 in a matter of minutes

1 banana (doesn't matter if it's past its prime)

juice of 1 lime

100ml/3½fl oz light rum

1 tablespoon light brown sugar, or more to taste

a large handful of ice

El Floridita in Havana, which is done out a bit like a posh bordello, is credited as the location where the daiquiri was invented. 'The Cradle of the Daiquiri', indeed, they call themselves. Hemingway knocked back a few there, as has every booze-loving tourist since the '50s.

In my view, the original is the best, but you can get that recipe anywhere, and I was quietly blown away by this version, served up to us by the sea near Hemingway's house on the outskirts of town.

Blend all the ingredients together for a few minutes and serve in fun glasses.

Blood Orange Margarita

Makes 4 in about 5 minutes

200ml/7fl oz silver tequila

100ml/3½fl oz Cointreau

300ml/½ pint blood orange juice, either freshly squeezed or from a carton

juice of 2 limes

a lime and a blood orange, to serve

For the rims of the glasses

2 teaspoons salt, preferably sea salt

2 teaspoons white sugar

about 1 tablespoon orange bitters, or fresh orange juice if you haven't got bitters

a couple of handfuls of ice cubes

In among all the faded glory of Havana, opposite the Parque Central, sits the 19th-century Hotel Inglaterra, with its famous café under the colonnaded entrance. We took to spending the sunset hours there, giving their cocktail waiter a bit of a workout as we watched the world go by.

First get the rims sorted: put the salt and sugar into a saucer and give it all a good rub together to mix it and break down any salt crystals. Pour the orange bitters (or orange juice) into another, smaller saucer.

Dip the rim of each glass into the bitters at an angle and rotate it all the way round, so that you get not just the rim wet, but also about 1cm/½ inch down the side of the glass. Shake off any excess, then roll the wet rim in the sugar and salt mix in a similar way, to coat it all the way round.

Now for the cocktail: half-fill the glasses with smashed ice (put your ice in a plastic bag and whack it with a rolling pin a few times). In a jug or cocktail shaker, mix together the tequila, Cointreau, blood orange juice and lime juice. Share between the glasses and give them a good swizzle to chill them. For the final touch, cut slices of lime and blood orange, and slot on to the rim side by side. Enjoy in the sun.

I went to Malawi, one of the poorest and most AIDS-ravaged countries in the world, on a whistle-stop trip to write about the newly available Fairtrade peanuts. The locals all giggled when I referred to peanuts - 'They don't look like peas!' was a phrase I heard more than once - whereas their eminently sensible name was groundnuts, because they grow in the ground. Having talked, laughed and cooked with the most impoverished people I've ever met, it's impossible not to admire their spirit, count your blessings and try to help just a little.

First off, to go to Malawi and not see the lake is like going to Paris and not seeing the Eiffel Tower - almost impossible, as it goes most of the length of the country and is far and away their most famous feature. But I missed it. What I did see was a country almost entirely dependent on agriculture, the vast majority of it in smallholdings of around a hectare. With a bit of help from the Norwegian government, a lot of the nut-growers were now organized so that they had one voice and with it stronger bargaining power at the market. And then they had opted to go Fairtrade, thus securing them a fair price for their hard-earned product, and a deserved bit of PR.

It's hard to not get annoyed at folk over here quibbling about how Fairtrade is more expensive, and how much of the extra goes to lining the supermarkets' pockets. From what I saw, if literally only tuppence extra makes it back to the farmers, then month on month, year on year, that changes lives: a secure, monsoon-proof house; a new bore-hole so they don't have to walk fifteen kilometres for clean water; the ability to care for sick relatives; the dream we all have of giving our kids a better future.

And the ridiculous thing is that it's only peanuts to us.

Malawi

Geographical summary: Shaped by the Rift Valley, Malawi is long, narrow and landlocked, with Lake Malawi as the dominant feature occupying 20% of the land. The tropical climate is defined in three seasons: cool and dry (mid-April to August); warm and dry (September to November); and a hefty monsoon season (December to April).

Population: 15.6 million.

Religion: Christian 79.9%, Muslim 12.8%, other or none 7.3%.

Ethnic make-up: Tribal, with a small handful of Asians & Europeans to round it off.

Life expectancy: 56 male, 57 female.

External influences: The Portuguese came first in the 16th century and brought maize, which turned into the major crop. Arab traders also making their presence known round this time, and both lots of visitors began trading in slaves. However, it wasn't until Victorian times that it got properly colonized, by the Brits who changed the name to Nyasaland (from the local word for 'lake'), and it didn't gain independence until 1964, when it became Malawi, referring to the Maravi Empire, whose reign preceded any foreigner visitations.

Essentials of their cooking: Plenty of carbs, protein where they can get it (poultry, nuts and the odd insect). Generally cook over coals/wood on the ground. Sweet tooth too, for jams and pastries.

Food they export: Tea, sugar, nuts, coffee.

Top 5 favourite ingredients: Fish (fresh and dried), sugar, maize/*ufa* (cornflour), kilombero rice, peanuts.

Most famous dish: *Nsima* (thick maize porridge).

What they drink: Water, be it clean or polluted. And Carlsberg is brewed in Blantyre.

Best thing I ate: A raw peanut, fresh from the ground.

Most breathtaking moment: When a large room of women hand-sorting nuts suddenly stood up with beaming smiles and spontaneously started singing a capella and dancing.

Don't Ask For…: Seconds.

Malawian Tea-tending Knife

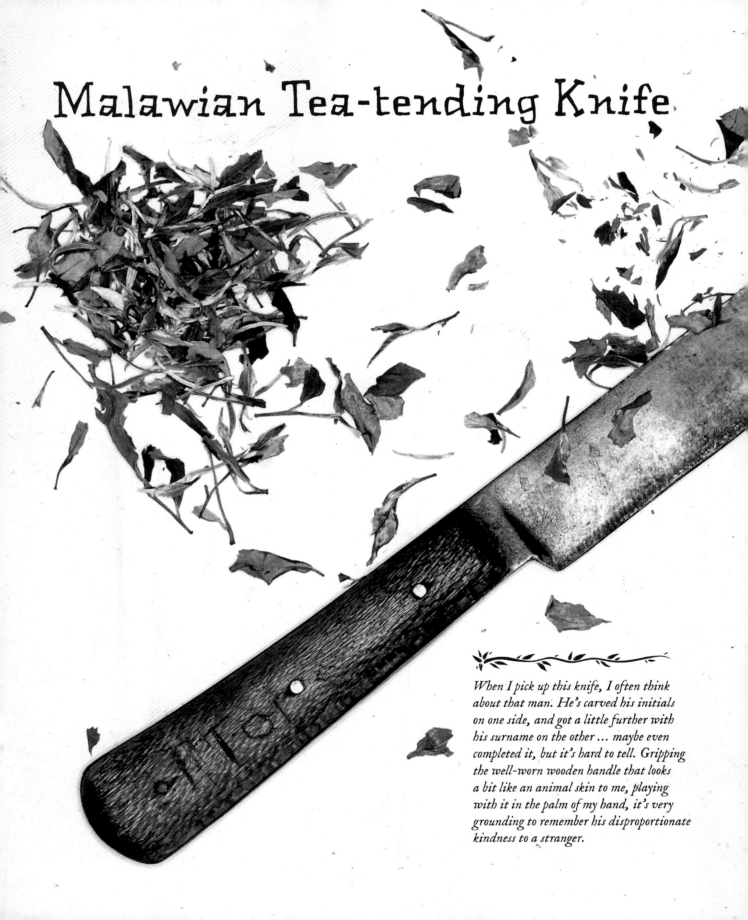

When I pick up this knife, I often think about that man. He's carved his initials on one side, and got a little further with his surname on the other ... maybe even completed it, but it's hard to tell. Gripping the well-worn wooden handle that looks a bit like an animal skin to me, playing with it in the palm of my hand, it's very grounding to remember his disproportionate kindness to a stranger.

Apart from the nuts, the other thing I saw a heck of a lot of on this trip was tea. It was the penultimate day, and come the evening I was more than a little bit wired through a tea-tasting earlier in the afternoon: I'd slurped my way (because slurping is an important part of the ancient art of tea-tasting) through forty little bowls, all brewed to a tannic-tastic strength, which was enough to make sandpaper of your tongue with a single sip.

We were to overnight at a lodge in our second tea estate of the day in Lujari, at the bottom of Mount Mulanji. We'd got a serious kind of lost on the way, so only arrived at dusk, and although I was a little bit nervous that we were going to have another tea-tasting, my mind cleared instantly when I saw the idyllic surroundings. Against a mountain background all you could see was rolling hills of dark green tea bushes, and as night started to fall (and we still couldn't find where we were going) we caught sight in the distance of the twinkling lights of the open-sided lodge.

The erstwhile English owners had organized a supper at their house where we could chat to about twenty of the guys and their wives at this landmark co-operative plantation. They were an enthusiastic, proud and chatty bunch, and the conversation flowed as freely as the wine. I remember talking to one bloke (I didn't catch his name) with an excellent face about the practicalities of tending such a large amount of bushes, and the hows of harvesting. He disappeared off in the middle of dinner and returned with a knife like this: a tea knife, with the main trunk of the blade for tougher parts of the plants, but the genius is the inner curved blade for light pruning and cutting off just the top leaves, which is the part used to make tea.

Of course, I got very excited, and although I desperately wanted it I knew better than to ask this of these kind and proud people - that would be so wrong.

Randomly for our location some grappa was drunk, and I just about remember the starlit descent down the hill back to the lodge, our stumbling and giggling the only sound to infect the total peacefulness. The next morning I came out of my room into bright sunlight with a tiny baby hangover, and there, on the table, was this knife. No note, just a word from one of the guys that it was for me.

So although I've never used it in the kitchen, you can understand why this knife makes me so very happy every time I hold it: it just has the best karma out of all and any of them.

NASFAM

Malawian Recipes

Chiponde
Homemade Peanut Butter

Nsomba zokazinga ndi ginja komanso anyezi
Ginger & Garlic Fried Fish

Mpunga wosakaniza ndi Nsinjiro
Chicken & Peanut Rice

Masamba amawungu omwe anaphikidwa ndi Rosemary
Rosemary's Pumpkin Curry

Lemon Iced Tea Lollies

Chiponde
Homemade Peanut Butter

Makes a small jar, which is enough, since it takes less than 30 minutes to make (most of which is nut-roasting time), is much nicer fresh and is best for about a week

150g/5oz salted peanuts (which are usually lightly roasted) or raw, preferably Fairtrade

Maldon sea salt, to taste (around ½ teaspoon, but maybe less for kiddy palattes)

Taste-wise you can totally tell the difference: less oily, less sweet, more savoury, and, unsurprisingly, less processed.

Over years of cooking with kids, I've noticed they tend to have a total disconnect over where their food comes from and how it became what it is. Peanuts, yes, peanut butter, yes, but how to make one from the other is a total blank, so take the few minutes needed to give them the simplest of lessons and sit back and watch the pleasure monster come to town.

Preheat the oven to 160°C/325°F/gas mark 3.

Spread the peanuts on a baking tray and, if they're ready-salted, roast them for 15 minutes, shuffling them halfway through. If you're starting from raw they will take more like 25-30 minutes to achieve the same deeper shade of golden; this not only heats their oils up and makes the result tastier and texturally better, but gives a nicer colour as well.

Cool for 5 minutes, then tip into a food processor and whiz. I like my peanut butter with some larger pieces of nut in, not all smooth - but essentially just keep blending until you get a consistency you like: something like biscuit crumbs, then add about 4 tablespoons of warm water and blitz again until it comes together. Tip it into a bowl and stir in salt and a bit more warm water - around 2 tablspoons: stop when you get a creaminess you enjoy, but bear in mind that until it stabilizes it'll probably seize a bit as it sits, so you may need to stir a bit more in later.

Transfer to a small, sterilized jar, give it a hearty bang on the table to knock the air out, and keep in the fridge.

Nsomba Zokazinga Ndi Ginja Komanso Anyezi
Ginger & Garlic Fried Fish

Serves 2. Prep takes about
30 minutes, cooking about 15

50g/2oz ginger, roughly chopped

2 bird's-eye chillies, roughly chopped

5 cloves of garlic, roughly chopped

3 spring onions, roughly chopped

½ teaspoon paprika

5 tablespoons groundnut oil

2 tablespoons white wine vinegar

2 portion-sized fish, line caught (red bream works well), about 700g/1½lb each (scaled and gutted weight)

around 750ml/1¼ pints light oil (groundnut is ideal), for frying

limes, to serve

salt and pepper

There are some table sauces that every nation takes to its heart - for us it's probably HP, Heinz ketchup and Colman's mustard, but in Malawi the market is pretty much sewn up by a brand called Nali, who make a tasty hot sauce with various intonations. My favourite was the ginger one, closely followed by the garlic, and I've kind of mixed and matched them together to come up with this recipe.

There are more species of fish in the Rift Valley than in any comparable area - that is to say, more freshwater fish in the lakes there than in all those of Europe and North America put together - so from teeny-weeny ones that get fermented and ground, to big mammas chopped up in the markets, you see a lot of fish in Malawi. Back home, I used red bream, but you can use any other portion-sized fish that's fresh and sustainable.

Apart from a maize porridge mush called *nsima* (not exactly yummy to me, but very cheap and useful for filling hungry tummies), rice is the other main carb of choice. They have a particularly delicious rice over there called Kilombero, with long and thickish grains. I was excited enough to carry 3kg (6lb) of the stuff back with me, but dismay doesn't touch the sides of what I felt when I opened it up and it was a bad batch alive with l'il critters. Over the years of bringing foodstuffs back home this has happened to me more times than I care to remember, and every time it still seems so unfair after one's gone to all that effort.

In a blender blitz up the ginger, chillies, garlic, spring onions, paprika and a teaspoon of salt with the groundnut oil and vinegar. Make some deep diagonal cuts across both sides of each fish - about 5 cuts along each side. Put about ½ teaspoon of ginger paste into each slit and smear the rest on the skin and in the cavity.

Pour oil to the depth of about 1.5cm/¾ inches into a frying pan large enough to hold both fish and shallow fry on medium high - the oil should be hot enough to make the fish fizzle when it goes in. Fry the fish fast for about 5-6 minutes on each side until golden. Serve straight away, with rice, salad and lime quarters.

Mpunga Wosakaniza Ndi Nsinjiro
Chicken & Peanut Rice

Serves 6, and takes 20 minutes activity then 20 minutes for the rice to cook

---

2 tablespoons groundnut oil or light olive oil or rapeseed oil

---

125g/4oz thick-cut streaky bacon, sliced

---

1 large onion, sliced (I use red for colour)

---

2 cloves of garlic, roughly chopped

---

1 green pepper, sliced

½ a green chilli, sliced (not for kids, though)

300g/10oz chicken breast, cut into medium-sized chunks

400g/13oz long-grain rice (though if you ever see 'Kilombero' rice from Malawi buy a load, as it's very specially fluffy)

700ml/1 pint 3fl oz chicken stock

---

a handful of coriander, roughly chopped

75g/3oz peanuts (e.g. salted), roughly chopped, preferably Fairtrade

---

2 spring onions, sliced

---

salt

As you'd expect from one of the poorest countries in the world, this is a simple dish but what you might not be expecting is quite how yummy it is.

Simple yes, but pleasingly so, and I've made kids and grown-ups alike happy with it.

In your favourite large cooking pot, heat the oil over a high heat and fry the bacon until crisping. Add the onions and carry on stirring for a couple of minutes before adding the garlic, pepper and green chilli.

Keeping the heat high, and the contents of the pan moving, lob in the chix chunks and rice and fry everybody for a few minutes, stirring all the time - don't worry if your pan is browning on the bottom as long as it doesn't actually burn.

Once it is all well coated, pour in the stock, season with a little salt and put a lid on the pot. From when it comes to a simmer, give it 10 minutes like that, then turn the heat off and leave to stand for another 10 minutes. Stir in most of the peanuts, the spring onions and half the coriander and give it a good taste for seasoning.

Serve hot or warm, finishing with the last of the corry and a final scattering of nuts.

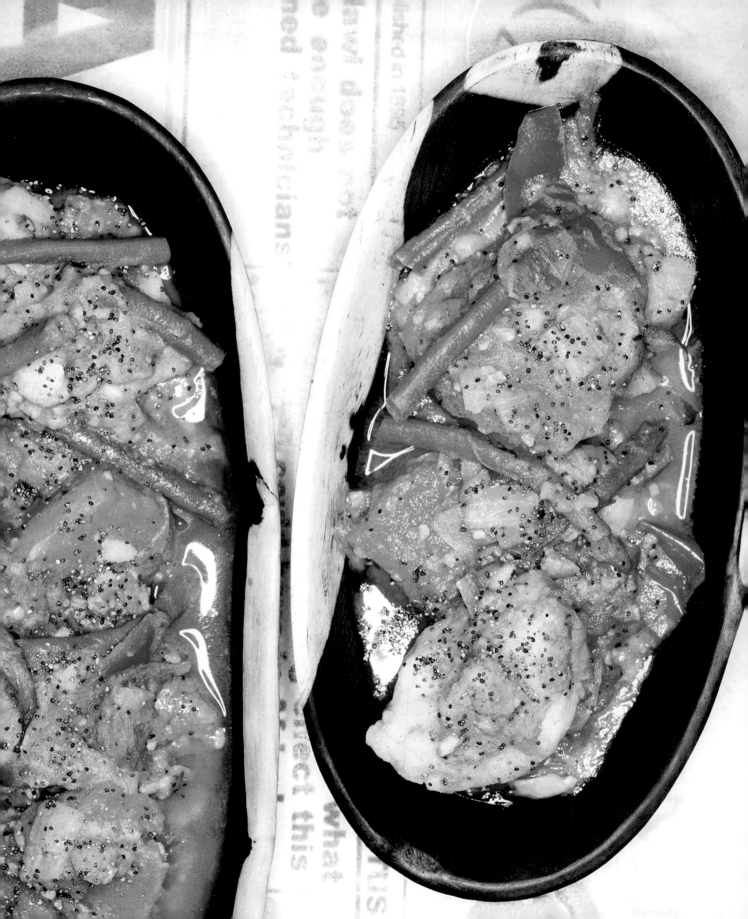

Masamba Amawungu Omwe Anaphikidwa Ndi Rosemary
Rosemary's Pumpkin Curry

Serves 6, and takes 20 minutes to get it going and then about the same again simmering time

---

75g/3oz salted peanuts, preferably Fairtrade

1kg/2lb pumpkin (or squash)

---

2 onions, coarsely diced

---

3 tablespoons groundnut oil

500g/1lb potatoes (about 3 medium), peeled and chopped into roughly 5cm/2 inch chunks

---

3 cloves of garlic, minced

---

3 bird's-eye chillies, finely chopped (with seeds), or more, to taste

---

2 teaspoons curry powder

---

a pinch of ground cloves

---

1 teaspoon turmeric

---

1 teaspoon (heaped) poppy seeds, plus a bit more for serving

200g/7oz French beans, topped (but not tailed) and halved

---

4 ripe tomatoes, cored and cut into wedges

---

salt

Rosemary was one of the lucky few I met in the peanut-growing region of Lilongwe who had a proper roof over her head; most lived under corrugated iron, which meant that every year when the fierce monsoon came, everything they owned got pretty drenched, much of it ruined, thus making it even harder to build for a better future.

Adjacent to Rosemary's simple living quarters was a little hut with a fire burning in the middle of it that was her kitchen. She made this curry in front of me using a memorably long wooden spoon, with more energy and smiles than I would have thought possible for one with such a gruelling life: peanuts are a bugger to harvest.

You also can use any squash for this, although the best are the starchy ones, like spaghetti or acorn squash.

Grind the peanuts in a food processor or pound with a pestle and mortar. Peel and deseed the pumpkin/squash and cut it into very large pieces, around 6 x 8cm/2½ x 3 inches, just to give you a rough guide.

In a wide, heavy pan, fry the onions in oil over a medium heat. Cook for a minute or two, then turn up the heat and add the potatoes. Cover with a lid, and stir from time to time until they are just starting to soften around the edges.

Turn the heat down a bit and mix in the garlic and chillies, followed a couple of minutes later by the ground peanuts, curry powder, cloves, turmeric, poppy seeds and a good pinch of salt. Put the kettle on.

Add the pumpkin to the pan, stir again and cook for a few minutes. Pour on enough boiling water to just cover the vegetables and put on the lid to bring it back to the boil quicker. Once it's bubbling fast, add the beans and tomatoes, give it all a prod, and simmer, uncovered, for about 20 minutes, or until it's reduced to a good curryish sauce consistency.

Sprinkle with poppy seeds and serve with rice.

Lemon Iced Tea Lollies

Makes 8, and takes 10 minutes to make (though there's 2 overnighters involved: one for infusing and the other for freezing)

15g/½oz loose-leaf tea (you're allowed to tear teabags open), preferably Fairtrade

juice of ½ a lemon

40g/1½oz sugar

lolly moulds and sticks

If central Malawi was all about peanuts, the south was all about tea. I visited a tea plantation called Satemwa, the first Fairtrade tea plantation in the country. Tea tastings are a surprisingly tannic affair, as you taste around forty at a time, all strong and black, which requires a lot of attention and stamina.

I didn't actually have these lollies over there, but when I was trying to think of a relevant tea recipe for this book, I thought they would have gone down a treat in the hot African sun.

I got my lolly moulds from Lakeland (www.lakeland.co.uk), and they also do cool rocket-shaped ones.

Infuse the tea overnight in 600ml/1 pint of cold water. The next day strain it, and stir in the lemon juice and sugar until dissolved. Taste and adjust with a bit more of either/both ingredients to suit your taste, bearing in mind that it will taste less sweet when it is frozen.

Pour into lolly moulds and put in the freezer.

Check the lollies after about an hour or so and push in the sticks; they should be just frozen enough to support the sticks, i.e. half in and half out of the moulds.

Pop them back into the freezer until hard.

To release the lollies, sit the moulds in warm water for just the briefest of moments.

If I could build a country to explore, it would look a lot like Mexico. Proper history, vibrant colour, great food, warm climate, natural beauty, lively fiesta - it really has got it all. On both trips I've driven over 2,000 miles in a fortnight, largely in a greedy effort to see as much as possible, and partly due to not looking at the map scale. The result of this kick-ass touring is that I know for sure that I really love this special place, and can't wait to see more.

The Mayan sites are a good place to start: Palenque, Tulum, Uxmal and the most famous, Chichén Itzá. Not only are they architecturally astounding, given that the builders had no metal tools and no wheel, but they're in such good nick for buildings 1,000 to 1,500 years old. Impressive and beautiful too, with all their geometric stone carving, but - and this is the really clever bit - they're also fun.

If you're going to build a pyramid to the sun it makes sense that you go as close to the object as possible - these temples are seriously high, and any more than five centimetres per step to balance your toes on is just modern extravagance. A lot of the sites are deep in tangled jungles, with a definite whiff of Indiana in the air: weirdly, despite their worldwide fame they never seem to be so busy that you can't still create an image of yourself as the great explorer, especially if you go early and wander off the beaten track. And the place gets even more Dr Jones when you read about the offerings of children's bones found at each base corner of the temple, as you're sitting on the low altar at the top where more human sacrifices had the beating hearts ripped out of their bodies. Gruesome but enthralling.

The second lot of residents to leave their mark are of course the Spanish: their over-the-top baroque churches are as much a part of the local furniture now as anything Mayan, and some of the old haciendas - in effect just slave plantations - are having an excellent renaissance as atmospheric hotels. The only place I came across where you can still find Mexicans who look like the stone carvings on the temples, that is to say not watered down with Spanish blood, is up in the mountains around the town of San Cristóbal de las Casas.

All of a sudden you start to see them on the roadside, wrapped in bright woollen overclothes: striking features with that characteristic hooked nose, though even shorter than the normal Mexicans and darker too. It seems quite sad that the only part they have left as their own is this small corner, but the balaclava'd cigar-toting legend that is Subcomandante Marcos, head of the freedom-fighting Zapatistas, whose base is hidden in these mountains, is on the case.

And then there's the food: market culture is still strong in Mexico, stronger than anywhere in Europe, with big market days in every town busting with freshness and noisy with banter. This is a country where the purchasing of food is a fun social event - so different from a trip round Tesco. The dishes that result from putting the ingredients centre stage are, of course, punchy with flavour. Their holy trinity of chilli, lime and salt (backed up usually by a handful of coriander) smacks of fresh zing, and the slow-cooked layers of a *mole* are smooth and complex. Put them together with a cold Corona and the heat of the sun and it's just one of my favourite cuisines in the world.

All of that against a backdrop of extreme natural beauty: too many folks go just for the beaches for me to waste space admiring them, but I will say that if you're ever round Oaxaca don't miss the Cactus National Park, which is so unreal looking you think you've stepped into a mescalated spaghetti Western.

FACT FILE

Geographical summary: Boundaries to the north over the Rio Grande with the United States and with Guatemala and Belize to the south. The Sierra Madre and Rocky Mountains run south from the border with the US. Northern Mexico is dry and desert-like, while the south is mountainous jungle, making it one of the world's most bio-diverse countries.

Population: 112 million.

Religion: Nearly everyone is Roman Catholic, 6% Protestant.

Ethnic make-up: 60% mestizo (Amerindian and Spanish), 30% Amerindian, 9% white, 1% other.

Life expectancy: 73 male, 77.5 female.

External influences: Got to give this one to the Spanish: Hernán Cortés arrived in 1519 with only 550 men and had the whole place sewn up and claimed for the Spanish throne just three years later. Controlled the territory pretty much until Independence in 1821, and even then it was the Mexican-born Spanish who stayed in charge.

Essentials of their cooking: They excel in all areas, from dishes that take days to cook (*cochinita in pibil*, or the ludicrously tasty *mole*), to ceviche, which is done in minutes. Bonus points for being able to wrap almost anything in a taco. Lots and lots of fresh fruit, veg and herbs.

Food they export: Beer, tomatoes, spirits (tequila and mescal), chillies and peppers, wheat, avocados.

Top 5 favourite ingredients: Corn, chillies, lime, pulses, coriander (and salt).

Most famous dish: Some might say chilli con carne, but I'm going for *mole*.

What they drink: Tequila or mescal (made from the same plant, the only difference being regional), sometimes with sangrita chasers (a shot of spicy tomato-based juice). Lots of light beer with lime, like Corona. Rich coffee. Plenty of delicious juices. Compulsory margaritas.

Best thing I ate: The best guacamole of my life, with crunchy little fried grasshoppers (*chapulines*) sprinkled on top: a slightly shocking reminder of what a ripe avocado that hasn't travelled the world actually tastes like. Also the never-ending joy of eating warm, freshly made corn tortillas – so different from anything we usually see.

Most breathtaking moment: The first time you walk into one of the old Mayan sites is one you'll never forget. Mine was Uxmal, which is impressively expansive and surprisingly quiet.

Don't ask for...: A race to the top.

OAXACAN WHACKER

The market in Oaxaca is legendary and world-class. It's so big you can get properly lost in it, but that's OK because there are little cafés at which to rest and re-orientate as you sample one of the many local moles (of the non-furry variety). It's impossible for any food-lover not to be wide-eyed and over-excited as you explore its alleyways: fruit and veg, pots and pans, chickens alive or dead, and more types of dried beans, chillies and corn than you knew existed.

You can buy any part of any animal you want, Day of the Dead sweets, honey rolls and many other kinds of attractive edibles, but there's also a fair amount of tat that reminded me fondly of my local market in Shepherd's Bush: '70s 'fashion' dresses, dodgy watches, voluminous, balloon-sized bras and a whole area dedicated to Tupperware.

But somewhere in among all of that there lurked my knife - she just had to be in there. It took the purchasing of an enormous pan for cooking tacos (imagine the sawn-off top of an oil drum beaten into a dome) to get the kitchen stall lady on side enough to show me to the knives - directions were never going to work in that rabbit warren - and after stopping at her friend's stall on the way to exact another compulsory purchase (a couple of gaudy plastic trays that I've since become quite fond of), we got to The Man who Sold The Knives.

The best thing about the buying of this knife was the way that as soon as I'd picked it the owner called over his mate, who got on his bicycle sharpener and pedalled as madly as he smiled, sparks flying everywhere, to make it properly sharp.

I like the mid-size of this cleaver: not as daunting, or in my hands as clumsy, as my enormous Chinese chopper, which I only use for the odd precision strike, not every day. But this has found a way into my regular armoury for the way it goes through chicken bones, pork ribs, racks of lamb, even fish steaks: anything that takes a bit of a knock, requiring more weight than a straight knife will give you - but not the wallop needed to get through big beef or any of the thicker meat bones.

No idea about those stripes though, but they work for me.

Mexican Recipes

Jugo Verde *Big Green Juice*

Chilaquiles *Mexican Breakfast*

Salsa Piccante Rojo
Charred Tomato & Chilli Salsa

Tequila Ceviche

Flores de Calabaza
Sautéed Courgette Flowers

Chicken Tostadas

Poc Chuc
Pork with Bitter Orange

Jugo Verde
Big Green Juice

**Makes a couple of glasses
in a couple of minutes**

3 apples

3 sticks of celery, with leaves
if possible

a bunch of spinach leaves

a few sprigs of mint

a handful of parsley

In Oaxaca we'd opted to stay in a hacienda right on the outskirts of town, on the grounds that it would be a calming respite from the busy city. How wrong we were, as the area our hacienda was in was celebrating their local patron saint's birthday for the entire four days of our visit, and every night we got involved in a mescal-fuelled messy fiesta with the rest of the town.

My Spanish is crap, they spoke no English, we were the only gringos there, but they just could not have been more welcoming and inclusive: They dragged us to dance to the tune of their 15-man brass band, fed us for free on long communal tables and bated us to shoot more Mezcal than I knew I could. At the end of the last night I was found next to the 20 foot papier maché effigy of St. Whomever-he-was of the Suburbs, both of us rather worse for wear, emotionally clutching him like a dear, dear friend I was about to leave. I loved Mexico before, but these few nights made me love the people in a whole new way.

This juice, served for breakfast, was the only way we got up and did anything the next day, reintroducing nutrition to our bodies in a vibrant, delicious, green way.

Just juice it all together.

*From the top: Chilaquiles; Big
Green Juice; Salsa Piccante Rojo.*

Chilaquiles
Mexican Breakfast

Breakfast for 2, or a kids supper for 3 or 4. Done and out of the oven in 15 minutes (once you've bought/made the salsa)

---

3 big handfuls of tortilla chips, plain as you can buy

---

1 recipe Salsa Piccante Rojo (see opposite), though if you're *really* hungover you could also use ready-made salsa, but you know it won't be quite the same

---

200g/7oz ricotta, or *queso fresco* if you can get hold of it

---

2 eggs

---

a knob of butter

---

a handful of coriander, chopped

---

extra virgin olive oil, to drizzle

---

salt

This dish is ubiquitous on Mexican breakfast menus, and comes in many shapes and guises. What we have here is a slightly simplified version that I ate in a truck stop on a very long, straight road between somewhere and another place really far away. I'm a pretty pushy, not very relaxing holidayer, but doing these killer drives was a great way to get to grips with the country at speed whilst eating where and what the workforce ate.

Along with nookie and a long bath, this is truly one of the Great Ways to Start the Day, though not in a Monday-Friday kind of way. Knock it up as an easy and fun brunch dish: it's spot-on with or without a hangover, and if you take the chilli in the salsa down (or even out) I predict a big hit for children's supper.

Preheat the oven to 180°C/350°F/gas mark 4.

Find a smallish ovenproof dish (I use a round one about 20cm/8 inches diameter and 6cm/2½ inches deep) and cover the bottom with about a third of the tortilla chips. Cover that with about a third of the salsa, then about a third of the ricotta. Repeat twice, not worrying about making perfect layers but just aiming to distribute the ingredients quite roughly, then cover the dish with a lid or foil and bake for 10 minutes.

A couple of minutes before times up, fry the eggs in butter then whip the lid/foil off the dish and lay them on top. Scatter on the chopped corry, and finish with a bit of sea salt and a splash of extra virgin.

Salsa Piccante Rojo
Charred Tomato & Chilli Salsa

Makes a medium bowlful, in under 30 minutes

---

1 red pepper

---

3 red chilli peppers, or 1 habanero

500g/1lb vine-ripened tomatoes

---

1 spring onion, finely chopped

---

a large handful of coriander, finely chopped

½-1 clove of garlic, finely chopped

---

juice of 1-2 limes

---

salt

To serve

---

tortilla chips (good with a sprinkling of smoked paprika)

It's worth making double quantities and freezing half to use for Chilaquiles (see opposite), which you definitely need to eat at least once in your life. Apart from that, you know what to do with this: you can hardly sit down anywhere in Mexico without a bowl of freshly fried tortilla triangles and a dish or two of salsa being put down in front of you.

Salsas can vary from tame to twitch-inducing: I'm pretty butch about my chilli and I've made this recipe how I like it - pleasantly shocking.

Char the skins of the pepper, chillies and tomatoes in any way that works for you: on a barbecue or a griddle on a high flame, or cut everything in half and whack them under the grill. Keep turning until most of the skin is blackened and blistered, and as each piece is ready drop them into a biggish bowl and cover with clingfilm. Leave until cool enough to handle (quicker if you put it outside).

Roughly peel the pepper, chillies and tomatoes, leaving on a little bit of the charred skin and keeping the seeds in the chillies but ditching them from the tomatoes and pepper.

Give it all a quick squeeze to get rid of some of the liquid, then pulse everything briefly three or four times in a food processor so it is combined but quite chunky, and tip into a mixing bowl.

Stir in the spring onion, coriander, garlic and lime juice, season well with salt, transfer to a colourful serving bowl, and serve with tortilla chips.

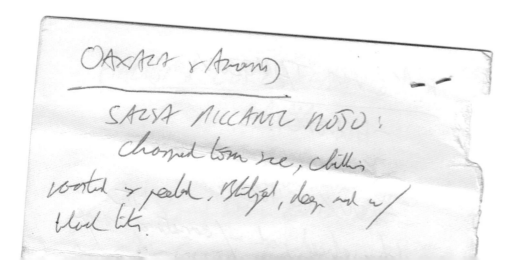

Tequila Ceviche

Serves 6, and takes 10 minutes to make then needs 20 minutes in the fridge

---

300g/10oz white fish (bass is ideal, anything cod-like also works but avoid thin flat fish like sole), trimmed, pinboned and with the blood line cut out if it's thick

---

a shot of tequila

---

juice of 2 limes

---

2 chillies (ideally 1 red, 1 green), seeds in and finely sliced

---

a small handful of fresh coriander, finely chopped

---

flaky sea salt

If the Holy Trinity of Mexican food is salt, lime and chilli, add tequila to the mix and now you've got a party.

Ridiculously easy, quick and tasty, the only thing that could go wrong is not using absolutely spanking fresh fish, so it's not a Monday dish. Nor is it a winter one, as the final necessary ingredient is sunshine.

Slice the fish as thinly as you can and lay the pieces so they just touch like a patchwork, either on one big shallow dish or individual plates. Pour over the tequila and the juice of 1 lime, then put it into the fridge for 20 minutes.

Just before serving, squeeze over the rest of the lime juice and scatter on the chillies and coriander, along with a couple of generous pinches of sea salt.

Enjoy with a cold beer, a glass of crisp white or more tequila.

Flores de Calabaza
Sautéed Courgette Flowers

Starters for 4 or a great veggie main for 2. Takes about 45 minutes but that's largely down to the cooking time for the kind of big grain polenta I like to use

---

300ml/½ pint milk

250ml/8fl oz water

---

1 clove of garlic, very finely chopped

---

1 whole chilli (dried works fine too)

100g/3½oz big grain, slow-cook polenta (see introduction)

---

a large knob of butter

100g/3½oz ricotta or Lancashire/Wensleydale (depending on whether you want the result to be creamier or saltier), or even a combination of both

---

40g/1½oz Parmesan, finely grated

6-8 courgette flowers (depending on size), with baby courgettes attached

---

2 tablespoons extra virgin olive oil

---

2 spring onions, cut into 5cm/2 inch pieces

---

a few leaves of oregano or thyme, just if you happen to have any in the fridge/garden

---

100ml/3½fl oz double cream

---

a handful of coriander, roughly chopped

---

1 lime

---

salt and pepper

The usual way we see courgette flowers on a menu is stuffed and deep-fried, which is a bit of a hassle to do at home. This recipe is typical of the Mexican attitude: a more relaxed, approachable way to cooking these beautiful blooms.

The flowery bit is very simple, and it's really your choice of polenta that will mark your dish out as different: the 5-minute-cook stuff is fine, though a bit pappy, whereas if you go for one with the coarser grains (which the Italians call Bramata) that take more like 30 minutes to cook you get a much richer, not to mention more authentic, result.

Put the milk and water in a pan with the garlic and chilli over a medium heat and season well with salt and pepper. When the milk starts to steam and bubble a little bit, tip in the polenta in a steady stream, whisking with one hand as you pour with the other. Cook very slowly (lowest setting on the smallest ring/flame), stirring occasionally, for the length of time specified on the packet: depending on the type of polenta used, it may need half a glass of hot water whisking in if it looks a bit solid - you're aiming for a consistency a bit like the porridge of your dreams. Once it's cooked, turn off the heat, stir in the butter and the cheese (saving a touch of Parmesan for the end), and cover.

Cut the flowers off the baby courgettes, slice them in half and set to one side. Warm the oil gently in a frying pan. Halve the little courgettes lengthwise and fry in the pan with the spring onions and herb leaves (not the corry yet); they should only just fizzle as they go in - this is not an aggressive cook. Stir over a low heat for a couple of minutes, then add the cream and turn the heat up so that it bubbles busily. Reduce it for a few minutes to the consistency of a thick sauce, seasoning as she goes.

Turn the heat off, toss in the flowers, put a lid on and let sit for a couple of minutes. Have a look at the polenta, which has probably seized up by now and formed a bit of a skin - nothing that half a glass of hot water and a brief whisk can't rejuvinate to its former creamy glory.

Take the lid off the courgette pan, stir the corry and the flowers so they are just wilted. Add a squeeze of lime juice and taste for seasoning. Share the polenta between warmed shallow bowls and spoon the sauce and bits over and around. Finish with a sprinkling of Parmesan and lime on the side.

Chicken Tostadas

Makes 8 fully loaded tostadas, in just over 1 hour

extra virgin olive oil

1 onion, chopped

7 cloves of garlic, finely chopped

1 teaspoon ground cumin

1 teaspoon chilli flakes

1 whole dried chilli

3 chicken breasts, cut into roughly 3cm/1¼ inch chunks

1 x 400g tin of tomatoes

½ teaspoon coriander seeds

2 x 400g tins of black beans

Tabasco

salt

For the salsa

3 large, ripe tomatoes

a handful of coriander, chopped

juice of 1-2 limes

1 head of baby gem, shredded (optional)

1 chilli, finely chopped

1 small red onion, diced

To serve

8 small corn tortillas, around 12cm

1 lime

plain oil (like veg) for shallow-frying

Nobody does party food better than those fiesta-loving Mexicans, and tortillas and their derivatives (tacos, tostadas, quesadillas, etc.) are some of the best (party-in-the-) street food I've ever eaten.

You can't go far in any Mexican city, town or village without seeing a tortilla-making machine, a contraption of dough hooks, conveyor belts and a cutting stamp, spitting them out at enormous speed. The joys of fresh corn tortillas are hard to come by here, but for the real McCoy email www.coolchile.co.uk, where a lady called Dodie will send you vac-packs of 10. They freeze well, so I'd advise getting a job lot in: I always do.

To cook the chicken, heat 3 tablespoons of oil in a frying pan and cook the onions over a high heat with 3 of the garlic cloves, the cumin, chilli flakes and whole chilli. Season with salt. When the onion has softened a bit, stir in the chicken and brown it for a few minutes. Add the tin of tomatoes with a splash more oil, bring to a simmer, then turn the heat down and cover with a lid.

To make the refried beans, use a heavy-bottomed frying pan (a cast-iron skillet is ideal) to fry the remaining garlic in 3 tablespoons of oil over a medium flame until golden, then add the coriander seeds. After a minute of two of brisk stirring, tip in the beans with their liquid from the tin and season with a hefty pinch of salt and as much Tabasco as you like. Let it bubble gently for about 10 minutes until thickened, then either mash by hand or blitz in a food processor.

For the salsa, core and deseed the tomatoes, emptying the seeds into the chicken, then dice the flesh finely. Mix in a bowl with the coriander, lime juice, chilli, red onion and a good pinch of salt.

When the chicken has been cooking for about 1 hour it should be really tender and falling apart. Take the lid off and use a wooden spoon to break up the chicken pieces, then simmer for another 5 minutes to get rid of some of the liquid - you want it to be a coating sauce.

Heat the oil in a wide frying pan and fry the tortillas in threes for about 30 seconds on each side, or until golden brown. Drain them briefly on kitchen paper, then put them on a suitably festive serving dish. Spread with the refried beans, then load up the chicken, lettuce (if using) and top with salsa. Finish with a squeeze of lime. Best. Party. Food. Ever.

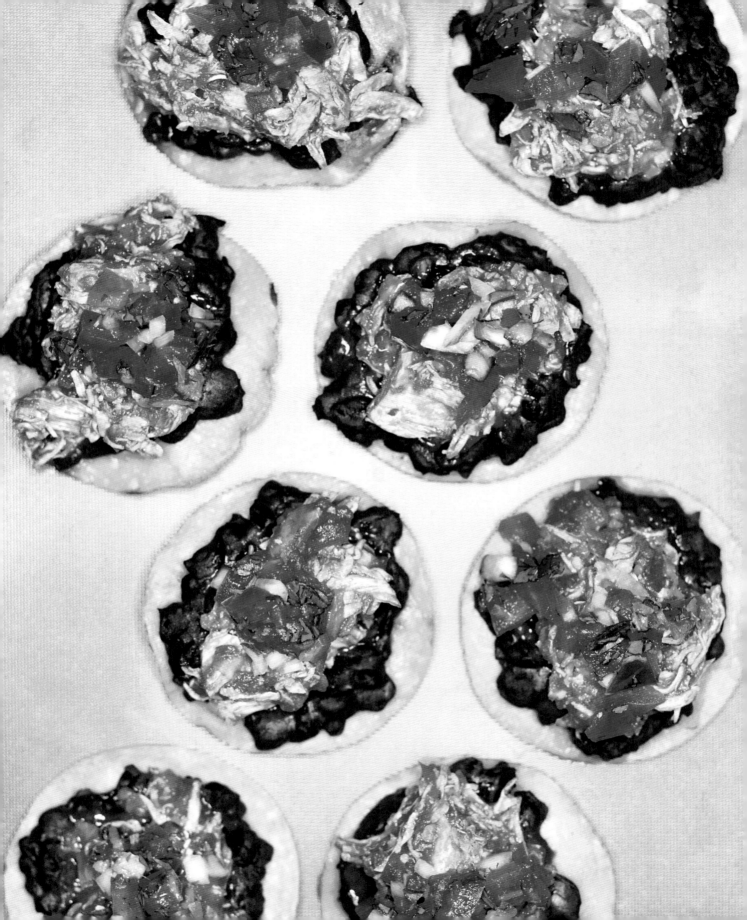

Poc Chuc
Pork with Bitter Orange

Serves 6, and takes around 1 hour
(not including the overnight
brine/marinade option)

700g/1lb 6oz pork loin

extra virgin olive oil

For the brine

75g/3oz salt

75g/3oz sugar

4 allspice berries

½ teaspoon black peppercorns

For the marinade

juice and zest of 6 Seville oranges
(OR juice and zest of 4 limes + juice
and zest of 2 oranges)

½ teaspoon dried oregano

3 cloves of garlic, crushed

lots of pepper (about ½ teaspoon)

For the onion salsa

1 small red onion, sliced thinly

1 chilli, thinly sliced

a handful of coriander, chopped

juice of 1-2 limes

a big pinch of salt

This real old timers' recipe is about two distinct flavours, and their effect on the meat as well as on each other: salt and bitter oranges. Long before the days of electricity and white goods, meat was brined or salted to help extend its life, but it could tend to leave its salty stamp on the end product.

Enter their native bitter oranges (*naranja agria* - we call them Seville orange), which form the backbone of the marinade: the juice not only has a fantastic, sharp and singing flavour but the acidity helps to de-salinate the meat. So for the authentic taste make this at the beginning of the year, in Seville orange season; the rest of the time a combo of limes and oranges gets pretty close.

The brining step is true to the past but, to be fair, optional now that we have fridges. It does, however, add tenderness: *poc chuc* must be grilled (literally the name means barbecued pork), and as tenderloin is a very lean cut, and the one I saw used most for this dish, the brining also helps it stay juicy.

This is great barbecue food for those fancying a diversion from burgers and drummers; but through the months where you need to cook inside, use a griddle or even a grill - the aim being to get an element of char.

If you're up for the brining, start the night before: either just by stirring or with a little gentle heat, dissolve the salt and sugar in 2 litres/3½ pints of cold water and put the brine in a container in which the pork will be completely submerged. Crush the allspice and peppercorns with the side of a knife (or with a pestle and mortar), and add to the completely cold brine along with the pork. Refrigerate overnight.

Next day, take the pork out of the brine (which you then throw away), and rinse it. Pat it dry and slice it into 6 equal portions. Lay the pork pieces 2 at a time between layers of clingfilm or waxed paper, and pound them with the flat side of a large knife/wooden mallet/anything flat and a bit heavy you have to hand, until they are a lot bigger and about 1cm/½ inch thick.

Mix together all the ingredients for the marinade. Lay the pork pieces on a baking tray, pour over the marinade and give it all a quick splash around. Leave at room temperature for an hour or two (though if you want you can also leave it overnight in the fridge).

For the yellow rice

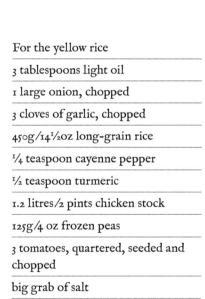

3 tablespoons light oil
1 large onion, chopped
3 cloves of garlic, chopped
450g/14½oz long-grain rice
¼ teaspoon cayenne pepper
½ teaspoon turmeric
1.2 litres/2 pints chicken stock
125g/4 oz frozen peas
3 tomatoes, quartered, seeded and chopped
big grab of salt

When you're about 45 minutes from serving, get the rice going: put a large frying pan over medium heat, pour in the oil and once it's hot add the onion and garlic. Cook until soft, then stir in the rice, cayenne, turmeric and some salt. Fry hard and fast for 30 seconds, stirring to coat the rice in the oil, then pour on the stock, bring to the boil, cover and simmer for 15-20 minutes.

Knock up the salsa by first soaking the onion slices in cold water for about 5-10 minutes. Chop the chilli and coriander and mix with the lime juice and salt, then drain and squeeze out the onion and stir into the other ingredients.

When the rice is cooked, stir in the peas and tomatoes and turn off the heat. Leave covered while you cook the pork.

Have your cooking method really good and hot: barbie fully fired up, griddle/grill both smoking. Pat the pork pieces dry, VERY lightly drizzle each one with a touch of olive oil (and if you didn't brine, sprinkle with a good pinch of salt).

Cook for about 2 minutes either side and no more, then let the meat rest for a couple of minutes before serving with the rice and salsa. And a few tortillas never go amiss.

Norwegian Arctic Circle

Geographical summary: About two-thirds mountains; some 50,000 islands off its much-indented coastline – one of the most rugged and longest coastlines in the world. The northern part of the country, within the Arctic Circle, has continuous daylight at midsummer and Arctic twilight all day in winter. Borders with Sweden, Russia and Finland.

Population: 4.9 million.

Religion: Nearly 90% Church of Norway (Evangelical Lutheran).

Ethnic make-up: 95% Norwegian (includes about 60,000 Sami), the rest v. minimal.

Life expectancy: 78 male, 83 female.

External influences: For nearly 450 years was in a union with Denmark until 1814, when it was made over to Sweden as war reparations on the Danes for siding with Napoleon. Independence came peacefully in 1905 after a referendum.

Essentials of their cooking: Curing is really what they're all about: pickling, salting and smoking. As well as fish, also fond of game, like deer and hare.

Food they export: Cheese, soybeans and soybean oil, waters and ice, chocolate.

Top 5 favourite ingredients: Stunning fish (salmon, herring, cod, halibut), dill, spuds, vinegar, salt.

Most famous dish: Gravlaks.

What they drink: Ringnes beer, aquavit, crystal clear water and a nice line in boozy coffee.

Best thing I ate: I ate the best spuds of my life right at the top of the world.

Most breathtaking moment: We didn't see the Northern Lights (well, not properly anyway) but we did rise before dawn once to see the fabled 'blue light', and as we glided into a fjord in the near dark, there was an eerie, peaceful aura that accompanied it.

Don't ask for…: A round of applause for Scott of the Antarctic: Roald Amundsen is Tromsø's most famous son, and he did actually get to the South Pole.

'Come on a cruise,' my brother-in-law Guy said. I'd been talking to him about how the missus had always wanted to see the Northern Lights, and it turned out he did a bit of work for a company that had some boats round there (and by 'there' I mean the part of Norway right up in the Arctic Circle, known as Finnmark). As I was to find out later, what he'd actually meant was come and hang out on a car ferry for four days; our boat being the sole weekly connection that the remote towns clinging to the edge of the snow-covered hills on icy fjords had with the rest of the world through the long winter months. So, not so much a cruise as a supply ship.

From the off it was clearly going to be a hilarious trip. Our landing at Tromsø was terrifying to the point of comical: we were diverted, re-routed and then sent back to the original destination as the pilots tried to fly around a blizzard, then they decided they really could land in it anyway - and all of this coming over the tannoy in jaunty Norse accents. Suffice to say that as we came in low, we really did knock the snow off the Christmas trees and didn't so much land on a runway as skid on a thick lane of ice. As we shuffled, shaking, off the plane, busy lads worked with spades a step ahead of us to make a path some one and a half metres deep through the snow.

But the adventure had begun, and once on our mighty ice-breaking ship, *Kong Harald*, we began to get used to the thirty minutes it took us to get dressed each day in preparation for minus 22°C/minus 7°F.

Over the course of our trip a pattern developed: breakfast followed by poker (Texas Hold'em) until we were pulling into the little town of the day.

Quick scrabble to put on as much of your wardrobe as possible, then skidding down the gangplank as the crew unloaded the post/fridge/unidentifiable bits of machinery/alcohol that said town needed to keep functioning. The rush was then on to find the bar in town, usually camouflaged under feet of snow, sink a few beers with aquavit chasers, then go and play in the snow until the *Kong Harald* sounded its mighty horn and we tottered back so as not to get marooned.

More poker and a nap, then supper, which was always interrupted by an announcement that the Northern Lights were clearly visible to the starboard side of the rear deck. But by the time we got there (remembering that we had to get togged up again) they were gone ... and by the time we got back to the dining room so was our dinner: it only took us until the last night to work out their ruse...

We went right over the top of Norway, to within twenty miles of the Russian border, where we celebrated our northernliness with a couple more shots in the Ice Hotel. It was our last day and the only thing left to do was drunken dog-sledging with some over-zealous huskies, which ended with growls and whines (us and the dogs) and that iconic shot of blood spots on snow.

Fisherman's Friend

Despite my optimistic character, I wasn't at all hopeful about finding a knife to bring back from this trip. For a start, we were on a boat most of the time, and when we did dock, these small towns looked so buttoned down for winter that shopping opportunities were virtually nil.

But our last stop was in Hammerfest, which was considerably larger than anywhere else we'd pulled in to - it had three bars, a small museum dedicated to the rebuilding of the town after the Germans had flattened it in World War II ... and a department store. But still my hopes did not rise, as I'm pretty particular about the knives I bring back - they have to meet my rather specific criteria (reflective of the place) rather than generically Global, Henckels, Wüsthof and the rest of the bad boys everyone knows. And, from experience, I knew they were not usually to be found in department stores. I had to hurry, as the *Kong Harald* had already blasted his horn, but as soon as I ran into the kitchen department and saw this on the wall I knew I had a winner: it's a design classic (and we all know how the Scandinavians love their design), it's extremely efficient at filleting fish (something they have to do a lot of in these parts), and it even had a silvery fishy, dare I say herringesque look to it. Or maybe I just had herrings on my mind through over-consumption.

Now you could quibble and say it's a German-designed boning knife made from Japanese steel, and I wouldn't be able to argue, but to me it just fitted with what I'd learnt of this country. I'd never seen a knife like it before, and had no idea Porsche made knives: Peugeot and peppermills yes, but this car-culinary hook-up was a new one on me, and in the light (sadly not Northern) of how fish-based this area is, both in terms of diet and the economy, this knife fitted my bill, and I've been filleting with it ever since.

The really genius thing about this knife is the way the blade is aligned while the handle sits flat across your palm, i.e. the opposite way to most knife handles. That's what those clever people at Porsche did so well: work out the comfiest way to hold a knife, and design around it. She is undoubtedly the sleekest and most ergonomic in my collection, and if all knives were made like this then chefs would no longer have calluses.

I TILFELLE REISE-SYKE
etter bruk vennligst
lukk posen og still den
på gulvet.

REISESYKEPOSE

IN CASE OF TRAVELSICKNESS
after use please close the
bag and place it on
the floor.

ÆKte

Lofottørr

R 0825

Norwegian Recipes

Polar Hotdogs
Arctic Dogs

Laks - og purresuppe
Salmon & Leek Soup with Crab Toast

Røkt and ned rødbet og pepperrot
Smoked Duck Breast with Beetroot, Horseradish & Rocket

Syltet ishavsrøye med norske poteter
Pickled Arctic Char & Norse Spuds

Emmas saltede torsk
Emmas Heart-warming Salt Cod Grill

Hurtigruten 365 dager i året

Hurtigruten har vært, og er fortsatt ett av de viktigs transportmiddel langs norskekysten. Skipene er fylt moderne teknologi som gjør reisen behagelig og t og den tar deg d

Daglig g   sør og
Kirke   ttsted
og   ortvei
på   lig bruk
m   t for de
D   lige måt
D   ts resta

Siden   e tjeneste
lokalbe   ger c

Om du reiser på ferie i vårt langstrakte land, br skipene som ren transport mellom havnene, el tilbringer en helg ombord sammen med familie venner, gjør vi det beste for at du skal føle deg velkommen.

Ruteplanen gjelder for et helt år, slik at det b for deg å planlegge reisen i god tid.

For mer informasjon besøk **www.hurtigrute** nærmeste reisebyrå eller vår booking på tlf. 8

Hurtigruten tar forbehold om endringer

Hurtigruten tar forbehold om endringer

Straight Flush

4 Kind

Full House

Flush

Straight

3 Kind

Arctic Dogs

Per person, done in the time it takes to cook the sausages

---

2 venison sausages

---

1 flour tortilla

---

mustard (the original Arctic dog was served with the kind of sweet mustard they're fond of in Scandinavia ... akin to American, but I think it's best with a big swoosh of English as well)

---

a couple of pickled gherkins, cut lengthwise

Outside the Ice Hotel we followed an eight-foot deep snow corridor to reach an unlikely looking teepee-type tent. Inside, I was surprised and grateful to see a pit-fire going in the middle, with sausages sizzling on it and tortilla-ish wraps warming on top. Hotdogs? And teepees? It all felt weirdly surreal, but that's what happens when you have shots for breakfast.

Due to the density of the meaty sausage and bread they feel much more like nourishing and sustainable food than the usual fluffy, processed version - just the snack you need to settle the tum before you go husky-sledging with a troop of six fired-up doggies who really hate each other!

Heat a griddle, grill or barbecue and cook the sausages over a medium heat for 15-20 minutes, turning from time to time.

Lightly grill the tortilla until warm, floppy and slightly marked, then spread it with mustard, lay down a couple of gherkin pieces and wrap up the sausages.

Salmon & Leek Soup with Crab Toast

Serves 6, and all done in around 40 minutes

For the soup

40g/1½oz butter

350g/11½oz new potatoes, diced

3 large leeks (about 600g/1lb 2oz), trimmed, thinly sliced and washed well

3 cloves of garlic, chopped

1.5 litres/2½ pints hot fish stock

4 tablespoons crème fraîche

300g/10oz piece of salmon, skinned, boned and cut into roughly 1cm/½ inch dice

1 tablespoon chopped dill

salt and pepper

For the crab toasts

200g/7oz crab meat, mostly white, but a bit of brown is nice too if possible

4 tablespoons crème fraîche

a large pinch of cayenne pepper

a handful of chives, chopped

6 slices of brown bread, toasted

salt and pepper

King crabs are not native to these Arctic waters, but were brought here from the Pacific by the Russians in the 60s as part of an experiment. Fifty years later they are the main source of industry for the local fishermen - the large baskets they're caught in are stacked up high at every port - and very tasty they are too.

I'm not suggesting that you use Norwegian king crab for this - our own native brown crab is king in our waters - but even with no crab at all, this soup is simple and nourishing for both body and soul: a good lunch dish.

However, if you fancy poshing it up a bit, embellish with the crab toasts and, for the investment of either your time (picking your own crab) or your money (getting someone else to do it for you), the dish gets elevated to dinner party status. You can do the work in advance, then when you're ready to eat just reheat the soup and drop the salmon in at the end so it's pink and perfect.

Melt the butter in a saucepan over a medium-high heat and before it starts to brown toss in the potatoes and leeks.

Add the garlic and let everything cook together for about 5-10 minutes, covered, without letting the vegetables colour.

Knock up the crab mix by putting the crab, crème fraîche, cayenne, chives and some seasoning into a bowl and giving it a good mix. Keep it aside, but not in the fridge.

Pour the hot fish stock on to the soup base and turn the heat up to full, leaving the lid off. Simmer fast and reduce, skimming from time to time, for about 20 minutes, or until the potatoes are tender. Turn the heat off, season well, stir in the crème fraîche, then distribute the salmon evenly over the soup and put the lid back on.

Finish the dish by magically turning bread into toast and dividing the crab mix between the slices. By the time you have assembled the toasts and organized hot bowls the salmon will be ready - just stir in the dill before serving.

Smoked Duck Breast with Beetroot, Horseradish & Rocket

Serves 4 as a starter, 2 as a main, and takes less than 20 minutes

---

3 tablespoons horseradish, peeled and finely grated (adjust according to taste and strength), or 3 tablespoons horseradish sauce

---

1 tablespoon lemon juice

90ml/3¼fl oz double cream

---

2 tablespoons red wine vinegar

½ teaspoon sugar

200g/7oz raw beetroot, peeled and coarsely grated

---

1 smoked duck breast (about 175-200g/6-7oz in weight), up to you if you want to trim off the fat

---

50g/2oz rocket

---

1 large sweet pickled gherkin, cut into strips

---

salt and pepper

We had this as fabulously fresh-tasting starter at The Corner Café in Honningsvåg - except for the minor liberty I've taken by swapping the smoked duck for smoked whale. The nice waitress assured us it wasn't on the endangered list, but couldn't remember the name in English so, wrongly assuming that we knew about whales, kindly went and printed a picture of it off the 'pooter for us to identify.

It's best to use fresh horseradish for this, but Polish horseradish in jars has an excellent, fiery quality - much better than the lame English ones.

Eat with heavy-duty rye bread/pumpernickel.

In a small bowl mix the horseradish with the lemon juice and half the cream and leave aside. In a large mixing bowl, combine the vinegar, sugar and some salt with the beetroot.

Slice the duck breast thinly. Stir the rest of the cream into the horseradish along with some seasoning, adding a splash of warm water if necessary to get it to a drizzling consistency.

Scatter the rocket on a large serving plate (or do individuals if you'd rather), then spoon on the beetroot, before laying down the duck and topping with the gherkin.

Swoosh over the dressing to finish and serve with a suitably hardy bread on the side.

The whale we ate!

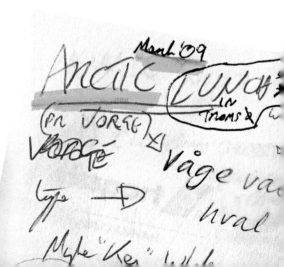

March '09
ARCTIC LUNCH
IN TROMSØ
(pr. VORGE)
VORGE
Våge va
type
hval
Myte "Ke"

Pickled Arctic Char & Norse Spuds

Serves 4 as a starter, and takes
10 minutes to get the cure on, then
6 days pickling and 30 minutes on the
day to pull the spud salad together

To cure the fish

45g/1¾oz salt

2 fillets of char or freshwater trout
around 275g/9oz each, pin-boned
(ask the fishmonger to do it)

250ml/8fl oz white wine vinegar

60g/2½oz sugar

3 bay leaves

5 juniper berries, crushed with the
side of a knife

1 tablespoon peppercorns

2 pinches of caraway seeds

1 small onion, sliced

a small handful of dill, chopped
(including stalks)

For the potatoes

400g/13oz new potatoes, washed

150ml/¼ pint soured cream

a small handful of dill, finely
chopped

3 spring onions, chopped

a squeeze of lemon juice

salt and pepper

Char is a good fish to know about - it's in the same family as trout and salmon, and can have a touch of the same attractive pinkiness, but isn't farmed and currently is in the lowest category for endangered species. If you don't have time to do the curing, shame and you will be missing out, but you can just knock up the easy salad and use rollmops.

This straightforward recipe plays to all the strengths of this region's produce and culinary tradition, and Norway being our closest neighbour to the north-east it really works in our climate too.

Once cured, the fish lasts a month in the fridge ... very handy.

To cure the fish, make a brine by dissolving the salt in 400ml/14fl oz of water. Trim the fish if necessary and lay it in a container just big enough to hold it. Cover completely with the brine and stick it in the fridge overnight.

Next day, put the vinegar, sugar, bay leaves, juniper, peppercorns, caraway seeds and onion in a pan with 150ml/¼ pint of water and bring to the boil. Cool completely, then add the dill. Take the fish out of the brine, cover with the cooled dill pickling liquid and refrigerate for 5 days.

On the day of eating, put the spuds into a pan of cold salted water, bring to the boil and simmer until tender. Drain and cool for a few minutes, then smash them up with a masher or fork along with the soured cream and seasoning. Stir in the dill and spring onions and finish with a squeeze of lemon (and a splash of water, if necessary) to keep a creamy consistency.

Slice each fillet of char into pieces and serve with the potato salad, preferably still slightly warm.

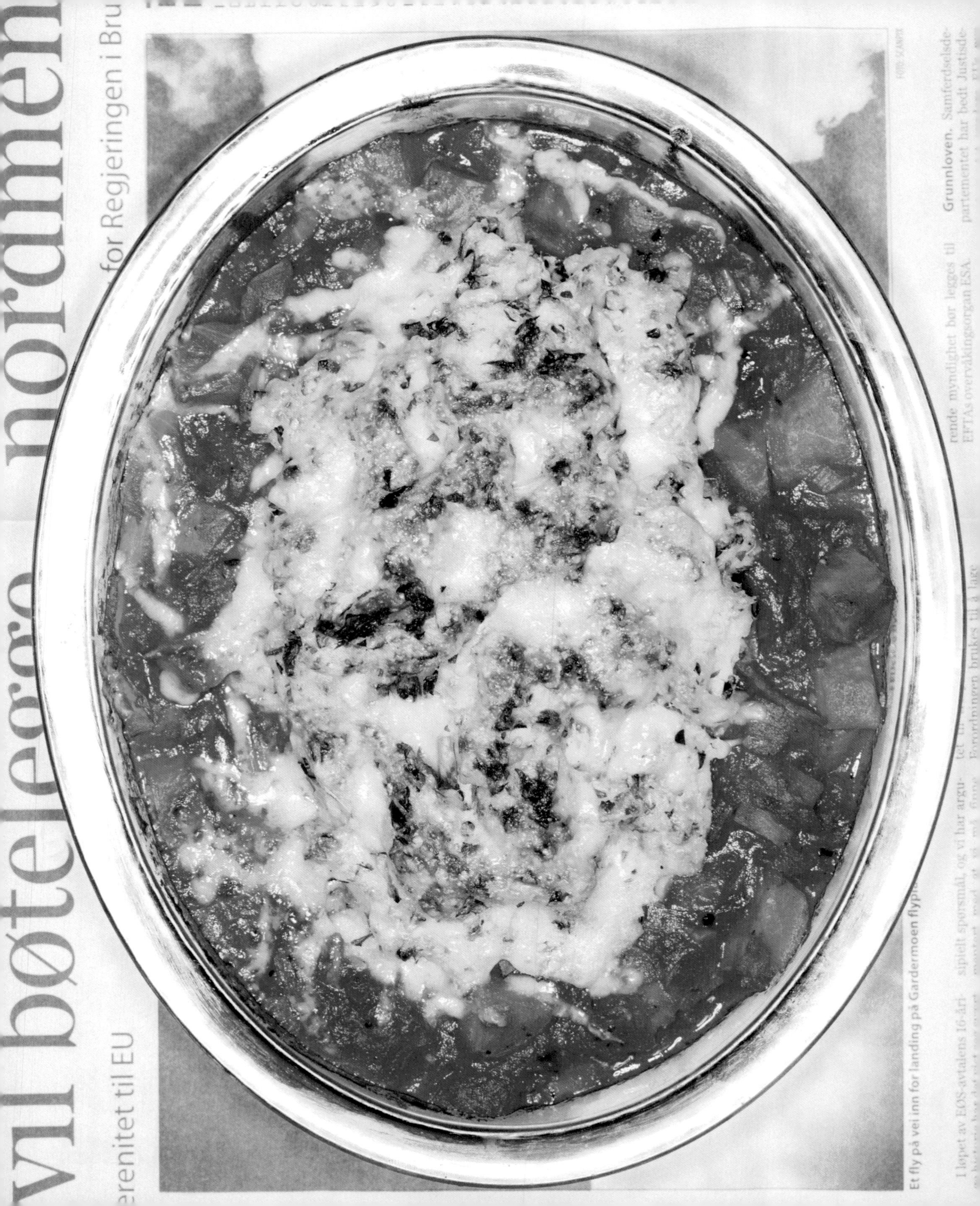

Emma's Heart-warming Salt Cod Grill

Serves 4, generously, and takes about 45 minutes once the cod is rehydrated

---

175g/6oz salt cod

625g/1¼lb mashing potatoes, peeled and halved

---

2 bay leaves

200ml/7fl oz milk

40g/1½oz butter

---

1 onion, chopped

---

2 carrots, diced

---

1 clove of garlic, finely chopped

---

a big pinch of dried oregano

½ teaspoon paprika

---

1 x 400g tin of chopped tomatoes

60ml/2½fl oz double cream

---

a handful of parsley, chopped

40g/1½oz Gruyère, grated

---

salt and pepper

My wife's birthday fell while we were in Tromsø, the capital city of Arctic Norway, and I'd been having a low-level panic about finding something fun to do. But as luck would have it, it turned out that the best restaurant in the whole top half of Norway was called Emma's Dream Kitchen and happened to be in Tromsø. Luckily the restaurant lived up to its other-worldly, Moomin-ish sounding name (helped along by a couple of shots of aquavit), and it was a close call with the cloudberry cheesecake, but we all agreed this was the best dish; just what you want to eat when it's minus 19°C/minus 2°F outside and blowing a blizzard.

As you'd expect with its warming, slightly nursery food qualities, it's really good for kids, too.

First you have to rehydrate the salt cod until it's bendy: this process is best kick-started by running it under cold water for 5 minutes, after which you can either leave it to soak in fresh water overnight, or if you're in a hurry change the water every half an hour or so for 2 hours.

Once your cod is ready for action, cover the potatoes with cold salted water and put on a high heat with a lid on the pan to boil.

Give the cod a squeeze and put it into a small pan with the bay and milk over a low heat. Cook gently for 30 minutes or until the fish start to fall apart.

Meanwhile, melt half the butter in a large frying pan and gently cook the onion, carrots, garlic, oregano and paprika with a lid for about 5 minutes. Tip the tomatoes into the pan, then half-fill the tomato tin with water, give it a swirl and pour that in as well. Turn up the heat, season, then put the lid back on, slightly squiffed, and leave to bubble for about 20 minutes, or until it has a good saucy consistency.

Take the fish out (chuck the milk - too salty) and peel off any skin and pick out the bones. When the potatoes are tender, drain and mash them, then put the fish bits in with the spuds, breaking them up a bit on the way in. Stir in the rest of the butter, the cream and parsley, and season well with pepper, and taste before adding any salt.

Preheat the grill to medium. Pour the tomato sauce into a baking dish and spoon the fishy mash in an island in the middle, leaving a bit of tomato sauce showing round the edge. Top with the cheese (mainly covering the mash) and put under the grill until golden brown.

Like anyone of my age, the journey through to the end of apartheid was a major part of my youthful political awareness, so although I didn't go there until just under twenty years after Nelson Mandela walked out of Robben Island, and fifteen years after the establishment of the first multi-racial government, I was still interested, and a little anxious, to see the actualities of this co-existence.

My primary purpose was in journalistic mode, to write about a Fairtrade vineyard, but I was keen to make sure that we didn't just get shown the pretty side of things, so at the airport I asked our guide if it was possible to visit one of the infamous townships, which the government has now renamed 'Informal Settlements'. Just ten minutes later we were right in the middle of one, with a fellow next to us pushing a shopping trolley of sheep's feet, quietly stinking in the sun.

It was and it wasn't what I was expecting: rows and rows of shacks as far as you could see in all directions, some of which were in fact businesses, like shops, identifiable by a stand of cabbages outside, and a telephone exchange (three ring-dial phones on a shelf). But most were homes: a single room with very little in it, often windowless, a corrugated iron roof and a padlock on the door. We had trouble keeping our expressions level as our guide then explained that this was the black settlement, and over there was 'the brown one'. It's easy to come in from the outside and pick holes in somebody else's culture, but even so this seemed wrong for the 21st century.

By contrast to the people we had just seen - not unhappy but aimless in its most basic sense, the folks working at the Fairtrade Fairhills vineyard in Du Toitskloof seemed so much more smiley (because, after all, a smile is the simplest human barometer for happiness) and switched on, keen to take advantage of the opportunities afforded to them. The Fairtrade Premium had started a kindergarten for the under-fives so that mum and dad could both go out and work, thus giving the children a better start in life: literacy and a down payment on further education.

South Africa

Also built with Premium money was a community café, craft shop and computer centre. Given the industry they're in, it's unsurprising that the biggest issue round here is alcoholism, so providing some after-work options and somewhere other than home to hang out is an easy and effective way to cut down boozing. Life there truly felt like a happy bubble squished between the fly-by at the settlement and a visit to the local town, which even in the daytime felt just a bit threatening, with people passed out drunk on the side of the main road.

After a few days at the vineyard, we left the happy land of Fairhills and headed deep into Boer country, to the picture-perfect town of Franschouk. It's a pretty place, slightly Californian-looking with its white picket fences and boutiques, but at dinner in the place we'd been told had the best food in town, we felt more than slightly uncomfortable to see that all of the diners were white, and the servers black. It just felt like too much of a shock now to be a part of this white culture (highlighted by the drunk, noisy Boers next to us, who were particularly boorish) so we left.

The final leg of our brief visit was a drive to Cape Town via some very pretty wineries. Table Mountain, white sand beaches and a gorgeous botanical garden made this a soul-soothing way to end the trip. We left as the preparations for the World Cup were busying all around, consciously aware that full integration was still a way away but hopeful that next time we came they'd be further down that road.

FACT FILE

Geographical summary: Africa's southernmost nation, with the Atlantic on the western side, and the Indian Ocean to the east. Landscape is dominated by a high plateau in the interior, surrounded by a narrow strip of coastal lowlands. Diverse climate, but generally tropical in the eastern part of the country, whereas the south-western part has a Mediterranean climate.

Population: 50 million.

Religion: Vast majority are Christians of some denomination (Zionist, Pentecostal/Charismatic, Catholic, Methodist, Dutch Reformed, Anglican), 3.8% Muslim.

Ethnic make-up: Roughly speaking 80% black, 10% mixed race, 10% white.

Life expectancy: 50 male, 53 female.

External influences: Dutch interest and then settlement in 17th century, joined later by some Germans and French Huguenots, but at the Congress of Vienna in 1815 the Cape came under British sovereignty. 19th-century discovery of gold and diamond mines brought in treasure seekers from all over the globe. Boers continued to dominate until 1994 with the election of the African National Congress.

Traditional cooking methods: Well, they don't half love a *braai* – their kind of barbecue.

Food they export: Wine, maize, oranges, grapes, apples.

Top 5 favourite ingredients: Big meat-eaters (chicken, beef, pork, springbok, lamb), fish (snoek, tuna, salmon, swordfish, kabeljou), squash, aubergines, *mielies* (corn on the cob).

Most famous dish: Biltong.

What they drink: Crisp whites, fruity reds and the only place on the planet to grow Pinotage grapes. Castle and Black Label lagers; Hansa Pilsner. Cider. Rooibos.

Best thing I ate: Might have to be a drink on this one: Boschendal Syrah 2001. Unsurpassable.

Most breathtaking moment: Standing on top of the Hawequas mountain range under a clear 360° African sky, marvelling at the natural beauty in all directions.

Don't ask for...: The good old days.

SLAGTERY GRUNTER

His name was Ockert, he was a butcher and he ran his business in a little town called Rawsonville. His business was called 'Chrisma Slagtery', and whereas the 'slagtery' bit I could have a jolly good guess at translating from Afrikaans, I was looking forward to watching a big chap break down a sheep with sparkle and wit. Turns out it refers more to his religious leanings, in the same way that we have Halal butchers over here - the Charisma Christians being part of the Pentecostal church in South Africa.

Finding a knife on this trip was always going to be tough as there was so little time for the usual necessary hunt. I was actually going to see Ockert to get a lesson in biltong (see page 266), as I'd been told that his self-named Safari Biltong was the best in the province. Prior to this trip, those sticks of dried cured meat had never really held much appeal to me, but they tasted different chewed on in situ, and seeing as they were pretty much South Africa's most famous culinarily export to the world, I felt I'd better get to the bottom of it.

Ockert was the first proper Boer I met on the trip, and he looked like he was born to be a butcher: large in all directions, rosy cheeks, jolly manner and bloody big moustache (it was only later that I realized most of the Boers looked like kids' drawings of butchers). He had a friendly manner and couldn't have been more helpful with my biltong mission, so I asked him where he got his knives, and, after the usual arched eyebrow, explained why. Straight away he went to the back and got this one: it's a pretty standard knife, but for the wicked shape where the blade gets wider at the top, which makes it unlike the tools generally used in butchery over here.

The handle is boring but honest - it's just what you'd see in any kitchen or butcher's in many parts of the world - but Ockert and his men have taken care of it: it's been sharpened literally hundreds of times over the years and was given to me with the kind of edge that a butcher needs to do his work well. And the name of the brand feels so appropriately Afrikaans: Grünter.

This knife is definitely real, not for show: it's not pretty, almost ugly in fact, and I find it weirdly aggressive to look at, though that could just be projection. I don't love it, but I use it from time to time and keep it to remind me of that trip, which it does in its vibe, as well as of Ockert.

It's not a knife that suits dressing up which is why I call it my utilitarian 'Slagtery Grunter'.

Fairhills

Fairhills is one of the largest Fairtrade projects worldwide to be accredited by FLO-Cert. Based in the scenic Breedekloof area in the Western Cape of South Africa, it is a joint venture between Origin Wine and Du Toitskloof Winery. All 14 producers of 22 farms that supply grapes to Du Toitskloof are part of the scheme. This means that over 800 farm employees and their family members benefit from this unique social development project.

It is a very dynamic project whereby the employees have full control through an elected Joint Body Committee. The Joint Body consists of 40 working members, 2 farm owners and one representative of Origin Wine. The decisions is split 80% work members and 20% owners (80:20)

Major funding
- Fairtrade premium,
- Additional contributions from Retail Groups
- 25% ownership of Fairhills brand.

South African Recipes

Venison Biltong

Potjie Brood
(Bread in a Pot)

Snail & Spinach Quiche

Lamb Loin Chops and
Butternut with
Tangy BBQ Sauce

Rooibos Malva Pudding

Berries in Shiraz Jelly

APPLES
BANANAS
BUTTERNUT
CABBAGE
CARROTS
GUAVAS
PEAR
POTATOES
ORANGES
ONIONS
TOMATOES
SPINACH

Ons Huisie
Traditional Cape Restaurant

TWENTY RAND

20

BOSCHE
2001
Syra

Wine of Sou

Venison Biltong

Makes enough to mean that you won't have to make biltong again for a while - and keeps for ever. Allow 15 minutes to knock it up, then an overnight stay in the fridge before hanging for up to a week

500g/1lb strip of lean haunch of venison

100ml/3½fl oz cider vinegar

2 level teaspoons salt

1 teaspoon sugar

1 tablespoon coriander seeds

2 teaspoons black peppercorns

5 juniper berries

1 teaspoon chilli flakes

a good grating of nutmeg

1 teaspoon bicarbonate of soda

It was impossible for me to come back from my first trip to South Africa without having the insider's tip on how to make biltong, so I forced an introduction to the town butcher, Ockert, and asked him to give me a lesson. In among the usual walk-in fridges of hanging carcasses there was one room that was temperate, with an electric fan blowing, and this was his pride and joy - his biltong room.

Trying to re-create this back in Shepherd's Bush was somewhere between a challenge and a load of laughs, involving an old cheese-storing box and daily checks on the internet for wind direction. But after a week, I had made biltong and I can thoroughly recommend this recipe for the culinary adventurers out there.

Cut the venison along the grain of the meat into strips a couple of centimetres/an inch thick. Lay the strips in a shallow dish, pour over the vinegar and leave for about 10 minutes, turning halfway through, while you prepare the spice mix.

Crush the salt, sugar and all the spices together coarsely in a spice grinder or pestle and mortar, then tip out on to a plate and stir in the bicarb. Take the strips out of the vinegar, give them a quick shake so the excess drips off, and touch in the spice mix so that all sides are coated. Lay the strips on a tray and refrigerate overnight.

Make a small hole with a skewer in one end of each strip of meat and feed some string through. Hang the meat up so that it can air in a warmish place (ideally somewhere it will be protected from flies - in the boiler or airing cupboard works well in winter) and with a bit of wind - remember Ockert's tip about fans. Depending on the season, it will take between 4 and 7 days to dry out. It's ready when it is dry nearly all the way through, but the middle is still just a bit soft, and thinner pieces will be done sooner.

Brush off the spices and, if it's still quite fresh, use a knife to slice it (with the grain). However, when it's well dried out you can just tear it apart. Ockert's recommended beer choice is a Hansa Pilsner, but he would say that.

Potjie Brood
Bread in a Pot

Makes 1 large loaf, and though you need to allow a few hours for all that rising and proving, the work input is minimal

---

10g/3½ teaspooons dried yeast

1½ tablespoons sugar

650g/1lb 5oz strong white flour

15g/½oz salt

---

light oil, for greasing the pot

I was complimenting Rowellen, the young chef at the Fairtrade community café, on his bread, and he explained how they bake it in a pot on the *braai* (a South African barbecue), which was a new one on me. Something about doing it in a pot made it seem so much less hassle, and I've done this a lot ever since: it makes a robust, crumbly, moist and slightly springy loaf that I've come to be rather fond of.

I used a cast-iron pot that I brought back from South Africa called a *potjie*, but you can use a Le Creuset casseroller or something similar - it just needs to have quite thick sides for even heat distribution.

In a big bowl mix the flour and salt, then add the dried yeast, along with the sugar and 500ml/17fl oz of warm water. Bring it all together, adding a bit more warm water or flour if you need it, to make it into one homogenous ball of dough. Tip it out on to a floured surface and knead with floured hands for 5 minutes, flouring the dough lightly whenever it gets sticky.

Oil a round lidded ovenproof pot around 25 x 10cm/10 x 4 inches, lid as well, then put the dough in, put the lid on and leave it to rise somewhere warm for 1-2 hours.

Take off the lid and use your fingertips to lightly spread the dough out so it covers the base of the pot, leaving a dimpled surface. Give it a second prove, lid on, for 30 minutes in the same warm place.

Now there are two ways of cooking this: the conventional oven and the less conventional but very South African *braai* option.

First the inside method: preheat the oven to 160°C/325°F/gas mark 3. Pop the bread into the oven, lid still on, for half an hour. After that, take the lid off, splash water lightly all over the surface and stick it in, uncovered, for another half hour, rotating it 180° halfway through.

And if you want to barbecue your bread: first get the coals good and hot, then push them round to the sides. Put the grill on the highest shelf, sit the pot on it above the cleared area so there are no coals directly below it, then use tongs to lift about 5 of the hot coals and put them on top of the lid. Turn it halfway through the 30-40 minutes it will take to cook; bear in mind that cooking over coals is all about heat spots, so be prepared for your bread to have a very artisanal, uneven crust!

Either which way, when you've finished cooking the bread turn it out and leave it to cool upside down in the pot for half an hour.

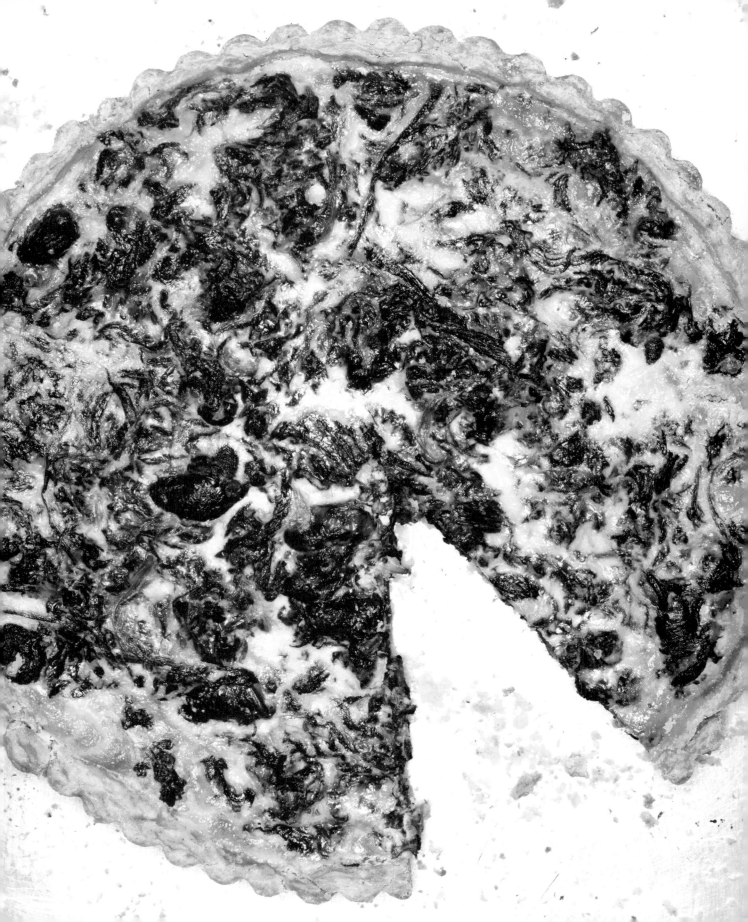

Snail & Spinach Quiche

Serves 6, and takes about 1 hours cooking then 45 in the oven

For the pastry

200g/7oz plain flour

100g/3½oz cold butter, cubed

2 egg yolks

2 tablespoons cold milk

salt and pepper

For the filling

20g/¾oz butter

8 cloves of garlic, finely chopped

1 x 250g tin of snails, drained and rinsed (get snails in tins from delis, posh food stores, the internet ... or there's always the garden)

a grating of nutmeg

400g/13oz frozen spinach, defrosted and squeezed out

a handful of flat-leaf parsley, finely chopped together with a big pinch of salt

50g/2oz Gruyère, grated

4 eggs

200ml/7fl oz double cream

salt and pepper

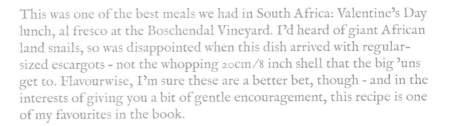

This was one of the best meals we had in South Africa: Valentine's Day lunch, al fresco at the Boschendal Vineyard. I'd heard of giant African land snails, so was disappointed when this dish arrived with regular-sized escargots - not the whopping 20cm/8 inch shell that the big 'uns get to. Flavourwise, I'm sure these are a better bet, though - and in the interests of giving you a bit of gentle encouragement, this recipe is one of my favourites in the book.

Pastry is easiest made in a food processor: start with the flour and some seasoning in the bowl and spin it for a few seconds to aerate. Add the butter quickly, piece by piece, and as soon as it's blended - just a minute or so - drop in the egg yolks and pulse for a moment.

Transfer to a bowl and bring together lightly with the milk - it may not form a ball of dough but that doesn't matter. Wrap it up tightly in clingfilm, squash it together through the clingfilm into a flattish shape, not a ball, and put it into the freezer for 15 minutes while you get on with the filling.

Heat the butter gently in a wide pan until it froths, then add the garlic and stir for a few minutes but don't let it brown. Tip in the snails and season with pepper and nutmeg. Sauté gently for a few minutes before adding the spinach, stirring well as it cooks for a few more minutes. Turn off the heat, stir in the parsley and cheese, then taste and season.

Preheat the oven to 180°C/350°F/gas mark 4. Locate a fluted tart tin 24cm/9½ inches in diameter with a push-up base. Unwrap your pastry and don't panic if it falls apart. Because it's so crumbly I like to grate it on the big holes and press it into the tin with my fingertips, but rolling it out between 2 pieces of clingfilm also works well. Any pastry left over will come in useful later. Put the tin into the freezer for 5 minutes.

When the pastry shell is firm, put it on a baking tray and bake blind (you don't need beans though) for 12-15 minutes, until it is golden brown. If any cracks have appeared you know what to do with that bit of leftover pastry.

Tip the snail mixture into the pastry shell, spreading it out evenly. Beat the eggs with the cream, season and pour carefully into the shell, turning over the filling with a fork as you pour so that everything is nicely distributed. Bake for 25-30 minutes, until golden brown and just set in the middle, and let it sit for 10 minutes before serving.

Lamb Loin Chops and Butternut with Tangy BBQ Sauce

Serves 4 in 1 hour

3 cloves of garlic, peeled

a few sprigs of rosemary, leaves picked

6 tablespoons olive oil (not extra virgin)

8 lamb loin chops (about 100g/3½oz each)

a butternut squash about 1.2kg/2lb 7oz

½ teaspoon cayenne pepper

1 teaspoon whole cumin seeds

salt and pepper

For the sauce

500g/1lb red onions, peeled and chopped

2 tablespoons olive oil, plus a bit more

3 tomatoes, halved

1½ tablespoons tomato purée

125ml/4fl oz red wine vinegar

2 bay leaves

500ml/17fl oz chicken stock

5 tablespoons runny honey

salt and pepper

In a little town called Rawsonville, in a courtyard filled with the Fairtrade grape pickers I'd gone to write about, we sampled South Africa's most famous bit of cooking equipment - the braai, a wood or charcoal barbecue - never gas (though for the purpose of indoor cooking I tried this back home just with a griddle over a gas flame and it was still a great supper).

It really was a perfect evening: we sat out under the great African sky, inhaling the smell of grilling lamb and getting familiar with the local wine (and by that I mean just the other side of the wall). The kids giggled as they sang pop songs to us, and the older folk told us the stories of their life, which they knew would be so different from their children's now that the vineyards had gone Fairtrade.

Chop the garlic and rosemary finely then stir in a couple of tablespoons of oil and a teaspoon of salt (or if you're fond of a pestle and mortar crush the garlic with roughly chopped rosemary and the salt, then stir in the oil). Rub the mixture on to the lamb chops and leave them to marinate.

Preheat the oven to 180°C/350°F/gas mark 4. Cut the squash in half lengthwise, then into quarters, leaving the peel on but taking out the seeds. Slice each quarter into thirds lengthwise so you have 12 long wedges.

Pour the rest of the oil (around 4 tablespoons) into a big baking tray with the cayenne, cumin, another teaspoon of salt and a good grinding of black pepper. Roll the wedges in the spices and bake in the oven for about 45 minutes, turning about halfway through or when properly browned on the first side. (Alternatively you can cook these on a cooler part of the braai/barbie, turning from time to time, until they are tender.)

Get the sauce going - in a wide pan, fry the onions in oil over a medium heat until softened: do the first few minutes without a lid then cover them, stirring from time to time, lowering the heat if they start to stick to the bottom of the pan.

Meanwhile heat a griddle on a medium high flame (or use the braai), season and lightly oil the halved tomatoes and put them on the griddle, cut side down. When they are charred on that side, turn them over and cook the rounded side, and when they have blackened all over you should be able to lift the skins off very easily with tongs.

Leave the griddle on for the chops, though if the tomatoes really stuck it may need a brisk wipe with a wet cloth.

When the onions are soft, stir in the tomato purée, then add 100ml/ 3½fl oz of the vinegar and the bay leaves, along with a good sprinkling of salt. Stir well and let the vinegar bubble away before adding the stock and honey. Plop in the charred, skinned tomatoes, break them up a bit and simmer fast for another 20-30 minutes or so, until you have a thick barbecue sauce. Turn off the heat, stir in the last of the vinegar and taste for seasoning. (This will probably make more than you need but it's a handy sauce to have around/freeze.)

Once blisteringly hot, put the chops on the griddle or braai. They should need about 3ish minutes on the first side and 2 on the second, depending on the thickness of your chops and how you like your lamb - these times are for a proper pink.

Serve it all up together, with a salad, and a gentle aside to the diners about how deliciously edible the squash skin is.

Rooibos Malva Pudding

Serves 6 plus, and takes 20 minutes to get it in the oven and 50 to cook

For the base

30g/1oz butter

120g/4oz caster sugar

2 eggs, beaten

2 tablespoons apricot jam

1 teaspoon bicarbonate of soda

120ml/4fl oz milk

180g/6oz plain flour

a pinch of salt

4 teaspoons white wine vinegar

For the sauce

2 rooibos teabags

140ml/5fl oz double cream

160g/5½oz caster sugar

60g/2½oz butter

2 tablespoons apricot jam

Malva pudding is a classic in the Cape and gets its name from Malvacea wine from Madeira, which was the tipple enjoyed with it. If you looked up 'nursery pudding' in the dictionary you might find this squished between the pages, but unlike most of the great ones we know, this is an easy make - no steaming required.

Usually it's served with custard, but that feels like a nursery too far for me - something like crème fraîche or Greek yoghurt works well, a little sharpness to cut through all that caramel ... though it's hard to beat a ball of ice cream with a hot pudding.

This crazily-easy cook isn't the prettiest of things, but you'd be mad to let that stop you: my sister loves a kiddy pudding, so I cooked a massive one for her birthday and it got hoofed down in seconds by oldies and youngies alike.

Preheat the oven to 190°C/375°F/gas mark 5 and grease a 2 litre/ 3½ pint ovenproof dish. In a medium-sized saucepan off the heat infuse the teabags in 140ml/5fl oz of boiling water.

To make the base, cream the butter and sugar, then beat in the eggs followed by the jam. Dissolve the bicarbonate of soda in the milk. Sift the flour with the salt and add it to the batter gradually, alternating with the milk and beating well between each addition. Stir in the vinegar and pour the batter into the dish - it should be only about a quarter-full at this stage.

For the sauce, fish the teabags out of the infusion and give them a quick squeeze, then stir in the cream and sugar. Add the butter and apricot jam and bring to the boil, then simmer for 2 minutes, stirring constantly.

Ladle half of the sauce over the batter, cover with foil and bake for 30 minutes, then lift the foil up, pour on the other half and bake uncovered for another 20 minutes.

Serve hot with your choice of dairy and preferably a glass of Madeira.

Berries in Shiraz Jelly

Serves 6, and takes about
30ish minutes to prep, plus
setting time

---

3 leaves (10g/⅓oz) gelatine

500ml/17fl oz shiraz (choose an
inexpensive bottle that describes
itself as 'full of fruit and spice' -
shouldn't be hard to find)

---

1 star anise

125g/4oz sugar

150g/5oz mixed blackberries and
raspberries (and blackcurrants
if available)

In the Boschendal Vineyard we took an entire afternoon reacquainting
ourselves with the shiraz grape, after an excessive Christmas on the cheap
stuff a couple of years back that had left our teeth and tongues stained
for days; henceforth shiraz was known in our house as 'shark wine'.

This recipe, unlike pretty much all the others in this book, isn't
something I actually ate over there, but an idea that came towards the
end of the third bottle. It uses the way shiraz is perennially described
as 'red berries and spice' to make a jelly deep in colour, flavour and
wine-writers' irony.

Soak the leaf gelatine in a basin of cold water and put a 1 litre/1¾ pint
jelly mould in the fridge with the berries scattered all over the bottom
of the mould. Warm the wine and star anise over a low heat until it is
starting to simmer, whisk in the sugar until properly dissolved, then
turn off the heat. Take out the star anise and whisk in the leaves of
gelatine one by one, chucking away the water.

Pour about a quarter of the jelly-to-be back into the basin and sit it
in a sink/larger bowl of cold water to cool it as quickly as possible.

When the quarter amount of wine is at room temperature (about
10 minutes), pour it over the berries so they are just covered and then
stick it back in the fridge.

Let the rest of the jelly mix cool to room temperature before putting
it in the fridge for an hour to get properly cold. Pour it on to the
now-solid berry base in the mould and put back into the fridge until
well set - you can do it in a day but overnight is always safest.

To unmould, dunk the base of the mould very quickly (just a couple
of seconds) into a bowl of hot water and turn the jelly out on to a very
flat dish/plate.

I absolutely knew I was going to love Lebanon: there's something about Arabic countries that gets right under my skin and, ironically considering their sometime attitude towards women, not to mention homosexuality, I just can't help feeling happy and at home. The call to prayer sounding from the minarets has an instantly relaxing effect on me, but when I heard it on my first morning in Beirut my state of calm was pricked by the next sound - that of church bells ringing. Which nicely sums up Lebanon: Christians and Muslims living together in not quite harmony.

And then there's the noisy neighbours: on the day I landed there was a newsflash to say that Israeli tanks were rolling across the southern border into Lebanon, but when I edgily asked my friend Kamal about it, he couldn't have been less bothered. Because, from those I spoke to, the people here are bored with both the international and the civil wars that have dominated their lives for too long. They're over fighting and just want to get on with living, and rebuilding their beautiful country.

I spent time in the two largest cities (Beirut, where half the population live, and Tripoli) as well as in the mountainous north, near the border with Syria, and inland in the Bekaa Valley. Laid on top of the ancient Arabic culture the whole place has an air of more recent faded glory: the architecture in Beirut, the clothes the glamorous older ladies wear, and the way a lot of the restaurants are done up all feel like they were put on hold some forty years ago, before the troubles kicked off and when Beirut was known as 'the Paris of the Middle East'.

With its fantastic food (the Bekaa Valley is hailed as the birthplace of mezze), its rip-roaring history of Romans, caliphates, crusaders and Ottomans, and its reputation for having some of the hottest nightclubs on the Med, there was no way I wasn't going to fall in love. It was just a question of looking past the bad press this bijou little country has had recently, because for column inches per square mile I doubt any country in the world could beat Lebanon - it's smaller than Wales, for God's sake ... just don't ask which God.

FACT FILE

Geographical summary: Narrow coastal plain bordering the Mediterranean, Israel and Syria. Mountainous spine through top half of country experiences heavy winter snows. Area a tiny 4,026 square miles.

Population: 4.3 million (not including est. 320,000 Palestinian refugees). Incidentally one of the oldest civilizations in the world, from around 10,000BC.

Religion: Muslim 60%, Christian 39% (but within these two there are a massive eighteen recognized religious sects), other 1.3% (including Judaism).

Ethnic make-up: Arab 95%, Armenian 4%, other 1% (many Christian Lebanese do not identify themselves as Arab but rather as descendants of the ancient Canaanites, and prefer to be called Phoenicians).

Life expectancy: 70 male, 74 female.

External influences: There was tag-teaming between Christians and Muslims from Constantine through to the crusaders being kicked out in the 13th century. From the 16th to the 20th century was part of the Ottoman Empire through to the end of World War II, when, with Syria, it came under French protectorate. Independence was granted in 1946.

Essentials of their cooking: Mezze is their masterpiece; also genius with pastry and a dab hand at kebabs. They grill over coals, bake in wood ovens, and also fry, braise and sometimes don't cook the meat at all (bit of a propensity for raw sheep).

Food they export: Various prepared foods (think tahini, pickles, falafel), soft drinks, preserved vegetables, confectionery and chocolate, nuts, potatoes.

Top 5 favourite ingredients: Pomegranate molasses, bulgar, chickpeas, parsley, olive oil.

Most Famous Dish: Kibbeh, and rather contentiously, hummus, which their friendly Jewish neighbours also claim.

What they drink: Being Arabic you wouldn't think they'd like their booze, but they do: arak (powerful and aniseedy), and wine from the Bekaa Valley.

Best thing I ate: It's a toss-up between the cedar honey (a cedar tree graces their flag) and a mind-blowing sweet cheese pastry called *halawet el jiben*.

Most breathtaking moment: Disengaging myself from a Hizbollah rally that I'd accidentally got swept up in to find myself looking up at the biggest colonnade in the world (literally), at the giant Roman ruins at Baalbek.

Don't ask for…: Anything kosher.

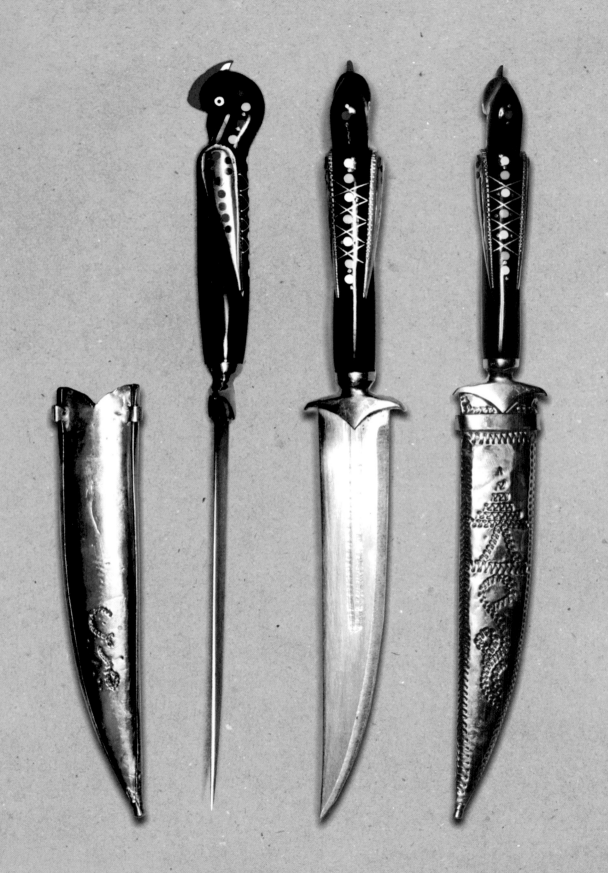

Phoenician Pheonix

Sometimes my quest for a knife that's typical of that country doesn't always work out how I expect ... Usually I start by asking a friend/ acquaintance/guide/bellboy/ butcher/random stranger where I might purchase such a thing, and from there on it involves a fair amount of blind stumbling, wild gesticulating in a foreign language, and a whack of good luck to secure my booty. But in the case of this bird-headed blade from Jezzine, it couldn't have been simpler. As soon as I explained my need, my friend Kamal knew instantly which knife I must have from the country of which he is so proud. Jezzine has a long history of avian cutlery: a 4,000-year-old knife with a duck's head was found in the tomb of King Ibshemuabi, who reigned at Byblos, just up the coast and supposedly the birthplace of modern writing.

Such a specimen sounded perfect, but it wasn't, however, within our reach, as these famous knives are made in a town fifty miles south of Beirut and we were heading the other way. And so I flew back to London knifeless and nervous and waited.

A couple of months later, I received word that my knife was at a fashion show in Paris (nice to see the French-Lebanese connection is still going strong) and from there it was just a hop and skip over the Channel to bring it safely home. I had no idea what to expect, but when I opened the box, and there it was in all its ornate, inlaid glory, I was somewhat taken aback. I've never had a decorative knife before, and the bit that completely nonplussed me was it had no edge on it to speak of, so I did the only sensible thing and called my knife sharpener, Mario, to whip this bird into shape.

Once I had it back, looking just as pretty but a bit more useful, it suddenly felt like a part of the group, and though I don't really use it in the kitchen it has become my picnic knife of choice. It feels perfectly decadent cutting hunks of bread and cheese in the sunshine with it, and if you're going to carry a knife around it's much safer, not to mention impressive, to have it cased in its own scabbard!

Lebanese Recipes

بيض بحامض
Lemon & Mint Eggs

خبز بجبن
Kibbeh with Tarator ... كبة بالطراطور

Managish
مناقيش

Roast Cauliflower
بطاطا مهروسة ومشوية بالثوم الحمص

Baked Potato Mash with Roast Garlic
قرنبيط مشوي

Lebanese Pizza
دجاج محشي بالصنوبر والجوز مع دبس الرمان

Stuffed Pot-Roast Chicken with Pine Nuts & Pomegranate Molasses
بقلاوة من طرابلس

Baklava from Tripoli

Kamal Mouzawak

Bayed Bi Hamod
Lemon & Mint Eggs

For 1, and 5 minutes from
start to finish

---

1 flatbread

---

1 tablespoon extra virgin olive oil

---

2 cloves of garlic, sliced

---

2 free-range eggs

---

a big handful of mint leaves, washed
and roughly chopped

---

a big squeeze of lemon juice

---

salt and pepper

Up in the mountainous north of the country, near the Syrian border, the grand dame of the family we were visiting cooked these eggs up for us in a flash.

So much fresher and lighter than the usual scrambled eggs, these are now my summer eggs of choice (though in winter I revert back to using double cream).

This is such a quick cook that you need to think through the heating of the flatbread first, by griddle, oven, or toaster, but don't actually launch it yet.

Get a small heavy-bottomed pan on a medium heat. Heat the oil, then fry the garlic gently, moving it around to keep the colour even. While that's happening, beat and season the eggs.

Now get your flatbread going - it'll take just a minute to get hot and floppy. Don't overdo it so it goes hard.

Pour the eggs into the pan and move them around with a spatula to scramble. Before they're set, stir in the mint and squeeze in the lemon.

Spoon on to a plate immediately with the flatbread, more lemon and a sprig of mint if you're feeling fancy.

Kibbeh with Tarator

Serves 4-6 (makes about 12 pieces) and takes a fun-filled 50 minutes

For the kibbeh shells

150g/5oz bulgar wheat

300g/10oz lamb mince

1 onion, chopped

a big pinch of ground cumin

For the kibbeh stuffing

1 small onion, finely chopped

a little light olive oil

2 heaped tablespoons pine nuts

250g/8oz lamb mince

a big pinch of ground cinnamon

salt and pepper

For the tarator

2 cloves of garlic, finely minced with a bit of salt

juice of 1 lemon

5 tablespoons tahini (stir it well before you use it)

75ml/3fl oz extra virgin olive oil

a good handful of green olives, stoned and roughly chopped

a handful of flat-leaf parsley, chopped

1 litre/1¾ pints of oil, for frying

Whichever Lebanese cook came up with the idea of stuffing lamb mince with lamb mince is a culinary genius. These are so yumtious for any occasion - supper, parties - and portable too for the office lunch. In their homeland, kibbeh come in lots of shapes and sizes (and even raw, made out of minced goat), but this is the enduring popular one.

Tip the bulgar into a small pan, pour on hot water until it sits about a centimetre/½ inch above the level of the grains and simmer for around 10 minutes over a low heat until the water is absorbed.

Now start working on the stuffing: in a wide frying pan sweat the onion in oil until soft, then add the pine nuts and fry until golden. Stir in the meat, breaking it up with a wooden spoon, then as it browns season with salt, pepper and cinnamon. Tip it on to a plate and spread it out to cool.

Back to the shells: in a food processor, blitz the mince, onion, cumin and some seasoning together for less than a minute, until smooth. Scrape back into the bowl and mix in the bulgar wheat thoroughly.

Now make your kibbeh: get a bowl of water, wet your hands and divide the shell mix into 12, putting an extra teaspoon of it aside to check the temperature of the oil later. Taking each one in turn, roll it into a firm ball, make a hole in the centre with your finger and work it up and around two fingers so that you have an elongated cavity, most of the length of your fingers. Fill this with stuffing, and, keeping your hands moist, pinch the top closed in a pointy way, in a lemon shape. Seal all the way round, repeat with the rest then put them all in the fridge.

For the tarator, mix the garlic, lemon and tahini together and add about 100ml/3½ fl oz warm water to loosen. Whisk the oil in slowly and season well with salt. Don't worry if it's a bit thin because it will thicken as it sits. Stir in the olives, sprinkle with parsley and finish with a pool of EVOO on top.

Heat the oil and see if it's up to temperature by dropping in the little bit of lamb mix and checking it floats to the surface, fizzling away. With wet hands, give your kibbeh a final compression squeeze and smooth over all the way round then deep-fry in batches of between 4 and 6, depending on the size of your pan, for about 5-8 minutes each, or until they are deep golden brown. Drain briefly on kitchen paper, then serve with the tarator: some over the top and a little dish to the side.

Manaqish

Serves 6. Takes 20 minutes to knock the dough up, 45 minutes rising time then a 5-minute cook

For the bread

500g/1lb plain flour (or a 50-50 combination of plain and bread flour)

1 teaspoon dried yeast

1 tablespoon sugar

1 teaspoon sea salt

For the za'atar mixture

4 tablespoons dried thyme

4 tablespoons sesame seeds

4 teaspoons sumac

6 tablespoons extra virgin olive oil

2 teaspoons sea salt

It was a sunny Saturday morning in Beirut, and there I was wandering around the Souk el Tayb, Lebanon's first and only farmers' market. It was filled with a fair old cornucopia: all manner of produce, including some truly world-class cabbages, stalls of local cedar honey in massive barrels, all shapes and kinds of kibbeh, and an odd amount of folks selling plant-related hair products. But the winner for me was the last stall I went to: sitting on a box in the furthest corner was a lady whose name turned out to be Nelly, knocking out these fine examples of tasty street food.

I use a combination of plain and bread flour, but just plain flour is fine.

Combine the flour, yeast, sugar and 1 teaspoon of salt in a bowl and use about 250-300ml/8-10fl oz of warm water to bring it together into a soft dough. Knead for a good few minutes until smooth and elastic, then divide into 6 and roll into balls. Leave them on a floured surface, covered with a damp cloth, to rise for about 45 minutes.

Preheat the oven to 240°C/475°F/gas mark 9 and put a baking tray in the oven to get hot. Roll the dough balls out into circles until they're about 3-5mm/¼ inch thick.

Mix together the za'atar ingredients. Dimple the breads all over with your fingers and spoon on the za'atar spreading it out with the back of a spoon, then transfer to the preheated tray and bake in the oven for 4-5 minutes.

Overleaf, clockwise from top right: Manaquish; Lebanese Pizza; Kibbeh with Tarator; Roast Cauliflower; Baked Potato Mash with Roast Garlic.

Earth&Co
شركاء الأرض

ABC Achrafieh, Parking L 3
Wednesdays from 4 till 8 pm

SAIFI
Saturdays, from 8 till 2 pm

Zouk Mikael
near Municipality
the rest of the week

نلّي شمالي
SAGAMINH NELLY CHEMALY
mobile: 03 814 341
e-mail: nellychemaly@yahoo.com

Roast Cauliflower

Good as a side for 6ish folks, and takes 5 minutes prep and around 45 minutes in the oven

---

2 small heads of cauliflower (each about 500g/1lb), outer leaves removed

extra virgin olive oil

sumac or ground cumin (Kamal did it with sumac, whose sourness works well with the sweetness of the roast cauli, but it's also good with cumin)

lemon juice

a handful of parsley, chopped

sea salt

It's just a regular, humble garden cauliflower, so who knew that roasting them whole made them this exciting and interesting? They sat on my friend Kamal's table as part of the spread - an edible centrepiece which we all hacked away at, cutting off chunks from the main stems and demolishing them entirely over a long Saturday lunch.

Preheat the oven to 190°C/375°F/gas mark 5.

Drizzle the caulis enthusiastically with oil, scatter them with salt and sprinkle over the sumac or cumin.

Roast them for about 45 minutes to 1 hour, keeping an eye on their colour and turning the temperature down if they are getting very dark: they're cooked when they're lightly browned and a skewer inserted meets with just a little resistance.

Before serving, drizzle again with good-quality olive oil and a fair squeeze of lemon, then scatter with parsley and a touch more sea salt.

Baked Potato Mash with Roast Garlic

Serves 4 with a good chef's snack. Takes about 1 hour to bake the spuds in the oven, followed by a bit of cooling time then 30 minutes input

---

6 baking potatoes (weighing about 1.75kg/3½lb), washed

1 head of garlic, broken up into cloves, unpeeled

125ml/4fl oz extra virgin olive oil

1 tablespoon thyme leaves, dried or fresh

salt

Back in Beirut, at the fantastic Halabi restaurant, this was served with a sprinkling of crispy deep-fried shallots (see page 55 for a quick recipe) as one of a 40 dish mezze assault. It's mash, but not like you've ever had it before. This is a version from a part of the world where dairy doesn't play such a crucial part, and much healthier it is too. Sublime with fish, chicken or anything that likes olive oil.

Preheat the oven to 200°C/400°F/gas mark 6. Put the wet potatoes around the edge of a baking tray with the garlic cloves in the middle, sprinkle with salt and put into the oven. After 20 minutes take out the garlic, turn the oven down to 180°C/350°F/gas mark 4, and bake the potatoes for another 45 minutes or so until the spuds are cooked. Take them out and let them cool.

Peel the potatoes and garlic and warm the oil. Fry the garlic cloves very gently with the thyme for a few minutes. One by one, drop in the potatoes and mash them with a fork, mixing them well with all the other ingredients. Season well with salt and serve with a splash more EVOO, warm or at room temperature, and don't forget those crispy shallots.

Lebanese Pizza

Makes 2 pizzas and all done in 30 minutes

---

a handful of pine nuts

1 onion, diced small

2 cloves of garlic, chopped

a glug of extra virgin olive oil

200g/7oz lamb mince

a big pinch of ground cumin

a big pinch of ground cinnamon

2 flatbreads (20cm/8 inches in diameter)

1 lemon

a handful of flat-leaf parsley, roughly chopped

a healthy pinch of paprika

salt and pepper

My first morning in Beirut I followed my nose to a bakery that did these kind of pizzas by the hundred every day: one bloke rolled the dough, another manned the wood-oven and the old lady took the money. Many a cold winter's day I have wished that bakery was magicked to the end of my road.

For reality's sake, the version here uses a pre-cooked flatbread like you get in packs of five in the supermarket/Middle Eastern shops, without much loss to the integrity of the dish, but if you are going to make your own flatbread, you can use the Manaqish dough recipe on page 287 and put the toppings on before you bake them.

Eat with a salad as a light lunch or slimmer's supper.

Preheat your oven to 200°C/400°F/gas mark 6, and while it is coming up to temperature put in the pine nuts on a really big baking tray to toast.

In a wide frying pan, preferably one with a thickish bottom, fry the onion and garlic with a good glug of extra virgin for a minute or two.

Tip the mince into the pan, breaking it up with a wooden spoon as you go, then add the cumin and cinnamon and give it a good stir. Fry the lamb mince until there is no pink left. Once it is starting to brown, some liquid will come out of the mince, and you want to keep frying over a high heat, giving it the odd stir, until this has all evaporated off - less than 10 minutes total cooking time.

When your pine nuts are golden, take them out and tip them into a mixing bowl (put the tray back in the oven) along with the mince when it's ready.

Taste for seasoning, then share the mix between the two flatbreads, spreading it out evenly. Run over both of them roughly with a rolling pin to push the meat into the bread a bit, then lift them on to the hot baking tray and bake for 7 minutes.

When they come out of the oven, hit them with a squeeze of lemon, a sprinkling of parsley and a good shake of paprika. Eat hot hot hot.

Stuffed Pot-Roast Chicken with Pine Nuts & Pomegranate Molasses

Serves 4-6, and takes 30 minutes to get it ready then 1 hour on the hob

around 100ml/3½fl oz extra virgin olive oil

70g/3oz bulgar wheat

1-2 cloves of garlic, finely chopped

50g/2oz pine nuts

1 teaspoon ground cumin or whole cumin seeds

½ teaspoon ground cinnamon

2 onions, cut into wedges

1 small butternut squash, peeled, the top part sliced in half lengthwise then into 2cm/¾ inch thick semi-circles, and the bulbous bottom cut into 5cm/2 inch chunks

2 bay leaves

a few sprigs of thyme leaves or a big pinch of dried thyme

300g/10oz beef mince

zest of 1 lemon

a handful of flat-leaf parsley, chopped

1 free-range chicken (weighing about 1.75kg/3½lb)

about 500ml/17fl oz hot chicken stock, or more as needed

125ml/4fl oz pomegranate molasses

salt and pepper

Pomegranate molasses is locally referred to as 'the balsamic of the Middle East', and this claim is not as aspirational as it sounds. Same syrupy dark appearance and similar sweetness, but the molasses has an added tangy fruitiness where the vinegar is just slightly sharp. It's also the backbone taste to this dish - a very old Lebanese recipe with a new attitude to stuffing your bird.

Heat 1 tablespoon of olive oil in a heavy-based pan large enough to hold the chicken and fry the bulgar, garlic, pinenuts and spices together, then pour on enough water just to cover the grains. Put a lid on and simmer for 5ish mins until the bulgar is cooked, then tip into a bowl to cool.

Wipe out the pan, put it back on a low-medium heat and pour in a healthy shot of olive oil. Tip the onions in and cook with a lid on for about 5 minutes, stirring from time to time.

Turn up the heat and mix the squash into the onions along with the bay leaves, thyme and some seasoning. Put a lid on and cook for 5-10 minutes, stirring, until the onions start to caramelize and the squash softens.

Meanwhile, in a big bowl mix the cooled bulgar with the beef mince, lemon zest, parsley and some seasoning. Stuff the chicken, closing the open end by folding over the flappy bits and securing with a couple of cocktail sticks (if you can't get all the stuffing in the bird, roll it into balls, drizzle with oil and bake in a hot oven for 15 minutes for a good cook's snack).

When the vegetables are on the way to being cooked, tip them into the ex-stuffing mixing bowl. For the second time wipe the pan out and put it back on to get good and hot with a splash of olive oil, then brown the chicken, breast-side down, one side at a time. Once both sides of the breast are appealingly browned, turn it over and fry it for a minute more.

Take out the chicken and put half the vegetables back into the pan. Nestle the chicken in the veg, breast-side up, and spoon the rest of the veg around it. Pour in the chicken stock so that it comes three-quarters of the way up the sides of the chicken, then drizzle the pomegranate molasses all over the bird and into the surrounding stock. Put a lid on, turn the heat down to low-medium and cook, bubbling gently, for about 1 hour - just push a thin knife into the thigh and make sure the tip of it is hot when it comes out. When it's done, leave it to rest for 10 minutes, and then serve with rice.

Baklava from Tripoli

Makes about 40 pieces, takes 40 minutes to put together and the same again to cook

200g/7oz shelled pistachios

125g/4oz caster sugar

3 tablespoons rose water

75g/3oz butter, melted

1 packet (around 300g/10oz) filo pastry (you will need this to be in 12 sheets, so you may need to halve them as sometimes they come as 6 large doubles instead).

250g/8oz honey

In the 8th century BC, traders from Tyre, Sidon and Arwad all arrived at this previously small town and each built themselves a walled city, hence the name: Tripoli means three cities. The things Lebanon's second largest city is most famous for are furniture and sweets, and clearly it was the latter I was more concerned with. The most famous location to sample these local delicacies is the six-floor Hallab & Sons: café on the bottom and busy factory above, which is currently in its fifth generation of sweetie-makers.

This recipe is easy, and impressive, though be sure to prepare yourself with a cool demeanour, as handling filo pastry can take a bit of patience.

Blitz the pistachios and half the sugar in a food processor until it looks powdery, with some small pieces, but no big bits. Take out a tablespoon (for later), put the rest in a bowl and stir in the rose water to make a paste.

Preheat the oven to 180°C/350°F/gas mark 4.

Brush a shallow 20 x 30cm/8 x 12 inch tin with melted butter and carefully lay a sheet of filo pastry flat on to it. You need each layer to touch the sides of the tin, so use a bit of another sheet as well if necessary. Brush the sheet with butter and lay down another sheet, pushing it into the corners and up the sides (though trim off any overhang with a knife). Repeat until you have 5 layers.

Spread half the pistachio paste on to the pastry, then use the back of a spoon to even it out and compress. Put on another sheet of pastry, brush with butter, lay another sheet on top and distribute the rest of the paste on top. Finally do another 5 layers of pastry, each brushed with melted butter.

Now cut about 8 slices, right down to the bottom, in diagonal lines both ways, so that you end up with diamonds. Bake in the oven for 40-45 minutes, until golden brown (you might want to turn the tin round during cooking so that the pastry browns evenly).

While it's cooking, knock up a syrup with the rest of the sugar and the honey: bring to the boil with 100ml/3½fl oz of water, then simmer on a low heat without stirring until reduced by just over half.

Spoon the syrup over the baklava as soon as it comes out of the oven, then sprinkle each diamond with a touch of the reserved ground pistachios. Cool and eat at room temperature - it's best not fridge cold.

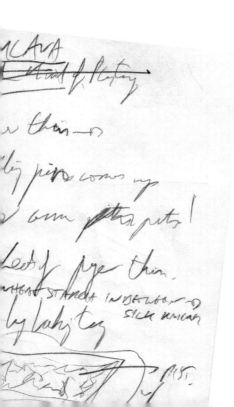

China always seemed so massive an undertaking, it was almost off-putting: the length of history and depth of culture, alien to ours in every way, over such a vast area, and home to a fifth of the world's population. But then an American friend of ours, Doug, married to the lovely (and Chinese) Alida, said they were planning a whistle-stop tour of her homeland for a few of their friends, and would we like to tag along. It was the in I'd been waiting for.

We flew to Shanghai and spent a couple of days getting over the lag before meeting up with the others. Immediately we were hit by the extent of how the cities in this country are all in a state of flux: off with the old and on with the spanking new. Yes, the skyline along the famous Bund and Huangpu River was impressive, but I counted 73 cranes from our hotel window and the old French Quarter had pretty much ceased to exist.

By far the best thing we did from here was a day trip out to Suzhou, where we passed a special afternoon walking around the serene and moving Humble Administrator's Garden. It was a perfect introduction to their historic talents: beauty and resonance, and a gentle lesson on how nobody in the world does an elegant curve like the Chinese of old.

In Beijing it was clear we'd missed the boat on the hutongs, as they'd been pretty much totalled for the Olympics, and all our guide wanted to show us was the new skyscrapers. The Forbidden City, with its vibrant yellow upturned roofs, 1,000 rooms and aura of a different age still stands firm, but for a people so proud of their past, it seemed staggering how little of it they were bothered with preserving.

Xi'an was the closest place to visit those unmissable warriors, as well as being the dumpling capital of China, but the city was in the process of building three new underground lines simultaneously, which literally meant it had ground to a halt. But the amazing Alida had connections, so the flashing blue lights of a police escort preceded our little mini-bus. Very fun.

China

Making our way further from the capital (and party headquarters), a tangible relaxedness came over the people. Lijiang in Yunnan province was my favourite place - charming, bustling and with a spirit to it that I hadn't seen so far on the trip. It also had one of the best food markets I've ever visited: fabulous fruits, amazing greens, 1,000-year-old eggs and chilli varieties new to me. Next door was the meat and fish market, and even though we'd missed the morning rush the place still reeked of fresh blood and had a lingering afterglow of good business done.

Our two last stops couldn't have been more different: first Shangri-La, up near to the Burmese border, where a walk down the pavement looking up at the atmospheric golden temples meant you risked tripping over either the indigenous tiny black hairy pigs or yaks the size of small houses. We were so high up here that they gave us oxygen canisters in our room, but we were so giggly on altitude we didn't even think to increase our buzz.

And finally to Hong Kong, which felt pretty rude after our peaceful time in the mountains but a couple of cocktails at the American Club in the harbour soon got us back into the swing of city life, and as we sipped away, looking across the bay at the famous nightly light show, the only thing on our minds was coming back soon. Next time, though, the accent would definitely be on trying to dig out more of Old China - less politicized, less revamped and more traditional. I've never been anywhere that is quite so aggressively pushing through its present to get to its future, and from what we'd seen, this was at a dear cost to character.

FACT FILE

Geographical summary: They've got it all: 9.5million square kilometres (3.7million square miles) of plains, mountains, coastline and desert. Third largest country in the world.

Population: 1.3 billion, and incidentally the oldest continual civilization on the planet.

Religion: Officially atheistic, but there are five State-registered religions: Daoism, Buddhism, Islam (1–2%), Catholic and Protestant Christianity (3–4%).

Ethnic make-up: 92% Han, with fifty-five 'minorities' making up the rest.

Life expectancy: 71 male, 75 female.

External influences: Mongols (Yuan dynasty 1260–1368 under Kublai Khan, Genghis's grandson); and some European trading posts in the 19th century on the coast, but basically everything inland was pretty much unpenetrated.

Essentials of their cooking: Searingly-hot woks, steamer baskets, over coals, big pots of slow-cooks to tenderize tough meats, deep-frying.

Food they export: Fruit and its derivatives (e.g. jam, marmalade, apple juice), preserved and frozen vegetables, tomato concentrates, dried pulses, tea.

Top 5 ingredients: Rice (and rice noodles), amazing greens, meat (especially piggy and poultry), ginger, eggs (and egg noodles), soy.

Most famous dish: Peking duck.

What they drink: Tea, beer, and homegrown wine.

Best thing I ate: *Xiao long bao* – soup dumplings – bite into them and sit tight for a little explosion of warm, pure liquid chickenness in your mouth.

Most breathtaking moment: Those terracotta warriors.

Don't ask for...: Pig's oesophagus – because they'll give it to you.

We were in a great big three-floor indoor market in Kowloon, Hong Kong, which had one level dedicated to meat, another to fruit and veg, and the basement for fish. As we wandered round between about 100 butcher's stalls, I noticed that all of them had the same knife: I'd never seen one quite like it before. It came in about four different sizes, but was the same knife: same ribbed wooden handle, same characteristic, imposing curve, with the area next to the long blade shaded where it had been ground down to make a thin cutting edge.

With no language in common, I flashed money at various butchers who looked bewildered and laughed in equal parts. I said I was *chu shi*, a chef. They laughed more. Hot, bothered and demoralized, we left, but in the spirit of never give up I tried asking the man who ran the place we were staying at where the Real Chefs went for their kit. Turned out he had a cousin who was a cook, so he called him up (in China everyone answers their mobile no matter what they're doing: it takes precedence), then pointed out a street on our map. Back we went into the driving rain - we were caught in the edge of a typhoon -

and walked and walked till we thought we must have got it wrong (because this was right at the end of our trip, and we'd worked out that there was a lot of getting it wrong here, and there wasn't a lot you could do about it), and then I saw gigantic steamer baskets hanging in front of a shop. We went inside - I drew the knife on a piece of paper and the lady disappeared. A few minutes later she reappeared saying, 'Lass one': the only one she had left was the daddy of the family, but if I'd had the choice I think I would have picked that one anyway. I was soaking and sweating in equal parts, but after three weeks of looking everywhere we went, all over China, on the last afternoon before we left this amazing country, I'd found my knife.

It's clearly a pretty serious butcher's knife, made of wood and stainless steel, with a ribbed handle for extra grip, and a beautiful, balanced weight for one so large. Love that killer curve, and the shaded part too. STRENGTH AND BEAUTY - two of my faves.

虾肉蒸饺
Corn Pancakes

四川辣排骨
Crispy Pork Ribs with Deep-Fried Garlic

蓉蓉西兰花炒饭
Crab Dumplings

油煎玉米饼
Hai Wan Ju's Busy Noodle Broth

海湾朱氏面
Egg-Fried Rice with Fragrant Ginger Broccoli

清 木雕彩漆地戏关羽面具 贵州 安顺
Painted and Carved Wooden Dixi
Mask of an Ancient Stage Figure, *Guan Yu*
Anshun, Guizhou Province
the Qing Dynasty

Chinese Recipes

Corn Pancakes

Makes 8 biggish pancakes (8-10cm/3½-4 inches), and easily done in 10 minutes

2 cobs of sweetcorn, shucked, or 275g/9oz corn kernals

1 or 2 spring onions, green part only, finely chopped

3 eggs

1 tablespoon light soy sauce

4 tablespoons plain flour

oil, for shallow-frying (groundnut is best, but sunflower or veg are also fine)

This is one of the best bits of street food I had in China, by a gurgling stream in a breathtaking mountain town not far from Tibet called Lijiang.

Quick as you like, simple, filling and, with a splodge of chilli sauce, totally moreish. It can usefully double up as a tasty kids' snack and for adults to have with, or after, drinks: I'd love to stumble across the cart that sold them after a few in my local.

If corn is out of season, frozen is better than tinned.

Mix the corn and spring onions together. Beat the eggs with the soy sauce and stir into the vegetables. Sift the flour into the mixture and gently fold in.

Heat a frying pan with oil to a depth of about 0.5cm/¼ inch until it is hot and fizzles when you throw a corn kernel into it. Using a small ladle (or about 2 tablespoons per pancake), fry in batches in the hot oil - stand back, as you have to beware of popping corn!

Cook for just a minute or two, until the edges are brown but the middle is still runny, then flip them over and brown the second side, which will be much quicker; more like 30 seconds.

Drain on kitchen paper and serve with an Asian chilli sauce; my favourite is Sriracha.

Szechuan Crispy Pork Ribs with Deep-Fried Garlic

Party food for 10 or starter for 4. Allow a minimum of 1 hour marinating time, then 20 minutes for the cooking (and if you're doing your own rib-chopping allow 15 minutes for that, too)

1.25kg/2½lb pork ribs, separated and chopped into 3-4cm/1¼-1½ inch bite-sized pieces (ask your butcher, or attack them yourself with a heavy knife)

---

2 teaspoons Chinese five-spice

---

1 tablespoons Szechuan peppercorns, pulverized in a pestle and mortar or ground in a coffee/spice grinder (optional but good for the true experience)

---

2 teaspoons chilli flakes

100ml/3½ fl oz light soy sauce

---

3 tablespoons fish sauce

---

2 tablespoons honey

---

about 1 litre/1¾ pints groundnut (or sunflower) oil, for deep-frying

---

6-10 cloves of garlic, cut into small shards

---

2 spring onions, green part only, thinly sliced

Twenty years ago British Chinese cooking was all about Cantonese, due to our relationship with Hong Kong. Nowadays Szechuan is the favoured region, an area famed for its love of chilli and spice.

Szechuan peppercorns are not like anything else you'll ever eat: they have a particularly assertive bite, but it's the mouth-numbing side-effect that makes them an eye-opening, slightly addictive experience.

Put the pork pieces into a large bowl, sprinkle with the five-spice, peppercorns and chilli flakes, then pour over the soy sauce, fish sauce and honey. Toss well with your hands until everything is coated, then leave to marinate at room temperature or put in the fridge overnight.

In a wide pan, heat the oil till it's hot but not smoking: chuck a nugget in and check that it fizzles fast but doesn't blacken too quickly - we need them to cook right through to the bone but the honey will cause them to darken quickly (you may have to sacrifice a couple this way, but it's worth it rather than burn a whole batch).

Once you've got your temperature sorted out, cook the riblets in 2-3 batches, carefully lowering the pork pieces separately into the oil. Move them around a bit during cooking, and after about 7 minutes, when they are a deep golden brown, take them out with a slotted spoon, drain them on kitchen paper and get the next lot going.

Once all the pork nuggets are done, put the garlic pieces into a metal sieve or colander, lower it into the hot oil and cook for a few minutes until light brown and crispy, stirring to ensure even coloration.

Serve sprinkled with the garlic shards and spring onions.

Crab Dumplings

Serves 6 as a starter (3 each), and only takes 30 minutes

200g/7oz crabmeat (freshly picked is so much better for this)

½ a thumb of ginger, trimmed (not peeled), washed and finely grated

---

1-2 chillies, very finely diced

---

zest of 1 lemon

---

handful of chives or 2-3 spring onions, finely chopped

½ a clove of garlic, finely minced

---

18 dumpling wrappers*

---

1 egg, beaten with a splash of water

For the dipping sauce

---

3 tablespoons light soy sauce

---

3 tablespoons rice wine vinegar

---

a scattering of very thin strips of ginger

---

* Available from Chinese supermarkets, or order from www.melburyandappleton.co.uk

Xi'an is widely known for being the dumpling capital of China, and indeed the eighteen-course dumpling feast we ate there was something to behold. Overwhelming, though, and we all felt some of their delicious nuances were lost in the sheer volume.

These, however, we had in Hong Kong, with no fanfare and no fuss. The signs were good, as the ratio of live fish outside on the pavement (in aerated tanks) to paying customers inside was about 2:1. I liked those odds, as it showed how seriously they took the freshness of their ingredients.

You can make these up an hour or two in advance and leave them in the fridge under a damp cloth.

Bring a wide pan of water up to a simmer.

Mix the crabmeat, ginger, chillies, lemon zest, chives and garlic together in a bowl.

Lay out 6 circles of dumpling pastry and brush with beaten egg. Dollop a teaspoonful of the crab mixture just below the middle, then fold the top over the crab mix to meet the other side. Seal up the edges with little pinches - a complete seal is really important or else they'll blow up in the water. Repeat in 2 more batches of 6, keeping the done ones under a lightly dampened tea towel.

Knock up the dipping sauce before you start cooking by mixing everything together. When you're ready to eat, drop the dumplings into the boiling water one by one and cook them for about 5 minutes, until they rise to the surface. Scoop them out with a slotted spoon and drain briefly on kitchen paper.

Serve immediately with the dipping sauce in little dishes, either individually or sharing one between two is dandy.

Hai Wan Ju's Busy Noodle Broth

Serves 2. The stock does its thing for 1 hour 30 minutes, then it's only 20 minutes for you to take it to the bridge

5 tablespoons light oil

4 cloves of garlic, chopped with a big pinch of salt

½ tablespoon chilli flakes

300g/10oz ready-to-use noodles (preferably udon, but any will do)

For the stock

500g/1lb chicken bones

500g/1lb pork bones

1-2 tomatoes

1 chilli

1 onion

2 star anise

2 cloves of garlic

1 carrot

2 sticks of celery

To serve

a small handful of beansprouts; a couple of handfuls of edamame beans, podded; a hunk of cucumber and a few radishes all thinly sliced; a wedge of Chinese cabbage, shredded; 1 stick of celery, finely sliced; a couple of spring onions, sliced; soy sauce

I have the good fortune of counting Chinese food guru Fuchsia Dunlop, author of *The Revolutionary Chinese Cookbook*, as a buddy, and so when my trip to China was on the cards I asked her to direct me to some proper places to eat the real stuff. This family-run noodle bar was just what I had in mind ... except they spoke no English, and we spoke no Mandarin, so it was a case of point and smile and see what turned up.

And we weren't disappointed, because the steaming, fun-filled bowls were just what we needed after the hour of walking round the same block, in the dark, on the edge of the eight-lane 3rd Ring Road trying to locate this strip-lit, inauspicious joint.

I particularly liked the way they served it, with the noodles in broth centre stage and all the bits and pieces arranged around the main dish, though we were a bit surprised when the waiter, having brought it to the table and showed it to us, then just dumped everything in and stirred it all up. He was right though - it was perfect just like that.

I'd recommend doubling the chilli oil ingredients and keeping the rest in an airtight jar at room temperature; it is a useful condiment to have around. Using pork bones for stock is refreshingly unEuropean and gives a very authentic whiff to your kitchen.

Put all the stock ingredients into a large pot with enough water to cover (probably about 2 litres/3½ pints). Bring to the boil, then turn the heat right down so that it is just steaming. Cook for about an hour and a half and strain, then bring back to a busy boil and reduce by about a third.

While the stock is reducing, make the chilli oil: heat the oil in a small pan on medium, and add the garlic, then the chilli flakes. Turn the heat down and fry gently for a few minutes, stirring until you get a lovely nutty colour, then pour it into a dish/jar straight away so that it stops cooking.

Prepare all the veggie bits.

When the stock has reduced, add the noodles and some salt to taste, and simmer for a few minutes.

Serve with the vegetables and chilli oil all in little dishes on the side, and have some soy sauce and a lot of napkins on the table.

Egg-Fried Rice
with Fragrant Ginger Broccoli

Serves 2, and takes 15 minutes (assuming the rice is already cooked)

400g/13oz cooked rice (or 160g/5½oz raw)

150g/5oz purple sprouting or long-stem broccoli, washed

25g/1oz unpeeled ginger, washed and grated

---

1 red chilli, sliced and with the seeds if you like it fiery (or use a good splash of chilli sauce)

2-3 tablespoons light soy sauce, and more to taste

---

1 tablespoon toasted sesame oil

---

3 eggs

---

3 tablespoons groundnut oil

---

4 spring onions, cut into 2cm/¾ inch batons

---

salt

This is such a simple eat that often in China a bowl of egg-fried rice was served as the last dish, once your tastebuds had been blown by the previous fourteen, just to make good and sure that you really were full.

The best way I know to use up leftover rice - needs to be no more than a day old, though.

Put a pan on the heat and add salted water to a depth of about 10cm/4 inches; stick on a lid and bring to the boil. Trim off the woody ends of the broccoli stems, and if they're thick, split the bottom 4cm/1½ inches in half.

In a small bowl mix the grated ginger, chilli, soy and toasted sesame oil. Drop the broccoli into the boiling water for 3-4 minutes, until cooked but still crunchy. Drain, tip the broccoli back into the pan, pour over the soy-ginger mix, give it a stir and stick the lid back on to infuse.

Beat the eggs with a pinch of salt. In a wok or frying pan heat the oil until just about smoking. Pour in the beaten eggs and half-scramble for around 20 seconds, then add the rice. Give it a good stir, and after a minute chuck in the spring onions. Keep moving everything regularly while the rice lightly fries for a further 6-8 minutes until it smells good and is beginning to get nice little brown crunchy bits.

Serve in bowls with the broccoli on top and spoon over the chilli, ginger and soy.

My feeling towards our closest neighbours roughly mimics our country's history with them: best of friends, with our Ententes *très* Cordiales, interspersed with times when they are nothing short of the Devil-in-a-beret. Like many of us, France is the country I've visited most: a family holiday to Normandy in the '70s; boozing and boys in Aix-en-Provence; gluttony in Gascony as a young chef; innumerable Parisian nip-overs; splashing with friends in the Dordogne; the not-so-high life of Biarritz, mountain crossing towards Spain; a pilgrimage with little ones to EuroDisney; and a memorable teenage trip which ended in me having to drive diagonally across the whole country throughout the night to catch an early morning ferry.

When I was younger I didn't have a problem with them - it was only when I entered my chosen profession that the French started to get on my wick. Such arrogance, and sexism too. Xenophobia. Michelin. Old school, fuddy-duddy, stuck up their own arses so far they couldn't see that the way people wanted to eat had moved on from the elitism of the 18th century. Such were the rantings of a healthily rebellious twenty-something.

But we all know that as we work our way towards the Great Profiterole in the Sky we temper our attitudes just a little, and my begrudging attitude lifted over the course of the next decade until all that's left is respect.

They do some things extremely well: cheese, pastry and boulangerie, wine and, of course, Champagne, which is where the knife came from. Not having been to those parts before, despite their obvious world status, I'd decided I needed a greater understanding of both the region and the Champagne-making process. My helpful friend Lorraine and I did a lot of work trying to secure various visits to my favourite Champagne houses, and all I can guess is that between us we slightly over-egged the pudding. For not only did we get shown round the unassailable Salon, the Howard Hughes of the Champagne world, but when we rocked up in Ay at Bollinger (our house Champagne) we were given a private tour, when they don't do tours, and then found ourselves having an intimate lunch with Monsieur le Président in Lily Bollinger's house.

To blag is human, but to get a result like that is truly Divine.

France

Fact File

Geographical summary: The largest country in western Europe. Mountains to the south (Pyrenees) and east (Alps). Atlantic to the west, a stretch of the Med in the south-east, and most of the inside is rolling plains. Temperate climate in the north, hotter down south.

Population: 62.6 million.

Religion: Roman Catholic 90%, Muslim (primarily North African) 8%, Protestants 2%, Jewish 1%.

Ethnic make-up: Celtic and Latin, with Teutonic, Slavic, North African, Indochinese, Basque minorities.

Life expectancy: 79 male, 85 female.

External influences: Don't be so ridiculous.

Essentials of their cooking: Reduction sauces, plenty of butter and perfectly cut vegetables.

Food they export: Wine and other boozy beverages, wheat, cheese, maize.

Top 5 favourite ingredients: Meat, fish, veg, dairy and pastry – they'll eat anything.

Most famous dish: Too many to mention … boeuf Bourguignon, snails, quiche Lorraine, steak tartare, tarte Tatin, frog's legs, crêpes Suzette, profiteroles and that onion soup.

What they drink: Light Euro-style beers and a lot of wine of varying quality. Strong spirits too, like marcs, eau-de-vie and the entire brandy family.

Best thing I ate: So many to choose from, but I guess the prize has got to go to the mussels I ate the first time we went to France. At 7, they were my first proper and true food love: unlike anything I'd ever eaten before and delicious beyond compare. Family legend has it that I ate nothing but mussels for the entire fortnight.

Most breathtaking moment: Walking the sacred cellars of Bollinger.

Don't ask for…: Return of the monarchy.

Pâtisserie
Chef's
Serrated
Palette

In my experience, the more Western the country, particularly if you're in a big city, the harder it is to find a knife of character. We were in Reims, and I wasn't particularly hopeful, but we'd had a good lunch at Au Cul de Poule, where they clearly took their cooking quite seriously, so I asked the waitress to ask the chef where they buy their knives. Reims is a city, but not such a large one that I thought we'd be looking for hours and then find the place only to be faced with the usual array of famous European brands.

The waitress reappeared with the name of a shop, so off we toddled (it had been a good lunch) and an hour later I was more than pleased when I found this. It's not so much a knife that has innate character, but it is so reflective of the French in all their pâtisserie and boulangerie glory. This is the country that gave us the croissant and the baguette, two international symbols for breakfast and lunch, as well as innumerable kinds of pastry and a cornucopia of different shapes, sizes and starter doughs of breads.

The tools of the pastry section are different from those of the main kitchen, where your chef's knife is replaced by a serrated, and your boner/filleter by a palette knife. Apart from a rolling pin and a pastry brush, these two are vital to anyone who spends their life devoted to flour. I don't like the handle, but it doesn't really matter because, as opposed to a chef's knife, which you grip for so long every shift that it becomes an extension of your hand, you wouldn't hold a knife that serves either of these dual functions for very long.

And that multi-purposefulness, which I'd never seen before, is why this caught my eye: the genius is in the practicality of combining two of the pastry section essentials into one. Simple, clever and very useful.

French Recipes

Warm Cheese Puffs

Salade d'Hareng

Steak Tartare avec
Moutarde et Raifort
(with mustard & horseradish)

Clafoutis aux Abricots

Roasted Raspberries

Warm Cheese Puffs

Makes about 45 in as many minutes ... and they're ludicrously easy to put away

125ml/4fl oz milk

65g/2½oz butter, cut into small pieces

125g/4oz plain flour

4 eggs

1 teaspoon Dijon mustard

a couple of pinches of grated nutmeg

50g/2oz Gruyère, grated

50g/2oz Parmesan, grated

salt and pepper

So there we were in Lily Bollinger's house, her *salon de thé*, to be more exact, sipping vintage Champagne with the president of Bollinger, and these little balls of loveliness were served alongside, to complete a perfect moment.

Although you MUST eat them straight out of the oven, you can prepare the mix in advance, pipe them out and put them in the fridge for a few hours: just add an extra 5 minutes to the cooking time.

Preheat the oven to 180°C/350°F/gas mark 4.

Heat the milk with an equal amount of water in a thick saucepan. Melt the butter into it as you bring it to the boil over a gentle heat.

Season with a few pinches of salt and as soon as the mixture begins to bubble, take the pan off the heat and beat in the flour with a wooden spoon, mixing quickly. Put the pan back on the heat and keep stirring until the paste comes away from the sides of the pan; it should take about a minute.

Turn off the heat and stir in 2 of the eggs (I find this stage easier with a whisk), then add the other 2 eggs one at a time, followed by the mustard, nutmeg, pepper and a touch more salt.

Chuck in all but half a handful of the cheeses and stir slowly until they've melted.

Lightly oil a sheet of greaseproof paper on a baking tray and use a teaspoon to make little piles of the mix, as upright as possible (easier if it's slightly chilled), about 3-4cm/1¼-1½ inches across and spaced out enough to allow for a bit of spread and rise.

Put a little grated cheese on each one and cook on the top shelf of the oven for about 15-20 minutes, turning the tray halfway through (bear in mind if you went on to a second tray that you need to cook them one tray at a time, as they need the top shelf to do their puffing).

Eat warm, with Champagne.

Salade d'Hareng

Serves 4 as a starter, and takes 40 minutes all told, including 20 minutes to boil the spuds

---

400g/13oz mashing potatoes, peeled and chopped roughly

---

4 tablespoons good-quality extra virgin olive oil

200ml/7fl oz crème fraîche

50g/2oz herring eggs

¼ an Iceberg lettuce, roughly shredded

4-6 pickled herring fillets ie rollmops (sweet or sharp cure, to your taste), gently squeezed then roughly sliced

---

juice of ½ a lemon

---

1 carrot, coarsely grated

---

salt and pepper

We were staying in the posh hotel in Reims where there was an uber-posh restaurant, and as is usually the case with such places the food was well executed but the atmosphere not much fun.

What *was* fun, however, was the brasserie down the end of the garden, where we had this salad, which I thought was about as much pleasure as you can have with a herring.

To get all the joy out of this you need that most French bit of kit, a mouli (or ricer as we less sexily call it). Regular mash will do of course, but the airiness the ricer brings does add to the result.

Put the potatoes into a pan of cold, salted water, bring to the boil and simmer until the potatoes are tender, then drain.

Push the potatoes through a ricer (or just mash them) and divide between 4 suitable and sizeable glasses (if you have a hand-held ricer, aim it directly into each glass in turn for maximum aeration; if not, just transfer the spuds carefully with a spoon).

Drizzle over the olive oil - half a tablespoon over each one - then mix the crème fraiche and fish eggs in a little bowl and spoon half of this over the potatoes too.

In another little bowl toss the lettuce with the sliced herring, along with a squeeze of lemon and some seasoning. Use a third of this mixture to make another layer in each glass, then go in with the grated carrot before layering on another third of the fishy lettuce, the rest of the eggy crème fraiche and the last of the herring on top.

Steak Tartare avec Moutarde et Raifort
with Mustard & Horseradish

Having always loved steak tartare, I now feel like I have been to its spiritual home: Au Cul de Poule is well worth a visit next time you're in Reims, as it has a blackboard menu of around eighteen different variations on the theme of hand-cut diced raw beef.

This well-established classic got its name from the Tartars of the 13th century, who according to legend didn't stop their charging around on horseback for anything - not even to eat. They would put a lump of meat under their saddle, ride hard all day, and by the time it came to eating it the meat was sufficiently tenderized by the repeated rubbing, the sinew having broken down from the pressure.

Even though it's one of those dishes that is ubiquitous in brasseries, there is absolutely no reason why it can't be done in the comfort of your own home; it's actually a very satisfying supper, though obviously you need good, fresh meat for this one, which means decent butcher not supermarket.

Sexy supper for 2:
light in quantity, but filling.
30 minutes max

400g/13oz piece of beef fillet, cut into small dice (not bigger than 1cm/½ inch-square - your butcher will do this for you)

---

1 level tablespoon Dijon mustard

---

2 tablespoons hot horseradish (fresh is best, pre-grated in jars is OK, but definitely not creamed)

---

1 shallot, very finely chopped

---

1 clove of garlic, finely minced

---

few drops of Tabasco

---

shot of Worcestershire sauce

---

4 slices of medium/thick sliced white bread

1-2 bulbs of chicory, cut into leaves, washed

---

good olive oil, for dressing

---

2 egg yolks

---

fleur du sel (or Maldon salt if you're feeling patriotic)

---

pepper

Preheat the oven to 180°C/350°F/gas mark 4.

Put the diced meat into a bowl and add the mustard, horseradish, shallot, garlic, Tabasco, Worcestershire sauce and generous seasoning. Mix together well but lightly, then taste and adjust as necessary.

Pack half the mixture into a ring-mould/pastry cutter sat on a board or large plate, press down with the back of a spoon and lift the ring off. Then do the same with the other half.

Lightly toast the bread in the toaster. Cut off the crusts, then split into two by cutting horizontally through the doughy middle - not as hard as it seems, as long as you have a long, sharpish serrated knife. Cut each piece into quarter triangles, arrange on a baking tray, untoasted side up, and stick in the oven on the top shelf.

In a mixing bowl dress the chicory lightly with good olive oil, a splash of red wine vinegar and some seasoning then stack the leaves architecturally on your serving dish/side plates.

Check the toasts after 2 minutes and every couple of minutes thereafter, taking any out that are ready. Separate a couple of eggs, sit a yolk atop each pile of beef and serve as soon as the toasts are good to go.

Clafoutis aux Abricots

Serves 6, and takes a mere 15 minutes to get in the oven and about 30 minutes to cook

350g/11½oz apricots or any other soft or stone fruit

80g/3oz sugar (you must taste your fruit - for the end result it doesn't matter if the apricots are underripe but if they are you'll need more sugar than this)

50g/2oz plain flour

50g/2oz ground almonds

a pinch of salt

2 eggs

½ teaspoon vanilla extract

3 tablespoons Amaretto or brandy

125ml/4fl oz milk

a handful of flaked almonds

Once you've undressed it, this is a batter pudding, but being French it's a bit smarter than it sounds. The word clafoutis comes from *clafir* (to fill), because you pack the fruit into your cooking vessel, pour on a batter to fill in the gaps, then bake till puffed and glorious. It's a French standard and with good reason: quick, easy, accessible and totally scrumptious with any stone or soft fruit - peaches, cherries, raspberries, etc.

If you're going to be totally proper about it, and you know what sticklers the Frogs are with their national dishes, this is supposed to be cooked in a *marmite* (pronounced mar-meet), a thick, cast-iron pot with a lid, ideal for a dish like this for its excellently even heat distribution - though I've never had any problems with any kind of ovenproof dish or even a frying pan.

I don't know if there is a connection with Marmite - I wanted to call it *Clafoutis aux Abricots en Marmite* as it was on the menu in Reims, but then I reckoned only Marmite lovers would make it and they'd be disappointed at the result, or confused to say the least.

Preheat the oven to 180°C/350°F/gas mark 4. Butter a baking dish or (ideally) an ovenproof cast-iron pot/pan about 25cm/10 inches across. Halve and pit the apricots and pack them closely into the bottom of the pan, curved side up, with half the sugar. Put into the oven for 5-ish minutes so that they start to soften.

Mix the rest of the sugar with the flour, almonds and salt. Beat the eggs with the vanilla, booze and milk, then pour gradually into the dry ingredients, stirring all the time, to make a thin batter.

When the apricots come out of the oven, give them a little shuffle and pour in the batter. Cook for about 25-30 minutes, scattering on the flaked almonds halfway through, until the batter is puffed up, golden and caramelizing a bit around the edge.

Tuck in straight away, with ice cream, cream or crème fraîche.

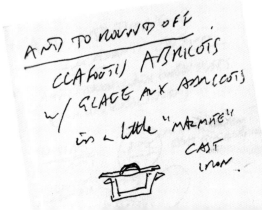

AND TO ROUND OFF . CLAFOUTI ABRICOTS w/ GLACE AUX ABRICOTS in a little "MARMITE" CAST IRON .

Roasting Raspberries
A Top Tip

Serves 2 in 15 minutes

200g/7oz raspberries

about 1 tablespoon caster sugar, more if the raspberries are tart

a bit of icing sugar

2 scoops of ice cream, to serve

We had this in a posh restaurant called Le Grand Cerf, halfway between the two great towns of the Champagne region, Reims and Epernay. It goes down in my memory as the only time I've found out after the meal that they had a Michelin star!

Out of the 100-plus recipes in each of my books, there is always one that just seems to grab people's imagination more than the others - a clear winner, if you like, and for years afterwards folks still talk excitedly to me about it. I've learnt to expect that now, in a resigned kind of way (a lot of love went into the other ninety-nine too, you know), but it's interesting that they're never the ones I imagine.

For this book, however, I'll give good odds on this being it. So simple, and yet there's a little bit of magic that happens in there ...

Preheat the oven to 200°C/400°F/gas mark 6.

Put the raspberries into an ovenproof dish that you're happy to serve them in and sprinkle on the sugar. Cook in the oven for about 15 minutes, so that some of the juices have come out of the raspberries but they are still holding their shape.

Dust with icing sugar (i.e. through a shaker or sieve) and serve with good-quality vanilla ice-cream.

FACT FILE

Geographical summary: Second most mountainous country in Europe after Switzerland. High plateau, lowland areas such as narrow coastal plains, and mountainous regions.

Population: 46.9 million.

Religion: 94% Catholic; 6% Protestant/other.

Ethnic make-up: Predominantly Basques, Catalans and Galicians.

Life expectancy: 78 male, 84 female.

External influences: The Moors invaded in 711AD, ruling for almost 800 years before Christian armies routed them.

The essentials of their cooking: They love to simmer quickly (i.e. clams) and slowly (i.e. tripe). The fast-serve nature of tapas means that much of the hot stuff is fried (and they have a tendency to throw it at the microwave a lot too). Grilling, for fish and steaks.

Food they export: Olive oil, wine, oranges of all shapes and sizes, tomatoes.

Top 5 favourite ingredients: Preserved pig (ham, chorizo, etc.), fish/seafood (especially *bacalau*, anchovies, clams), the pepper family (chillies, capsicums, pimentos, piquillos, paprika), pulses, olive oil.

Most famous dish: Paella.

What to drink: Lots of Rioja (white and red), Estrella Dam on tap, fruit juices in cans, strong coffee.

Best thing I ate: Spit-roasted kid in Majorca.

Most breathtaking moment: My first walk around the Alhambra – never seen anything like it in my life.

Don't ask for…: Melon and Parma ham.

Spain

Spain is like Italy without the pretensions: diverse north and south, interesting regional identities, strong arm of the Lord and heavy on the culture, but in a less self-aware way than their easterly neighbours. It is a country obsessed with food: good *mercados* exist in nearly every town and city for fresh meat, fish, produce and general provisions, but interestingly there's plenty of fun to be had in their supermarkets too, so often a soulless place for a food-lover. How many kinds of *bacalao* (salt cod) do you really need? And their obsession with preserving, canning in particular, is impressive: any veg you can think of you can find in a tin or a jar.

Spain and I share the same overview for life: a bit of culture, a lot of fun, with a large portion given over to eating and drinking ... and conveniently they're predisposed to liking me, as my name means 'Happy'. We share the same character trait of not doing things by half and are prone to almost unhealthy obsessions, in their case Catholicism, anchovies, love, the colour black, *jamón* ...

It's got a rough side - I've had more incidents there than anywhere else per visit: two muggings, one car broken into, multiple flashings, and in Madrid our hotel room was even rented out in the daytime to a prostitute. But there's also high art, a lot of it in high churches, and it plays an important part of their culture. It's admirable how Gaudí was allowed to make Barcelona his plaything and hard to think of any other city that is so synonymous with one modern architect.

And then there's the Moorish south, the least European place on the mainland. A trip round the Andalusian cities of Córdoba, Seville and Granada when I was 18 was the first time I'd really connected emotionally with a particular time, place and people in history: it was just so jaw-droppingly impressive, and a world apart from all the other really old stuff I'd seen - try it on your stroppy teenagers.

Unlike the Italians, the Spanish are not a vain lot: the inevitability of gorgeous young women turning into something a bit different once they hit fifty knocks that on the head, and once they've crossed that threshold they get a new lease of life as matriarchs - respected and untouchable, as opposed to in our country where we just get old.

El JaMonero

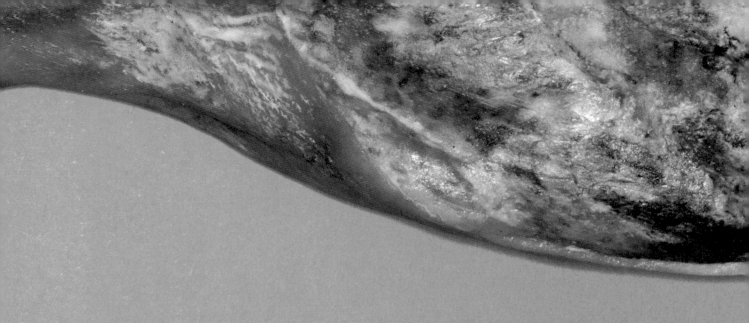

This a job-specific knife - like my Japanese eel-filleting knife, but a lot more useful. Being from Spain, there are no prizes for guessing what my *jamónero* is for: all twenty-five centimetres of it are designed solely for the purpose of slicing their beloved ham.

The Spanish take ham to a whole new level: for me *jamón ibérico de bellota* (acorn-fed piggies) trounces the better-known Parma ham of Italy, with its darker, richer meat.

We'd been directed to the best knife shop in Barcelona by our friend Oli, who lives there, and once we'd breezed past the machine-guns in the window and other general death-inducing weaponry I spotted this straight away: fastest knife in the book.

A whole cured pig's leg is quite an undertaking, not to mention anywhere from expensive to ridiculous, so we generally only get one in for parties, though memorably we took a whole *jamón*, complete with shrivelled trotter, to Glastonbury a couple of years

ago as any-time sustenance. One of my best bits of the whole festival was when a cross-eyed party reveller fell into the wrong caravan (ours), screeching 'What's that pig's leg doing in here?' before falling out again.

As knives go it's pretty straightforward: came out of a factory in south-east Spain, made by Arcos, one of Spain's best-known knife producers. The handle is simple, cool to hold and functional, and there's a weight to it that makes you feel confident about getting through that beast of a thigh ...or thigh of a beast. Those dimples down both sides of the blade are for ease of slicing this dense meat, letting the air get in, and therefore less pressure is needed, so you can keep your strokes smooth. Ham carving is a real art, and one that's taken very seriously in their part of the world. I like that the Spanish still do it by hand, whereas the Italians have given in to the slicer. It's actually surprisingly difficult, especially when you start getting down to the bone; I even went to a ham-carving class once ... with my new knife, of course.

Spanish Recipes

Pan con Tomate e Anchoas

Pea & Ham Croquetas

Solomillo de Ternera
(Veal Tenderloin on Toast)

Goats' Cheese, Confit Tomatoes
& Basil Oil

Piquillo Peppers Stuffed
with Brandada de Bacalao

Tortilla di Butifarra
(Catalan Sausage Tortilla)

Fried Eggs, Salt Cod
& Black Pudding

Pan con Tomate e Anchoas

Nibbles for 4 (8 pieces),
and a 10-minute make

---

4 large slices of sourdough, halved

---

1 clove of garlic, peeled

---

2 really juicy, vine-ripened tomatoes
(or if the big ones are no good, a few
more cherries), halved

---

several splashes of extra virgin
olive oil

---

a small handful of basil leaves,
roughly torn

---

anchoas (if you have plumped for the
ones packed in salt, remember
to rinse them well before using)

---

a few twists of the peppermill

You need decent anchovies for this - I'd go so far as to say it's not worth making it without them. That doesn't mean posh delis and big bucks, just a decent jar from the supermarket, not the cheapest little tin. Personally I think the ones preserved in salt are consistently the best of those available in the UK, though the quality of those in oil in little jars has soared recently.

In Spain they take their anchovying so seriously that you'll see two kinds on nearly every tapas menu: *anchoas* (brown, and cured with salt) and *boquerones* (white, and cured in vinegar, i.e. pickled), not to mention fresh, grilled or fried, in season. Pound for pound their anchovies are so much better than ours that to me carting back a 500g/1lb tin is muscle well spent.

Perfect for drinks.

Preheat the oven to 180°C/350°F/gas mark 4. Spread the bread out on a tray, drizzle with extra virgin olive oil and bake for 5-7 minutes, until going golden round the edge and crisping but not desiccated.

Rub each piece of toast with the garlic clove - an 'X' usually does it, though feel free to scribble furiously if you love the stuff. Holding on to the outside of the halved tomatoes, press the cut side into the toasts and rub and squidge them all over.

Season with pepper and drizzle with a healthy splash more olive oil. Finish with some basil and the little fishies.

Opposite from the top:
Pan con Tomate e Anchoas;
Pea & Ham Croquetas;
Sollomillo de Ternera.

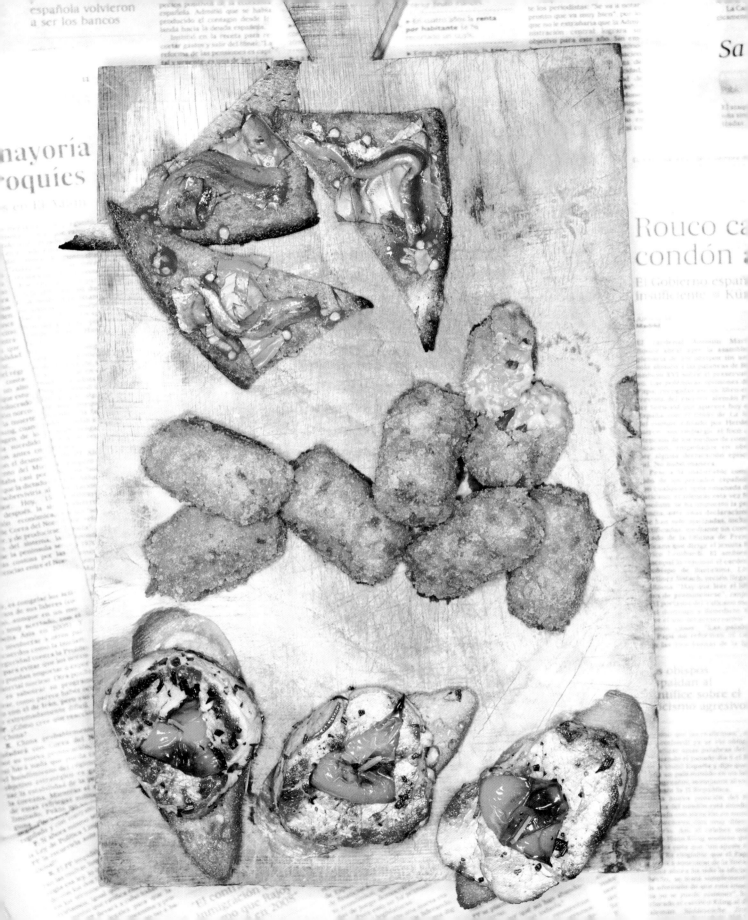

Pea & Ham Croquetas

Makes about 16, and takes about 1 hour from start to finish

For the roux

40g/1½oz butter

5 tablespoons plain flour

250ml/8fl oz chicken stock

25g/1oz Parmesan, finely grated

130g *jamón* (Spanish ham, which is cured and dried. You can also use a British cooked ham but the flavour is much less intense so go for 150g ham and 180g peas), thick sliced and then cut into small dice

200g/7oz frozen peas, defrosted

around 1 litre/1¾ pints vegetable/sunflower/frying oil

salt and pepper

For the coating

a handful of flour seasoned with salt and pepper

1 egg, beaten with 2 tablespoons water

100g/3½oz fine breadcrumbs

Mmmmm ... *croquetas*: possibly the most moreish food to have rolled out of the Iberian peninsula, and if the aim of our culinary efforts is to bring pleasure to those we love, watch these little cylinders of scrumptiousness enrich their souls. They may not be the fastest make in the world, but my God, are they worth it.

One last thought: although they are best eaten there and then, you can let them cool and blast them briefly through a very hot oven the next day. Some of the best party food ever.

Melt the butter in a thick-bottomed pan then add the flour and stir for a few minutes on a medium heat. Slowly pour in the chicken stock, whisking to get all the lumps out until it becomes a thick paste.

Turn the heat off, mix in the Parmesan, ham, and some seasoning (only pepper and no salt if you're using *jamón*), then spread thinly on a small baking tray to cool it down (if you're in a hurry you can put it outside or in the fridge until it's cold and solid).

Now set up your breadcrumbing station: a small tray with seasoned flour, a wide bowl with the beaten watered egg, another tray for the breadcrumbs and a big plate at the end to put the finished ones on.

Blitz the peas in a food processor to break them up, squeeze any excess water out of them and stir well into the now cold gluey paste.

Dampen the palms of your hands, then pick up a couple of tablespoons of the paste and roll into thickish thumb-sized cylinders. Shape all the *croquetas* first on the floured tray, making sure they are well covered with flour on all sides and both ends. If they are uncomfortably soft to work with, put the *croquetas* into the freezer for 15 minutes until firmer, and re-roll them in the flour. Then in 4 batches coat them completely with the egg mix, then roll in the breadcrumbs.

Pour the oil into a wide saucepan to a depth of about 3-4cm/1¼-1½ inches, making sure that the level comes nowhere near the top of the pan so there's room for it to bubble up. Fry the *croquetas* in 2-3 batches for 3-4 minutes, or until golden brown and crispy. Sit them on some kitchen paper to soak up excess oil before tucking in. Irresistible.

Solomillo de Ternera
Veal Tenderloin on Toast

Makes 6 pieces, and takes about 15 minutes after marinating time

350g/11½oz veal or pork fillet

2 sprigs of rosemary, leaves picked and chopped

2 cloves of garlic, chopped

2 tablespoons extra virgin olive oil

6 slices of baguette, about 1cm/½ inch thick

½ a green pepper, cut into 12 random triangles

salt and pepper

There are some social occasions that call for something greater than a canapé but smaller than a starter, like anything from a few friends over for drinks to a full-on party. What are tapas to the Spanish we have no good single word for in English, and yet the fashion now is very much for this size of nibble: canapés being a little bit fussy and plates being a bit much of a commitment.

Veal tenderloin can be a bit pricey, so you can also make this scrummy no-brainer with pork fillet (another name for the same cut of meat) without losing flavour or authenticity points.

Ciudad Comtal, at the bottom of the Rambla de Catalunuya, arguably has the best tapas in Barcelona, and this manages to be both sophisticated and rustic; tasty and somehow endemically Iberian.

Slice the veal into 6 mini-steaks and put them into a dish with the rosemary, garlic and olive oil. Give them a roll around and leave to marinate for a while - a few hours at room temperature or overnight in the fridge, in which case take out an hour before needed to bring up to room temperature.

Preheat the oven to 180°C/350°F/gas mark 4 and put a skillet or frying pan on to get good and hot.

Splash some olive oil on to the slices of bread and sit them in the middle of a baking tray, leaving a space all round the edge. Put the green pepper pieces skin side down around the sides (you want them to feel more of the heat, hence this arrangement) and cook in the oven for 10 minutes, or until the toasts have turned golden-brown.

Turn the oven off, leaving the tray inside to stay warm, and then get started on the veal.

Season one side of the meat with salt and pepper, and lay them in the hot dry skillet/frying pan seasoning side down. After 2-3 minutes season the other side, flip them over and cook for another 2-3 minutes.

Take the toasts out of the oven, put a piece of veal on to each one and top with 2 pieces of roast pepper, using a cocktail stick to secure the stack.

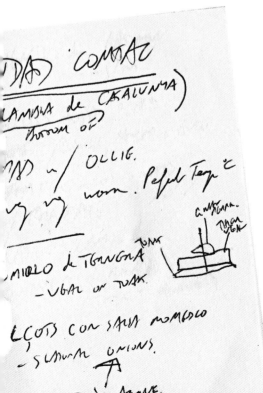

Goats' Cheese, Confit Tomatoes & Basil Oil

Serves 4, and all done
in 30 minutes

a large bunch of basil (40g/1½oz),
leaves and stalks separated

a whole dried chilli (optional)

125ml/4fl oz extra virgin olive oil

2 cloves of garlic, peeled and
smashed

300g/10oz very ripe cherry tomatoes

2 large handfuls of rocket

a few drops of sherry vinegar

100g/3½oz goats' cheese, cut into
4 slices

salt and pepper

We had this at one of Barcelona's most trendy (as in El Bulli inspired) restaurants, called Cinc Sentits, and though the rest of the meal was a phantasmagorical whirlwind, it was this simple dish, served as a cheese course, that I woke up thinking of the next day. They did it with a local, very artisanal, almost hairy-tasting sheep's cheese, and though I encourage you to do the same, a good goat is easier to come by in our land and fits the bill just as well.

It's really important that the tomatoes should be flavoursome - that is, vine-ripened, good and smelly and somewhere in the boundaries of seasonal.

In a small pan, gently heat the basil stalks with the chilli, olive oil and garlic.

Make a little cross on the base of each tomato with the tip of a sharp knife. When the oil in the pan starts to fizzle around the garlic and basil stalks, drop in the tomatoes and cook over a low heat for about 4 minutes. Take the tomatoes out with a slotted spoon and set aside, chuck out the chilli, garlic and basil stalks and let the oil cool down.

Dress the rocket with the vinegar, 1-2 tablespoons of the cooled basil oil and some seasoning. Make a little rocket mountain on each of the plates and put a slice of goat's cheese on top. Pop the tomatoes out of their skins and share between the plates.

Roughly chop the basil leaves and blend for 10 seconds with the rest of the oil (or you can just stir it in but you won't get that vibrant green colour). Taste and season carefully with salt and pepper, then use a teaspoon to distribute the green oil over and around the other ingredients.

Piquillo Peppers Stuffed with Brandada de Bacalao

Makes 16ish, and takes about 1 hour after an overnight soaking

175g/6oz salt cod

400g/13oz mashing potatoes, peeled

4 tablespoons extra virgin olive oil

3 small shallots (or 1 banana shallot), finely sliced

2-3 cloves of garlic, minced

2 pinches of smoked paprika, preferably the hot one but sweet will do

3 tablespoons double cream

a squeeze of lemon, if you fancy it

a tin or jar of piquillo peppers with at least 16 pieces in it, drained

pepper

This is one of my all-time favourite tapas - the saltiness of the fish, the creaminess from the mash and the slight piquancy of the peppers all come together perfectly in every bite ... shame I always seem to be half-cut when I have them and those nuances pass me by.

As with most tapas, these are great party food, but I've also done a couple with a bit of rocket as a damn fine starter.

Soak the salt cod overnight, changing the water a few times.

Next day, first get your mash going: quarter the spuds into cold salted water, bring to the boil, simmer until tender, then drain.

While the spuds are going, lift the cod out of the water, pick/cut out any bones and peel off the skin, then roughly chop the flesh.

Preheat the oven to 180°C/350°F/gas mark 4. Heat the oil in a medium-sized frying pan and fry the cod, shallots, garlic and smoked paprika for a few minutes until the cod is opaque and the shallots have softened, then turn the heat off. Once the spuds are well-drained mash them into the cod with the cream. Season well with pepper and a squeeze of lemon, and let the mix cool a little by spreading it out on a plate.

Stuff the peppers, put them on a small, baking tray, then brush them lightly all over with water. Bake in the oven for 10ish minutes until hot but not collapsing; you can give them a splash of extra virgin olive oil when they come out of the oven if you want, but in Spain they are usually served matt.

Tortilla de Butifarra
Catalan Sausage Tortilla

Makes 8 nice slices, and takes 30 minutes to make, 30 minutes to cook

---

2 potatoes (about 500g/1lb), washed, unpeeled, cut into rough 3cm/1¼ inch chunks (I like the red-skinned ones for this but they're not strictly necessary)

---

4 raw fat sausages, cut into 3cm/1¼ inch pieces

---

2 tablespoons extra virgin olive oil

---

2 white onions, sliced

---

2 cloves of garlic, roughly chopped

---

2 ripe tomatoes, sliced

8-10 eggs (depending on size), beaten and seasoned

---

a pinch of dried oregano

---

salt and pepper

Butifarra is the typical sausage of Catalonia and can come in many forms, such as black and white, raw or cooked. Seeing as they are so lax with their terminology, I see no reason why we need to specify any particular kind of sausage, other than it being of decent quality, and on the fat side.

We had this halfway up the long outdoor escalators that take you up to the top of Parc Güell, Gaudi's fantastical vision of future living. It was New Year's Day and biting cold, and in a packed bar of local folk having a day off, this straightforward plate of Spanishness and a couple of Estrella Dams with Veterano chasers sorted us right out.

Preheat the oven to 170°C/340°F/gas mark 3½.

Bring a pan of salted water to the boil with the spud chunks in it and a lid on. Simmer for about 8 minutes, until the potato pieces are just cooked, then drain.

In a frying pan (around 25 x 5cm/10 x 2 inches) that can go in the oven, fry the sausage chunks in the oil over a pretty high heat until they are lightly browned. Keeping the pan on the heat, lift them out and put to one side. Fry the onions in the same pan, stirring regularly - you don't want too much colour on them. As the onions begin to soften, stir in the garlic, followed shortly by the sausages and potatoes.

The pan should be pretty full now, so very gently turn them all over so they are well mixed, then turn off the heat. Pour the beaten, seasoned eggs into the pan - you need all the solids to be covered by egg mix, so you might need to add another one or two, depending on your pan/eggs.

Arrange the tomatoes over the top, season with salt, pepper and oregano, then take a palette knife or spatula and push the tomatoes down into the surface of the tortilla a bit.

Cook in the oven for 30-40 minutes - you want it to be set round the edge, and ever so slightly runny in the middle. Leave to sit for 5-10 minutes before running a palette knife round the edge and flipping, but when you choose your receiving dish, bear in mind you have to flip this one twice so that the tomatoes stay on top.

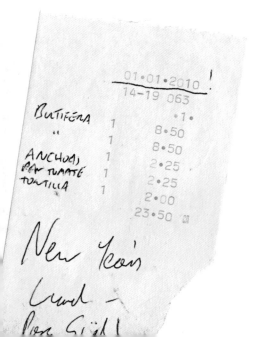

Fried Eggs, Salt Cod & Black Pudding

Serves 2, and after you've soaked the cod only takes 15 minutes

---

100g/3½oz salt cod

---

2 tablespoons extra virgin olive oil

---

1 clove of garlic, chopped

75g/3oz black pudding (or one sausage of *morcilla*, the Spanish kind), sliced or diced

---

a small handful (6-ish) of cherry tomatoes, halved

---

2 eggs

---

a small handful of chives or spring onions, sliced

---

pepper

The idea was a four-day romantic New Year's getaway; the reality was somewhat different ...

Day 1 we met up with our great friend and bon viveur, Oli, and he and the wife went on a ten-hour bender that, given my state of pregnancy at the time, meant that the ensuing row ('It's my holiday too, you know') became a foregone conclusion.

Day 2 was New Year's Eve, and we got mugged (though Susi held on to her handbag for dear life, growling, for some reason, like a small dog, so they got away with nothing).

Day 3 was spent driving up to southern France to hook up with some friends; nice idea, but it happened to coincide with the one and only day in my pregnancy of gut-wrenching vomming.

Day 4 we headed back to Barcelona for our evening flight, stopping for lunch in Girona, and came across this revelation of a dish - the highlight of the trip (though it has to be said, the competition was a bit thin).

Unfortunately there was also an unscheduled Day 5: stuck in the airport due to snow in Gatwick for thirty-six hours. Pregnant, with no fresh air and only airport food for a day and a half. Worst Trip Ever.

First you have to rehydrate the cod (see page 200), which, just to warn you, is easiest done overnight.

If the fish still has skin and bones, get rid of them, then cut it up into rough 1cm/½ inch dice.

Preheat the oven to 170°C/340°F/gas mark 3½. Using a pan that can go into the oven, heat the oil over a medium flame and fry the pieces of cod and the garlic. Cook for about 5 minutes, until it all begins to get golden and crunchy and starts sticking to the bottom of the pan, then add the black pudding and the tomato halves.

After another 5 minutes, evenly distribute the contents around the pan, then crack the eggs in and tip it so that the whites run all around. Give it a few grinds of the peppermill and put the pan into the oven for about 3-ish minutes, until the eggs are set.

Sprinkle with chives and eat immediately - toast is good.

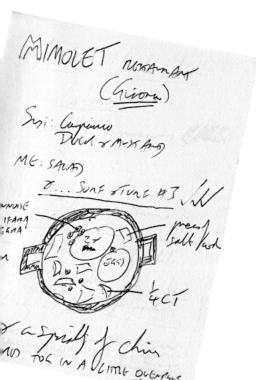

345

Index

THANK YOU

This is a book that I've been working towards writing for 20 years, and really gearing up for over the last five, so you'd think that given all that preparation time I would be reasonably across the research and necessary detail. But maybe it's precisely because it's been a long time coming and came to mean so much to me that infact it turned out I needed more back-up than I ever have done to fill in the picture that I'd painted in my mind.

Specifically on the recipes, I have of course credited in the intro those dishes that I've recreated knowing who first made them. But there are a few folks who helped with the authentication of others, namely that I had made something that tasted like it did in their respective homelands: Simone Shagam, for biltong assistance; Juliana's mum, Fatima Zachi, for her fejouada recipe; and Vhal Bustamente for his verification of my Filipino dishes.

Like any decent cook, I'm continually indebted to my suppliers, not only for the excellent quality of ingredients, but also for their patience with my random questions: Veronica at Chef's Connection; Rodney at Macken's Butchers; Tony at Fishmonger's Kitchen; Tim Wesch at Weschenfelder Sausage Making Supplies; and as ever, the Batman and Robin of Shepherd's Bush Butchers, John & Perry at Stentons (especially when it came to giving my Hong Kong chopper the proper work out it deserved, as well as trying to get our heads round that Brazilian Pig Leg Boning knife).

Staying with the knives, I owe an enormous debt of gratitude to Henrietta Lovell, aka The Tea Lady of the Rare Tea Company. We both know what you did and neither of us can ever talk about it in public! Kamal Mouzawak not only knew what knife I should have from his country but then purchased it on my behalf, and arranged shipment ... as far as Paris, anyway ...

Where I was lacking a few collected bits from various countries, some of my friends were amazingly helpful in gathering the necessary cornucopia to complete the collages: Margaret Rooke, Andrew Emmott and his mum, Sue, all came together to colour in my Malawi. Xander and Christoffer van Tulleken ransacked their garage for things Burmese; Maria Graça Fish of the Brazilian Embassy kindly lent me her moquecas and figurines, and Sarah Hatcher and Peter Robertson who, whilst not really understanding what the brief was, fulfilled it perfectly from St Lucia.

Photographing some of the dishes against newspapers from their respective country was an idea of mine that if I'd known the issues involved I might have been persuaded to walk away from. To that end I'd like to give gracious thanks to Mercy Tahuna, at The High Commission of Malawi; Her Excellency Ruth E. Rouse, The High Commissioner of Grenada; Feona Sandy, at The High Commission of Grenada, and Berit Scott, at The Royal Norwegian Embassy. Also to Richard Gush and Tobin Shackleford for their assistance with South African newspapers, as well as other specifics from the Cape.

Another layer of complication I inserted was having the recipe titles in their indigenous language, where it made sense, and as I'd mainly failed to note these in my Food Diaries, a certain amount of retrospective translating of my dish names back into their original language had to occur. The following kind people humoured me with this activity: Revd. Torbjørn Holt of the Norwegian Church, London; Mariko Otake (Japanese recipe titles); Selin Kiazim and Sinem Kiazim-Hassan (Turkish recipe titles); Basel Abbas (Lebanese and Moroccan recipe titles); Lucy Lee (for China and Hong Kong into Mandarin); Siphiwe Jere (for Malawian recipes); Austin & Catherine Tan at Mum's House (Burmese Supplies) and lastly to my friend Rosangela Nunes Pereira, who not only helped with the Brazilian names but also the hilarious translation from Tramontina, the Brazilian knife-makers regarding the finer design points of their Pig Leg Boning Knife.

Nicola Wissbrock also had a hand in that very high-maintenance Brazilian knife, as well as general support on a gamut of needs from sodium nitrite to newspapers to bicycling over an emergency loaf of rye for the shoot: your labours were very appreciated - thank you.

The first shout-out on the photos is of course to Andrew Montgomery, whose eye for detail and need for perfection is responsible for this book's arresting visuals. His food photographs manage to look both retro and slightly futuristic in a way that I hope will make them timeless. In any case, I'm truly enjoying them in the here and now.

But a book with this many shots in it over so many years and locations obviously has had a paparazzi of photographers contribute to it. None more so than Susi Smither, always the official photographer for our trips, and whose shots are so much more than holiday snaps. Also to Gill McEvedy, whose pics of Burma I found colourful, useful and touching; Luiz C. Ribeiro of the New York Post, for digging out his excellent photographs of our Brazilian trip, and to Martin Thompson for the fast fling we did round the Philippines; Juloo Oliver, for still having those snaps from the Meatpackers, and to Alison Darren and Lorraine Martin for their iconic shots of 'Frisco; Tess's Aunty Pina was unbelieveably kind and took a 4 hour bus ride in the Philippines to get me a shot of some knives that I wanted; my brother in law, Guy Sellers, for that atmospheric, chilly seascape in the Arctic, and Cousin Henry for the warmth of his shots in the Spanish sun. Pro photographer Circe kindly spent half a day on her Vespa whizzing round Manhattan shooting my fave food joints and eating bad food on my behalf at the Grand Central Oyster Bar. And Wendy Millyard got snap happy in sunny St Lucia, tracking down the best bouillon on the island. Lastly to my sister Floss, whose old pics of Ma and Pa in this book make it a much more meaningful one for me.

In terms of the team that actually made the book happen, it really all came down to three people from my side: chronologically, Natalie Hume had the first shift, from January to July, sitting at my kitchen table and typing as I cooked and talked through what I was doing. We were working up against a hard deadline to get all the recipes finished: the birth of my baby, and just managed it, finishing the last 3 recipes on my due date (and Delilah helpfully obliged by being a week late). But more than just typing, Natalie was a friend as I got fatter, having done it three times herself for her gorgeous daughters, as well as having a palette that I came to respect and trust.

Then as I concentrated on first motherhood, and then the text, the recipes went to the one and only Kate McCullough to test, which she did with such focus and accuracy that I then asked her to come and cook the book a second time alongside me for the shoot. She worked tirelessly, and managed to get so much done whilst maintaining her cool, Irish nerve as opposed to my natural tactic of sweaty hysteria. (And on recipe testing, quick thanks too to Ben Whitehouse and Angelina Harrisson for picking up the stragglers).

Natasha Coverdale has been involved in this book from first conception: we worked on the initial proposal that went out to publishers and she did a truly visionary job in bringing together all the thoughts that had been rattling round my head for years and making sense of them on paper. But more than that she brought her own ideas to the party (and at times it was a real party) and it's her creativity, not to mention huge amount of hard work, that has made this book the stunner that it is.

Thanks too to the inimitable Mr Dominic Minns, whose flair and filigree have added style and smiles to these pages.

It's been the pleasure I knew it would be to work with the team at Conran Octopus again - like slipping into a bath of goose fat: comforting, slick and supportive. Sybella Stephens has coped with my words and rewriting like a stoic trooper, Jonathan Christie in the design department is just happy to have got out less scarred than on our last encounter, backed up by the thoroughly helpful and helpfully thorough Jaz Bahra. Letting go is always hard but I know that production is safe in Katherine Hockley's hands. And when the time comes to it, I'm looking forward to blazing the publicity trail again with Fiona Smith. But really my heart lies with Lorraine Dickey: I know this will be pretty much her last book at CO, which means we can never bring the band together again, but I've loved playing alongside her, and wish her so much love and luck with the next chapter of her life.

My agent, Rosemary Scoular at United Agents, has always been a supporter of this eccentric project, even when I was madly gabbling the initial concept over a glass of vino. She then guided it from over-excited chat to saleable idea skilfully and respectfully, and was there as a back-up brain when I wasn't sure. Wendy Millyard, her trusty and kind PA, is one in a zillion, and I always come out of any interaction I have with her feeling smilier and more sorted than before.

No book of mine is ever complete without a huge plate of thanks being handed to Lorraine Martin, my friend and PA of 11 years. If I were to detail all the different tasks and contributions she has made to this book it genuinely would take another double page spread, but suffice it to say, again, that I could not do it without you (life, not just the book), and that goes for the friend stuff as much as the work.

And lastly to the home front, well not strictly the home front but the one next door as neighbour Liz needs to be thanked for well, just being there. From needing caraway seeds in a hurry to eating not one but two shiraz jellies, she's just the best friend a chef could have whilst living less far away than you could spit an olive stone.

I have Sarah Smither to thank for those great trips to China, Turkey and the Caribbean: not only are you now officially the matriarch of our all-female tribe, but also Best Grammy in the World.

And to Tess, who did the most important job in the book: loved and looked after the baby whilst I got on with the small matter of getting it written, shot, edited and proofed. I am so grateful and proud that you are a part of our little family.

Also to my old mucker DanDan, whose Monday specials with the little one were not only vital but also deeply enjoyable for both me & D.

Susi - we did so many of these trips together, ate that amazing food, saw those beautiful things and had all the fun. We've travelled the world hand in hand and I've loved every minute of it. Writing a book that was so important to me was always going to take a lot of graft, so thank-you for your patience, encouragement and love.

And lastly to Delilah, whose newborn presence demanded me in the wee hours thus making this the first book that I've largely written in daylight hours ... and sober, too.

Acknowledgements

First published in UK in 2011 by Conran Octopus Ltd,
an imprint of Octopus Publishing Group Ltd,
Endeavour House, 189 Shaftesbury Avenue, London WC2H 8JY
www.octopusbooks.co.uk

An Hachette UK Company
www.hachette.co.uk

Distributed in the United States and Canada by Hachette Book Group USA,
237 Park Avenue, New York, NY 10017 USA

British Library Cataloguing-in-Publication Data.
A catalogue record for this book is available from the British Library.

Publisher: Lorraine Dickey
Art Director: Jonathan Christie
Photography: Andrew Montgomery
Design & Art Direction: Natasha Coverdale
Design Assistant: Jaz Bahra
Senior Editor: Sybella Stephens
Copy Editor: Annie Lee
Production Manager: Katherine Hockley

ISBN: 978 1 84091 577 8
Printed and bound in China